ASK JERRY BAKER

● ●

—What is the most durable of the bulb-type plants?
—When is the best time to plant perennials?
—Do you really need to "feed" houseplants?
—Does it matter when you mow the lawn?
—Which groundcover will flourish in the shade?
—Does talking to your plants really work?

America's Master Gardener® has the answers to these and hundreds of other questions about how to start and maintain a healthy, productive garden. Long an advocate of the five P's of gardening—Pride, Patience, Persistence, Practice, and a little bit of Prayer—Jerry Baker provides the nuts-and-bolts information that America's gardeners have come to rely on. Filled with dozens of homegrown remedies for ailing plants and Jerry's special secrets for sustained gardening success, this wise, witty, and highly readable guide puts everything you need to know about the loving care of your garden at your fingertips.

PLANTS ARE *STILL* LIKE PEOPLE

JERRY BAKER, America's Master Gardener®, is known to millions as the gardening spokesperson for K Mart and for his daily show on Cable Health Network. The bestselling author of PLANTS ARE LIKE PEOPLE, TALK TO YOUR PLANTS, and THE IMPATIENT GARDENER, he has educated and entertained millions with his simple, down-to-earth, step-by-step approach to gardening.

JERRY BAKER

AMERICA'S MASTER GARDENER®

PLANTS ARE
STILL LIKE PEOPLE

ⓟ

A PLUME BOOK

PLUME
Published by the Penguin Group
Penguin Putnam Inc., 375 Hudson Street,
New York, New York 10014, U.S.A.
Penguin Books Ltd, 27 Wrights Lane, London W8 5TZ, England
Penguin Books Australia Ltd, Ringwood, Victoria, Australia
Penguin Books Canada Ltd, 10 Alcorn Avenue, Toronto, Ontario,
Canada M4V 3B2
Penguin Books (N.Z.) Ltd, 182–190 Wairau Road, Auckland 10,
New Zealand

Penguin Books Ltd, Registered Offices: Harmondsworth, Middlesex,
England

First published by Plume, a member of Penguin Putnam Inc.
An earlier edition was published as Plants Are Like People

First Printing, May, 1992
23   24   22

 REGISTERED TRADEMARK—MARCA REGISTRADA

LIBRARY OF CONGRESS CATALOGING-IN-PUBLICATION DATA
Baker, Jerry.
  Plants are still like people / Jerry Baker.
    p.   cm.
  Updated ed. of: Plants are like people, 1972.
  "A Plume book."
  Includes index.
  ISBN 0-452-28105-9
  1. Gardening.   I. Baker, Jerry. Plants are like people.   II. Title.
SB453.B3175   1992
635—dc20   91-42460
                                                              CIP

Printed in the United States of America
Set in New Century Schoolbook and Futura

Designed by Steven N. Stathakis

PUBLISHER'S NOTE
Some of the ingredients recommended in this book are chemicals. Follow
manufacturer's directions and read warning labels carefully before using these
products.

To my wife Ilene,
who is the sunshine of my life

CONTENTS

FOREWORD

∙∙

"I haven't changed much over the years. I have just learned to live and garden smarter."

When *Plants Are Like People* was first published, comparing plants to people was considered novel and unique and my commonsense remedies were considered old-fashioned, passé, and, in some cases, completely nuts. I'm sure that over the last twenty years that opinion has not altered much among those intent on making a buck at the expense of our health and the safety of our planet by manufacturing or recommending the use of old, outdated, and untested lawn and garden chemicals as the only way to control insects.

But to several million of you, *Plants Are Like People* and her sister were a return to the saner practices of good old-fashioned home gardening techniques found true by our forefathers and—in my case and for many of you—passed on by our grandparents. I did not in the first edition of this book nor have I ever since indicated that insecticides, pesticides, or weed killers should never be used. On the contrary, these home garden helpers are necessary to protect our food sources and the plant life we need to produce the very air we breathe.

I object to our misuse and abuse of these scientific wonders; then we lay the blame on the chemicals for the result. We have, in fact, made a junkyard out of the environment just as we've done to our bodies. We take pills to get up, to get down, to get skinny and to get brown, looking for the magic motions, potions, or lotions. There are none, folks.

Scientists have found dozens upon dozens of organic, biological, and biodegradable insect and disease controls for many lawns and garden problems and will continue to discover more. In the meantime, you and I can continue to use the commonsense approach of using safe, simple, economical materials that are readily available around our homes first, just as our forefathers did, and then using the proper chemical controls, recommended in the prescribed quantity and for the proper length of time, in a safe manner and using the mildest form first.

Don't use an atom bomb when you need a fly swatter.

Yes, these pages are still filled with my oddball collections of tonics, tricks, and concoctions, and a few new ones to boot.

To my old friends who have tried them and found them to be true, thank you. To you new fans of home gardening: try a few and see the differences.

I have changed only what I thought necessary to keep you and your garden on a straight, healthy, pretty, and productive path.

LAWNS

···

THE HEAD OF
THE GARDEN

···

My lawn and this book have one thing in common: they are now both over twenty years old. As I revise and update *Plants Are Like People*, I'm about to do the same to my lawn.

Those of you who have accompanied me along my career's path have often seen my yard in photos or on TV and have watched it grow older, maturing into a warm and comfortable haven for me to work and play.

Our relationship—not yours and mine, but mine and my lawn and garden's—has not always been peaches and cream. As a matter of fact, there's been a little sour milk on the scene from time to time. But by practicing the formula for successful living and gardening from Grandma Putt, we have grown to better understand each other and appreciate what each one contributes to the other's comfort and well-being.

Grandma Putt, my Grandmother Putnam, the lady you've come to know over the years through my books, originally gave me the formula on her lap and in her arms. The formula is to practice the three P's—pride, patience, and persistence. Through the years I have learned that there were two more to add; those were practice and prayer. Along the way I've discovered this formula is the basis for success in marriage, a career, and in raising children and pets as well as plants.

There is no one who tires of an attractive lawn, except perhaps the guy or gal who works at keeping it that way. Don't look so shocked. An average to better-than-average lawn takes work, lots of work. But that doesn't mean it can't be fun as well as rewarding. As we mature, we must have exercise to stay healthy, and there's nothing like a good workout or two in your backyard each week to keep fit—and that goes for both you and your "yarden."

I haven't changed much over the years; I've just learned to live and garden smarter. I am still a great believer in the old-fashioned, easy, safe, and economical ways of gardening. Yes, I still wear my golf shoes whenever I go into the yard, and soap and water are my first line of defense for insect and disease problems.

I have always believed that you should think of your lawn as if it were the hair on your head. People judge your hair, or your lawn, by its appearance. Your lawn is the first thing a stranger sees when he approaches your house. He can't know if you have fine furniture or nice clothes or even if you have a fancy car in the garage. What he *can* see is your lawn, so make your lawn look like it

"A formula of Pride, Patience, Persistence— plus Practice and Prayer—is the basis for a good marriage, a good career, and raising children, pets, and plants."

"Think of your lawn as if it were the hair on your head."

just came back from the barber—clean, combed and well cut. Good grooming is as important for your garden as it is for you.

LAWN DANDRUFF TREATMENT

Lawn dandruff is known as thatch. It's an accumulation of grass clippings and debris that builds up over a period of time. When it's not removed, thatch becomes a breeding place for various lawn diseases caused by fungus. If the fungus diseases are not curbed, the grass will simply fade away, and your lawn will become bald.

This lawn dandruff, or thatch, is also a thief. It robs your lawn of food, air, and water. As it gets thicker and tighter packed, it sheds water and won't let the weed killers and lawn medicines you apply get down to the roots of the grass where they're needed. You must dethatch before you do any other job on your lawn, or the others will be for nothing.

There are several ways to eliminate and remove this dandruff, and the first is to catch all of your grass clippings when mowing. The type of grass doesn't mean a thing; catch the clippings of them all.

You can remove the existing thatch by using any one of three methods.

The first method is to use a lawn groom rake. This rake, especially designed to pull up thatch, consists of many fine half-moon-shaped blades with very sharp edges and a small bar at the top of each to allow the rake to clean itself as you go. This is a hand method, and the one recommended for small lawns.

The second method is to purchase a roto-rake bar, an attachment that converts your power mower into a power dethatcher. This is usually a blade that replaces your mowing blade, which you must remove. I would like to caution you on the use of this tool. Start your lawn mower on a concrete or other hard surface and then proceed back and forth across the lawn at a normal pace. Do not stop on the turf as doing so will cause extensive root damage. When you've done the entire lawn back and forth in one direction, then do the whole lawn in a cross direction.

The third method is to use a power rake or power renovator, which can be rented from tool rental companies and some nurseries. The power machines are extremely effective, but they need your complete concentration. Don't try to use them on hills or uneven ground; use a hand rake there instead. Follow the directions that come with the machine.

Each of these methods does for your lawn what a scalp treatment does for your hair, and the result is the same: improved circulation to the roots produces fatter, stronger, greener, healthier grass.

Don't be shocked to find that you've collected seven or eight twenty-gallon garbage cans full of thatch for each one thousand square feet of lawn. Now what are you going to do with all this excess grass? Start your first compost pile (to be discussed on pages 406–407). Remember, ecology has to do with the methods by which we return to the earth, in one form or another, what we have removed.

The best time to give your lawn its dandruff treatment is just before each shampoo. In the cool weather states, that means April, June, and September; in the West and South it means October.

SHAMPOO
YOUR LAWN

Since we're comparing lawn care to a scalp treatment that we'd give ourselves, the next logical step after removing dandruff from our scalps would be shampooing. Why not do the same to your lawn? That's just what I'm recommending: shampoo your lawn with soap and water.

Professionally, we refer to this soap treatment as applying a surfactant and using it regularly on greens and fairways to relieve surface tension, the invisible barrier that keeps water and food from penetrating. To understand the effects of surface tension, you need only recall your childhood days when you would sit and spit into the dust. You'd watch the spit just sit there in a ball and not soak into the dust. The surface tension of the water droplet kept it a droplet and prevented it from penetrating.

"A clean lawn is a healthy lawn."

When we spray our lawn with a mild solution of soap and water, we break down this invisible barrier which causes lawns to burn up in hot weather and makes us disappointed with the brand of fertilizer we use. But we shouldn't blame the fertilizer. The surface tension of the water droplets prevents the nitrogen from being absorbed by the grass and getting down to the roots. Instead, the water droplets and the nitrogen dissolved in them are going down into the sewers, causing algae and weeds in our rivers, ponds, lakes, and streams.

Since soap is sort of sticky and constantly moist, it holds water moisture longer. This means we do not need to water our lawn as often, even in hot weather.

Lawn shampooing makes your garden dollar stretch because soap is a spreader-sticker; it catches the nitrogen in your fertilizer when it is washed out of its regular carrier. By regular carrier I mean the type of material onto which the manufacturer sprays the nitrogen so that the bag is full, and which holds the nitrogen before it can wash down the sewer.

The presence of soap makes your weed killer more effective by helping it to stick to the foliage where it belongs.

Shampoo will also wash off the airborne soot and dust that attaches itself to the surface of the blades, clogging up the pores and cells that permit the plants to manufacture their own food through the process known as photosynthesis. When these cells are plugged up, the plant becomes anemic, turns yellow and pale (as we do when we have anemia) and, if the condition is not checked, will die.

We certainly can't forget insects. Yes, the simple lawn shampoo will act as a preventive insecticide against soil insects: bugs aren't too much different from us humans when it comes to taste. Soap wasn't designed to eat, and neither of us cares for the taste of it. When it's necessary to use an insecticide, this same soap will hold it in place to do the job effectively.

The term "biodegradable" should be explained here, so that you will understand that by using soap you are not adding to pollution but improving the environment. A biodegradable substance is one that will break down and become an active part of the soil, instead of causing damage. All these soap solutions decompose and none will cause algae or weeds in our rivers, ponds, lakes, and streams.

I have found over the years that different kinds of soap products do different jobs better. All these

"A lawn is like wall-to-wall carpeting in your living room."

solutions will break up surface tension, but some will do more. For instance:

1. *Ordinary liquid dish detergent,* under any brand name, is great for an early spring lawn bath applied from your hose-end lawn sprayer at a rate of one cup per twenty gallons of water to cover 2500 square feet.

2. *Bar laundry soap,* such as Fels-Naphtha or Octagon, can be made into an all-purpose lawn and garden shampoo by dissolving a quarter of a bar of soap—shaved or pulverized very fine—into a quart of boiling water. When the soap is completely dissolved, add four ounces of one of the liquid dish detergents, which will emulsify the mixture and prevent it from gelling. Pour this mixture into a three-quart container, add two cans of beer and cover the container. Use one cup of the mixture per twenty gallons of water for every 2500 square feet every two weeks, after you mow the lawn. This solution will discourage insects and diseases and encourage deeper, healthier soil and better foliage color and growth. We'll use this bar soap solution with some changes for other jobs in the yard as we go on. For instance, you can add tobacco juice.

To make tobacco juice, put a third of a pouch of chewing tobacco into the toe of a nylon stocking. Put the tobacco into a quart of boiling water into which you have dissolved a package of Knox gelatin. Allow it to steep and then throw away the tobacco. Use 1:1 with the bar laundry soap solution—a cup of each per twenty gallons of water; a tablespoon of each per gallon of water.

3. *Children's shampoo* is a very mild surfactant used to improve the appearance of your grass when you're about to have company and want your yard to look its best. Children's shampoos are not for cleaning heavy duty pollution; for that you use the liquid dish detergent, which cuts the dirt, dust and airborne solution from industrial fallout and auto emissions. Use a cup per twenty gallons of water for 2500 square feet.

4. *Flea and tick shampoo* is a mild form of soap a little stronger than children's shampoo, but the manufacturers have added a very safe and mild solution of pyrethrum and insecticide made from a member of the chrysanthemum family. Flea and tick shampoo is used instead of children's shampoo for the same purpose, but it has the ability to discourage mosquitoes and other bugs from joining your party. Use a cup of shampoo per twenty gallons of water to cover 2500 square feet.

5. *Insecticidal soaps* are a perfect example of the old saying, "What goes around comes around." Soapy water as an insect deterrent has been recommended and used for hundreds of years, and now that old wives' tale is applauded as a scientific breakthrough. They are effective at keeping insects away and are good surfactants.

6. *Powdered laundry soap* can destroy toadstools and fairy rings as well as reduce surface tension. To get rid of toadstools and fairy rings, sprinkle a cup over each ten square feet of affected area, after you've punched dozens upon dozens of holes with a nail or sharp stick over the same area. Water in well and then in a week add a cup of liquid dish detergent and one-half cup of ordinary brown mouthwash to a gallon of warm water and drench the same area.

Shampoo the lawn after the snows melt in the North and East and as soon as the rains stop in the West. In the southern states, begin any time. Lawn shampooing should be repeated at least once a month throughout the growing season.

Believe it or not, your lawn will fairly sparkle

like your favorite crystal and china when it has been washed properly. Remember, a clean lawn is a healthy lawn.

You are probably wondering how long this lawn-washing procedure has been used and recommended. At least the sixty-eight years that Grandma Putnam was alive. And I'll just bet that a lot of you can recall your parents and grandparents pouring dish and wash water—that did not contain grease or bleach—over the roses and other plants as well as the lawn. They were just reusing the water and may not have been aware of the benefits of the soap—but good ecological practice had extra benefits then, too.

JOG YOUR LAWN TO GLORY

To prevent the dandruff from building up and the surface tension from returning, you need to massage the turf area, to give it a little exercise. No, I'm not going to suggest that you get down on your hands and knees and literally massage your grass with your hands; I suggest that you stand up and use your feet. Many of today's doctors recommend—and with good reason—that we jog every day. So what do we do? We don our sweatsuits each morning and run up and down the roadside, when what we really should do is put on a pair of track spikes or baseball or golf shoes and run around our own yards. The spikes are the secret. They punch holes in the soil that let water and air down to the roots and let fertilizer get deeper into the soil. Jogging or walking on your lawn breaks up compaction, the pressing down of the soil that crushes and smothers the roots. If you're reluctant to engage in this strenuous activity just for your lawn's sake, I suggest that you wear your golf spikes whenever you're working in your yard and take a walk each evening through your garden and say goodnight to the many friends that you've invited to live permanently in your garden. If you have small children in the neighborhood, encourage them to stop by to play a little catch with you—but make sure they wear spikes. (And remember, no sliding.)

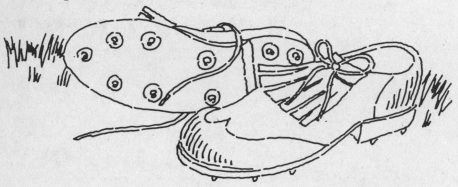

What we're really after is aeration, which is an important factor for root structure. You can also rent a machine, called a lawn plugger, that will remove two- or three-inch plugs from your lawn, or you can purchase a hand tool called a plugger. Your lawn would appreciate this treatment once a year in the late spring after you have dethatched and shampooed for the first time. When you use a lawn plugger, leave the plugs of soil on the lawn. When you're finished, go back and break them up with the back of a rake and spread them around. They then act as a top dressing. You can see that you're promoting sound ecology by returning to the good earth what might well have been thrown away. If you'll just relax and tune in to Mother Nature's frequency, you'll find that your gardening can keep you as healthy as your garden. Most professional lawn services do lawn plugging, as well as dethatching.

LAWN ROLLING: I HAVEN'T CHANGED MY MIND!

• •

If you can shut your eyes and picture those big, heavy wagons rolling across Flanders Field, each loaded with the massive weight of a cannon, you can imagine the damage done to the poor earth below.

Mother Nature does not send a huge log rolling across a meadow to flatten it out just because it has a hump or two, nor does she hurtle a huge rock around to pound a knoll or two back into place. No, she gently nudges them back into place with a few light rains and sends the gophers, moles, or angleworms over to undermine the humps, so there's room for them to settle down.

I am by no means suggesting that you call the moles and gophers over, and the worms don't understand your lingo, so you must do the job for them—but not with a roller. Rollers are built and designed to compact surfaces for reinforcement and to eliminate the possibility of soil expansion. Let's look at parking lots—they're hard, strong, and firm. If you want your lawn to be a parking lot, use a roller. If not, go the gentle way.

If, after a hard winter, you have some humps

and lumps, use a plugger and remove some of the surplus soil so that when you water, the remaining surface will have somewhere to expand to. Sort of like letting the air out of a balloon.

Or you might use a sod spade and cut around the ground, lift off the turf, remove the surplus soil and replace the turf cover.

Gullies and tire tracks are repaired in reverse: lift the turf, refill the soil and replace the turf cover.

On an established lawn, the weight of a roller causes the soil to be packed down, thus shutting out water penetration when warm weather comes, and it crushes the roots, causing them to suffocate.

Almost the only time I recommend the use of a lawn roller is when you're seeding a brand-new lawn. And this is an empty roller, used only to seat the seed in the newly prepared soil, so that it can get a firmer grip. The other use is when laying sod, and again, only enough weight should be added to the roller to allow the roots of the new sod to touch the soil beneath firmly and push the joints and butt ends together to insure a good knit.

I am sure that I will not win the lawn roller manufacturers' award again this year.

TO CUT OR NOT TO CUT, THAT IS THE QUESTION

Lawn cutting is probably the most taken-for-granted job around the yard. It is also the most begrudged. What most people don't know is that there is a right time and a right way to cut any type of turf, and if you do not adhere to these rules, you can defeat your whole purpose.

We do not cut a lawn just to make it look nice. The major reason to cut your lawn is to stimulate branching. When there are more plant surfaces, more photosynthesis can take place, thus enabling the rhizome, or growing factory, to utilize food. This food is then changed into chlorophyll, which is sent back through the system, giving the grass a rich green color.

The second reason we cut is to keep the blades standing tall and straight. No one likes to see a proud person—or plant—stoop shouldered. And when grass is allowed to grow too tall, it bends over onto the blade next to it, shading its neighbor's roots and causing the neighbor to get tired and lean on the next. You end up with everybody lying down on the job.

Yet another reason for cutting the turf is to stimulate the chlorophyll (blood) flow. When you cut the tops off the blades, the rhizome sends a rush of fluid way up top to seal the fresh cut, and the fluid contains chlorophyll. Again, more chlorophyll means more green color.

By the way, never think of a blade of grass as being a weakling. It is probably stronger than you or me. It is said that a blade of grass forcing its way through the soil exerts the equivalent of 4600 pounds per square inch of thrust. That is probably an amount similar to the power of a spaceshot.

N O   B R U S H   C U T S

Who would ever think there's a right or a wrong time to cut a lawn? Any good grass grower! Let's cover the why first. When grass is cut, the cut surface is exposed to elements that the grass has thus far been protected from, namely heat and surface winds. Secondly, the tunnels to the roots are also exposed for a brief period to these same elements, which comes as a shock and a surprise. It is like working in an air-conditioned office all day and walking outside into ninety-degree weather. It shocks your system and takes your breath away for a moment or two.

I have found that the best time for cutting the lawn is in the evening when the weather has cooled down some and the dry winds have subsided. The grass will then have several hours to adjust to the new haircut before the noonday sun reaches its peak. Evening mowing will also be more comfortable for you.

The best days to cut your lawn are Mondays and Thursdays, which leaves you free to enjoy the weekend. If you only cut once a week, Thursday evening is best for the same reason.

Another thing to take into consideration when attempting to mow is the moisture content in both the soil and the blade. A barber wants your hair dry when he cuts, so that it doesn't mat down or stick together, either of which would cause pulling and pinching, and you'd end up with festered hairs at the roots. Grass will have the same problems if you attempt to cut it when it's wet. It'll mat down, sticking to the blades and inside the machine, thus causing the lawn mower to pull the ends off instead of cutting them clean. Pulling grass dislodges the roots or runners, as the case may be, and causes a festering condition, thus causing the rhizome to die. And you end up with what looks like lawn mange. The grass will drop out just as your hair would. The lawn should be dry when cut, and you should water it early the next morning.

The frequency with which you cut your lawn is another factor that will determine both its quality and density. The bluegrasses, Merion and Kentucky, will be at their greenest and healthiest if they're cut one-and-a-half to two inches every two days and the clippings removed each time. The ryes and fescues should be cut twice a week, bent grasses every other day, and Dichondra once a week. That's right, once a week. Some think that Dichondra should be cut only once a month, but that is not so.

There are commercial growth inhibitors available, but I recommend them only for commercial use. And at no time do I recommend that you lower a blade in season and give your lawn a brush cut.

HOW TO MOW

Have you heard that you can mow a lawn in any direction you want? I'm sure this is right to some extent. However, for the sake of the grass's health and your lawn's appearance, I suggest that we copy the approved method of the greens' superintendents and the sod growers.

It is important that you not walk on the grass area you're about to mow, as this tends to make it lie down, and you won't get an even cut.

Mow around the exterior of your lawn area first, perhaps two mower widths. Mow around the flower beds that border your lawn. Do not enter the center yet. Each time you cut your lawn, reverse the starting direction of this exterior cut.

Now begin a normal across-the-lawn cut. As you approach tree wells and center beds, mow two mower-width circles around these and proceed with your normal cutting practice until you've finished.

The next time you cut the lawn you'll cut in a totally different direction so that the grass is never forced to grow in one direction. There are eight directions to cut: from north to south, south to north, west to east, east to west, southwest to northeast, northeast to southwest, northwest to southeast, and from southeast to northwest.

If you alternate your mowing pattern, your lawn will look picture perfect.

The type of machine you use to cut your lawn will also affect the health and appearance of the grass plants themselves.

It is important to understand that you must use a sharp blade at all times. A dull blade will rip, tear, and beat the grass to death, shattering the ends of the blades and leaving the lawn with a tannish, filmy appearance where the ends have dried out.

I suggest that you buy a new blade for rotary mowers each year, alternating the new blade with last year's blade every month. Have the spare one sharpened when you change. A reel type mower presents a different problem; I run a flat stone over the blade edges before I begin to mow, to take off the nicks and bumps that could cause tearing, and I have it sharpened once a month by a professional.

There are now plastic blades on the market for rotary lawn mowers that are just as effective as steel—and safer. Again, I'd advise you to buy two and switch off, sharpening the one you're not using. These blades can also be sharpened and balanced in the normal manner by a professional mower shop.

The argument about which is best, rotary or reel, power or hand, will not be settled by my opinion or this book. However, I do intend to give my opinion. I recommend, for the sake of saving time, a self-propelled machine, no matter what type you use. Next, I do not drive or fly blind. I like to see what's coming or going, so I use a reel type, as do most golf courses and sod growers.

Rotary lawn mowers do a fine job if they are sharp, well tuned and balanced, and if you keep the undercarriage free of grass. Do not stop and start any more often than necessary, and then only on solid surface that's free of stones (when possible). Stopping while mowing may create settling circles where the mower is allowed to sit with the blade rotating.

Bent grass must be cut with a special reel mower that has seven blades, as must most southern and western grasses.

Do not allow grass clippings to lie on the lawn, as they'll just increase the thatch buildup that you will need to remove later.

Grass clippings can be added to your compost pile (see pages 406–407) or given to a farmer who is fattening up cattle. In either case, you are again practicing sound ecology.

R E M E M B E R : G R A S S C A N ' T S W I M

The most important ingredient for proper growth of any plant is water. Without it, we all know that plants, like people, would dehydrate or dry up. Too much water, on the other hand, tends to make us blow up or bloat. It will do the same to grass, making it fat, soft, and tender, just as your hands will be after they've been in dishwater too long.

In this bloated state, both your hands and your lawn can easily be injured because the tissue is soft. The secret: keep your lawn strong, firm, and healthy with proper watering.

TYPES OF WATER
· ·

Oh, yes! There are different types of water. The basic scientific formula is H_2O, but then we go on from there as natural trace elements are added as the moisture falls in the form of rain or snow. For instance, during an electrical storm, rain particles are charged with as much as 78 percent nitrogen, and it's the nitrogen that accounts for the fresh, green look of a lawn after a thunderstorm. Its high nitrogen content means that rainwater is best for your lawn.

Well water has trace elements that it picks up from the soil, like iron, the blood builder for you and me; but it does not pick up as much nitrogen as rainwater.

Last we have tap water. This has many, many trace elements and chemical additives. One of these trace elements is fluoride, which, in small amounts, helps build strong teeth. One of the chemical additives is chlorine, which helps to purify the water. Some chemical additives hurt plants, and there is one that especially harms them and also bothers the human system—namely, salt. Who would ever water with salt you say? You do, every time you turn on a hose attached to a normal faucet. Sodium salts are added to our public water systems, for our good health—to promote strong teeth, strong bones, and so on. Some salt is necessary for good health in people, but not for plants. As a matter of fact, salt kills more lawns than anything else.

"Grass can't swim."

So what we look for in water is purity. Of course, the best water we could get is water collected in cisterns or a rain barrel. As a matter of fact, I don't know why, with the antique-collecting rage that's going on right now, we couldn't all just as easily have a rain barrel. I have one. Rainwater is so pure that it not only does it not have the impurities or trace elements that plants don't like, but, as a bonus, it contains the purest and mildest yet strongest fertilizer that there possibly is—nitrogen. That's right, that's what is in the air right now above your heads: one pound of actual nitrogen for one cubic foot of air or 78 percent nitrogen, 21 percent oxygen, one percent inert matter (78:21:1).

If we could collect enough rainwater we wouldn't need to use any other water. But since we can't, we try to achieve the same results the best way we can. Therefore, we must depend on Jupiter Fluvius, Mother Nature's right-hand man, god of the rains, and on our own ability to use filtered water wherever possible.

THE TIME TO WATER

It's been argued by many experts in many ways, but, judging from my experience, I would say that there is a right time and a wrong time to water. The best time is just after the sun comes up. While the dew is still on your lawn, turn on your sprinkler and water. You should allow the water to run long enough to get deep penetration, because deep penetration means deep roots. Shallow watering or shallow penetration means that the roots will stay close to the surface of the soil. When you stop watering, the soil will dry out very quickly, and the roots will also dry out. When the roots dry out, the rhizomes are injured, and when that happens, the top of the plant dies. Soon you have a brown lawn.

You water early to permit the lawn to dry out slowly so it will be dry by the time evening comes when the night dews and coolness sets in. If your lawn is wet when the evening dew comes on, it doesn't have a chance to dry out. When the lawn is continually soggy, there's a great probability that fungi or other lawn diseases will develop. The top of the grass is cool, and the earth, down inside, stays warm. Fertilizer, which has nitrogen in it, makes the soil warm. So if you add water late in the afternoon or evening, you create ideal incubating conditions for lawn diseases. My advice is to go a little out of your way to make sure that somebody's responsible for early morning watering.

A very good comparison and, I think, one that we can easily understand, would be the following: suppose on a very hot summer night, before you went to bed, your wife took off your bed sheets, soaked them in a bathtub of cold water, threw a couple of buckets of ice water on the mattress, took your pajamas and made them soaking wet, and put all of that back on the bed. Then, you climbed into bed in wet pajamas, pulled the covers over you, leaving the windows open (we're trying to duplicate your lawn's living conditions), and went to sleep. I'll bet by the end of three days you'd have a little fungus-amungus, too! Because you couldn't dry out, your skin would get soft and vulnerable, then it would itch, and you would scratch. That's what happens to the plant tissue. It itches, scratches, and catches all of the diseases there are.

The argument that I receive most often on my opinion of early-morning watering is, "How come the golf courses water all night long and don't have a lot of diseases?" Well, I think that's relatively simple. We don't collect green fees, so we don't have to worry about when the lawn is being watered. And, besides that, golf courses spend a great deal of money spraying with fungicides, once or even twice a week, to combat the fungus diseases. So that's not much of an argument.

HOW TO WATER

• •

The job of watering seems simple, but it's misunderstood in many cases. I said earlier that we want to water deep. Well, how deep is deep?

For the average lawn, the cool grasses, such as Merion and Kentucky blue, the ryes (which are both cool and warm), the red fescues, *Poa trivialis*, or any other cool grass: water to a depth of about three inches. For Dichondra, zoysia, and Bermuda, it's a good idea to water to a depth of two inches. Even if you have sandy soil, water deep so that the roots get used to staying down there.

How do you know when you have two, three, or four inches? That's simple. Take an empty coffee can or a fruit can and place it at the farthest point that the water reaches. When the water level in the can is three or four inches—or whatever you've determined you want—stop watering. The can acts as a homemade water meter.

It's a good idea to do this at least twice a week. It isn't going to do your lawn any good if you water a little every day, because a little every day doesn't help at all. As a matter of fact, it harms, because that's shallow watering, and the lawn will react by growing shallow roots, which weakens it and makes it susceptible to all sorts of damage.

PICK A
SPRINKLER
• •

There are all kinds of lawn sprinklers, and for me to list or illustrate every type on the market today would take up the greater part of this book. The best system, if you can afford it, is an automatic one, with a water meter and timer that goes on at a set time. It waters for a given period at a constant pressure, until the lawn gets a certain amount of water to the depth that you indicate. That's the best, and it's also the most expensive. But it may not be feasible, and a lot of people don't want to tear up their lawns. So they go to a regular sprinkler.

There are some automatic home watering systems at your local department store or garden center that come in do-it-yourself kits. They're very effective and very good, and they cost only about a tenth of what the professionally installed system costs.

What type of sprinkler do you use if you can't afford the first and don't want to bother with the second? You use a regular lawn sprinkler. I've found that the one that puts down the most water and gets it out there the fastest and heaviest is the pulsator that goes "chicka-chicka-chicka-chicka-chicka." You can regulate the spray to a small circle or a large one. They cover a large area, and four of them will do approximately 5000 square feet at a time.

The wand sprinklers are good for those hard-to-get-at places. There are some with adjustable heads that do an oblong, square, circle, or rectangle. There are all kinds of them, and any of them will work. It's just a matter of economics and how long you want to wait to get the water down

Feeding with liquids at the same time you water is not recommended, at least not in my book, because I find that people have a tendency to forget or overfeed, and this causes the lawn to burn. However, feeding with a hose-end sprayer is highly recommended. That's the jaw that fits on the end of the hose, and you put the liquid fertilizer into it. That is a very good way to fertilize, but it's not to be considered watering of the lawn. It would be considered a light daily sprinkling, and fertilizing should be done after the lawn has been watered. Automatic feeders are definitely not for the amateur. I have never found them used successfully by an amateur.

I say "Grass can't swim" to make you realize that plants, especially grass plants, are just like human beings. We all need a certain amount of water to keep ourselves healthy but too much will get us in trouble. We humans, since we breathe, drown. Grass is the same way: dependent on oxygen. If too much water is used and the roots are kept under water or are submerged for a period of time, or if the top of the grass plant is submerged, then the plant smothers. Therefore we have to remember not to put down too much water.

You can probably recall seeing light yellow or soggy spots in a lawn that have become off-color as a result of drowning. So it's a good idea not to water all day and all night in soil that isn't well drained.

Clay soils, as a rule, are not well drained. Grass will drown in clay soil where there are pockets in the ground and where the ground is not level or has not been graded to let water run off. You can't make a swimming pool out of your yard and expect the grass to live.

FERTILIZING: FEED YOUR LAWN OR FORGET IT

As to the best kind of fertilizer, there are no "best kinds." I'm sorry, Jupiter Fluvius, mighty mythical rain god, your thunder brew—78:21:1—is by far the best, but then, it's not always available. I'm referring to a manufactured product.

Your lawn doesn't give a tinker's darn what you feed it. It just wants to eat—for as long as possible and as often as possible.

The three most common trace elements that all plants need are nitrogen, phosphorus, and potash. The numbers on the front of most lawn food bags indicate the percentage of each of these three elements contained in the particular product. You need only multiply each of these numbers by the weight of the bag to find out, in weight, what you're getting for your money. In most cases we're after all the nitrogen we can get. You may be wondering what the rest of the bag is full of. It's the carrier or filler that the manufacturer uses to fill up the bag so you can safely put it through your spreader. Unless you have a lawn that can read, the three numbers on the bag don't mean a thing to anybody but you, and that's just to make sure you get your money's worth.

I said earlier that there are no best kinds, but

that's not quite true. If you're willing to pay for the best combinations of growing elements your grass needs, then you'd best invest in a material like Scott's turf builder. Their combinations and special manufacturing method make them the leader in professional turf management.

Next, the organically based lawn products, such as professionally processed sludge and recycled trash-base granular lawn products that will soon be available in most large cities as they build new, environmentally safe garbage and trash-processing plants, are all very good supplemental lawn foods for the warmer summer months. But when it comes right down to feeding the average lawn, let economics dictate your selection. Super K-Gro or Scott's lawn foods will provide you with a winner.

Here is my lawn feeding system and timing:

1. In the very early spring in the north and in late January in the south and west, purchase a bag of lawn food that indicates it covers 2500 square feet of lawn.

2. Next step is to buy a four-pound box of Epsom salts in the health and beauty aid department of your grocery store. When you get home, mix the Epsom salts and your lawn food together and apply using a setting of 4 medium open on a hand-held spreader (either Precision broadcast or Ortho whirley spreader are fine) over five thousand square feet. Of course, adjust the amounts for your lawn size.

3. Water in the dry lawn food and Epsom salts with this lawn tonic. Into the quart jar part of your hose-end lawn sprayer pour:

1 can of beer
1 cup of liquid dish detergent

Fill to the top with household ammonia. This mixture in twenty gallons of water covers 2500 square feet.

4. After your second true mowing—that's when you have more green blades than brown in the grass catcher—mix together a bag of Milorganite and the same size bag of ammonium sulphate and apply the mixture using a number 2 medium spreader setting. Treat with the Milorganite mixture every week, and always wear your golf shoes as you do. You can use a liquid feeding program for the summer in place of, or in addition to, the Milorganite mix if you wish. For liquid feeding, put into your hose-end quart jar:

1 cup of liquid lawn food
1 can of beer
1 cup of flea and tick shampoo

Fill to the top with household ammonia. This mixture in twenty gallons of water covers 2500 square feet.

5. In the fall of the year, repeat the first mix of lawn food and Epsom salts.

Whenever I'm down at the garden store, I always look for broken bags of lawn or garden food that are marked down for quick sale. I bring them home, mix them all together (though not weed killers), and then from time to time I give my lawn and garden a picnic by applying this mixture using setting 3 on the whirley spreader.

BEAT THE WEEDS

The dictionary sums up the situation as it presently pertains to our precious lawn: "Weed, *n*. Any plant

"Weeds are not all bad. As a matter of fact, I haven't found a weed I couldn't like."

growing uncultivated, useless or troublesome, offensive or hurtful." If there is anything in this whole wide world that will make the hair stand up on the back of my neck, it is to come out into the yard some bright, sunny morning and find a fresh, fluffy yellow head poking its way through the blades of a bright green lawn. Today one dandelion, tomorrow hundreds. What's a green thumb to do?

The first thing to do is relax. All too often we get so upset that we begin to run around like a chicken with its head cut off, and we end up wasting time, effort, and money.

Weeds are not all bad. As a matter of fact, I haven't found a weed I couldn't like. I don't always like it where I find it, but eventually we reach a mutual understanding on where we will both enjoy the other's company.

I grow, cultivate, feed, harvest, and eat dandelion greens. I grow, cultivate, feed, and harvest the yellow flowers of the dandelion, then brew them and drink their golden nectar. So 'tain't all bad having such a versatile weed handy. I might also remind you that some of our ancestors worshipped weeds. Their gospel was called *Herbal*, and one of the most sacred of the weeds was the one we call plantain because it brought the bad spirits out of a person. So you see, you're not just dealing with any old stray cat: some of the weeds in your garden played a part in our history.

When a sod grower is looking for additional land to plant or a golf course designer is seeking a location for a new course, they both look for land with a good weed cover, because this tells them that the soil is fertile and that they can overcome the unwanted weeds without much difficulty by using any one of the modern herbicides or weed killers.

Next, you should know what you are looking

for and at. Many a poor soul has completely destroyed his lawn by purchasing the wrong type of control, one which destroyed the good grasses and left the unwanted plants to thrive.

IDENTIFYING WEEDS

For the sake of simplification, let's concentrate on the two categories that you'll meet on your journey with Mother Nature.

The first will be the "monocot" or grassy weeds, such as goose grass, crabgrass, nut grass, foxtail, Dallis grass, and witch grass. These few, the annual monocots, live one full season and reseed themselves. Then the old foliage dies, never to return. But the new seed sprouts a hundred-thousandfold, which can cause one heck of an Excedrin headache for someone who's trying to grow a good-looking lawn. Tall fescues, timothy, orchard grass, and nimble-will are perennial monocots, and they return each year from the rhizome.

The secondary category is the "dicot" or broad-leafed weed. In this category we find our most persistent pests. Purslane, chickweed, dandelion, henbit, oxalis, thistle, plantain, buckhorn, clover, ground ivy, and knotweed are all dicots.

Now walk out and look at your lawn and its weedy inhabitants. Can you recognize them? What next?

CONTROL

I have found that when a lawn is properly dethatched and shampooed often, aerated, well fed, watered properly and mowed often, weeds are at a minimum and very few chemical controls are necessary. So obviously prevention is the best method of control.

Proper use of weed killers seems to be a big stumbling block for many of you. Liquid weed killers are by far the most effective and efficient way to eradicate weeds from your lawn, and if they're applied between 1 and 3 P.M. on a bright sunny day when the temperature is over 50 degrees and under 80 degrees, they will destroy the plants they are designed to affect. There are, however, a couple of steps you can take to increase the efficiency of any weed killer.

1. Prewash the area where the weeds are with a cup of liquid dish detergent per twenty gallons of water over 2500 square feet.

2. Mix and spray your weed killer as recommended in a hose-end sprayer that has red paint or nail polish marks on the head and jar, as well as an orange or red golf ball inside to warn you and others that this is a sprayer that is to be used for weed killers only. The golf ball also acts as a stirring device.

3. Mix only enough weed killer to spray the weeds; do not spray the entire yard. Spraying weed killer everywhere upsets ordinary grass growth and in many cases gets on the foliage of shrubs, flowers, evergreens, and vegetables, harming or even killing these plants.

4. Do not spray anything but the weeds under the drip line of trees.

5. Add a tablespoon of liquid dish detergent to the weed killer mix, no matter how large the quantity (one tablespoon, that's all!).

6. Clean and store the weed killer sprayer and

weed killer banded together on a high and inside wall shelf.

7. A week after first applying weed killer, mix weed killer in an old sprayer bottle that was used for window spray or prespot laundry spray. Add the amount of weed killer needed for the amount of water the bottle holds, plus a tablespoon of liquid dish detergent. Attach the handle to your belt when you mow the lawn. Then when you pass over the weeds with the mower, stop and spray the weeds that still look too healthy. Destroy the hand sprayer when finished.

In both the North and South, weeds are best destroyed in either spring or fall when they're growing their very best.

Dry weed-and-feeds are effective but inefficient because of the way they're used. Most homeowners use them as a miracle cure, when in fact they're really a mild dose of both weed killer and lawn feeder.

1. Apply a dry weed-and-feed two days after you've fed the entire lawn, at the same time of the year as you'd apply liquid lawn food and weed killer.

2. Prewater the turf area with a cup of liquid dish detergent per twenty gallons of water to cover 2500 square feet. While the grass is damp, apply the weed-and-feed over the weeds only, with your spreader set on setting 2. Do not water in for twenty-four hours.

3. Spot spray a week later as recommended in step 7 of the liquid program.

4. Avoid spreading weed-and-feed mixture on gardens, trees, and shrubs.

5. Wash your spreader out with soap and water, rinse, and wash again.

The monocots or annual grassy weeds are best controlled with a pre-emergent treatment that kills the seed when it is dormant, before it can germinate or sprout in the spring. Pre-emergent weed killers are available in both dry applications or liquid, and both are very effective.

But beware! Not all lawns are grass, as some unsuspecting Easterners have discovered when they moved west and south and met Dichondra, a ground cover substitute for grass and a member of the morning-glory family. If you use a common weed killer on this type of lawn, you can kiss it all good-bye.

When you move in and can't identify your variety of lawn, visit a local nursery with a sample of the turf to find out what it is. It sure is better to be safe than sorry.

Time is of the essence. The secret to successful weed control is timing. You must also check the label on bottles and bags of weed control products for warnings or special handling.

For spot weed killing on lawns, patios, walks, and near pools, I mix 1 ounce of vinegar, 1 ounce of liquid dish soap and half a shot of gin in 32 ounces of warm water. Apply with a squeeze sprayer.

LAWN
DISEASES

Most lawns are grown under unnatural conditions. That is, they're expected to perform in soil, light, and moisture conditions that are totally foreign to their natural habitat. These conditions make your lawn an ideal target for the many fungus diseases that attack a weak strand of grass.

The best defense against these lawn diseases is, of course, the good cultural practices that we've already discussed. Dethatch and shampoo regularly to destroy destructive spores. Aerate the soil with spikes whenever you're working on the lawn. Always remove the grass clippings when mowing.

I have found that an application of garden gypsum—a natural soil conditioner, salt neutralizer, clay breaker-upper, nitrogen catcher, dog-urine-damage preventative and repairer, dry spot firmer, and alkaline soil neutralizer—certainly saves a lot of grief and aggravation. Treating with gypsum will halt many of the problems that are often mistaken for lawn diseases, as well as counteract fertilizer burn.

Most lawn diseases are the direct result of improper watering. If you'll just water as early as possible in the morning and have the job done between 9:00 and 9:30 A.M., you'll seldom (notice I did not say never) have to deal with severe lawn disease problems.

There are about ten common turf diseases that you could face in the middle of your yard anyplace in North America. And when one shows up, it's usually on the rampage, like a forest fire in tinder box trees. When you first see signs of disease, your first reaction is to blame the neighbor's dog, a faulty spreader (or spreador), or bugs, or a careless gas can that went for a walk when you weren't looking. Oh, it's true, one of these *could* be the culprit, but odds are the cause is on the ten most dreaded lawn disease list, and the first thing you can do is haul out the liquid dish detergent and a bottle of Listerine. Mix together a cup of the detergent and a cup of mouthwash in your quart hose-end jar (the twenty-gallon one) and fill the balance of the jar with water and let it rip; twenty gallons covers 2500 square feet. That's like taking double the dose of medicine to begin treating a disease—it weakens the disease agents' resistance, so that when you apply a dry disease control or liquid disease control, they will react much faster.

If I've learned nothing else about counseling the home gardener in twenty years, I've learned not to put into print any recommendation for using specific chemicals. Over 60 percent of those I recommended in the original *Plants Are Like People* have changed, been discontinued, or are outlawed. Don't panic! I *will* give you a categorical control recommendation, which means that whether you're reading this for the first time in 1992 or 2050, the current chemical might change but the category won't.* All lawn disease can be prevented or controlled with either a dry disease control or a liquid disease control. Both types are expensive and should be used *as recommended*, not double dosed or half dosed.

Your very first step, however, should be to consider all of the possibilities before you begin treatment. Treating fungus diseases can be expensive, my friend, since you use the same type of medicine on the lawn as your doctor uses to cure a fungus you might get. Check the disease descriptions below to determine what ails your lawn. Or take a turf sample to your local nurseryman or county extension agent to be sure of what you've got.

Last, but not least, check for insect damage, which might be the cause of spots, specks, patches, and bruises. The next section tells you how to check.

Here's my ten-least-wanted list for lawn diseases.

Leaf spot: This attacks Kentucky bluegrass in the early spring and fall when the weather is cool and

*I'm as earth-friendly as the next guy, but sometimes you've just *got* to use chemicals for the life of your garden—and this is one of those times.

damp. Reddish brown to purplish spots appear on the leaf stem. Wash your lawn with liquid dish soap and water following the instructions on page 7. Remove grass clippings and stop heavy feedings until the lawn is cured.

Fading out: This attacks fescues, Kentucky blue, Merion blue, and bent grass lawns. It occurs in hot, humid weather. Lawns having this disease begin to turn yellow-green, as though they need iron or a good fertilizing. Dethatch and aerate your lawn, then shampoo following instructions on pages 5–9.

Brown patch: Brown patch attacks St. Augustine grass, rye, Kentucky and Merion blue, fescue, bent, and centipede grasses. It occurs in humid regions during hot, wet weather right after a heavy application of fertilizer as it attacks lush new growth. The grass will turn a brownish color in narrow streaks. Do not feed during hot, wet weather; water early in the day.

Rust: Rust attacks Merion and Kentucky bluegrass in the late summer, when heavy dew is present, and continues until frost. Reddish brown or yellow-orange pustules develop on the leaf and stem. To control, shampoo as directed on page 7.

Grease spot: This attacks 'most all grasses on poorly drained soil. It is most noticeable in the early morning when you can see circular spots, black in color and slimy, on the lawn. Cut down on your watering and apply gypsum as on page 49.

Dollar spot: Attacks bent grass and fescue in the humid northern part of the country, but also occurs farther south and in northern California. It occurs in cool, wet weather and on turf that is low in nitrogen. The grass will look bleached out, like it's been damaged by a dull lawnmower blade. When the disease is at its peak, a white web will be visible on the grass early in the morning when the dew is on the lawn. Shampoo with liquid dish detergent, and water as on page 7.

Snow mold: This disease naturally attacks the grasses of the North. Greenskeepers dread it, as it loves the bent grasses, although it also attacks most of the blue grasses. It occurs when snow covers the turf for a long period of time under drifts and where poor surface drainage is present. Snow mold looks like cotton on the leaves, or a slimy, pink growth. Apply gypsum in the fall and feed heavily in October with Milorganite. Aerate and shampoo as on page 5.

Toadstools: These will grow wherever decayed organic material is buried. Tree stumps, builders' refuse, and peat moss deposits are some of the toadstools' food supplies. To control, you should, if possible, remove the source of food. Next, punch holes eight to ten inches deep all around the area and water well. Spray with a cup of liquid dish detergent to twenty gallons of water and follow with a spraying of turf fungicide, applied directly down the holes. At least two applications will be necessary.

Fairy rings: These occur coast-to-coast, border-to-border, and get to about all the grasses. The rings continue to expand two to three feet a year, with toadstools growing at the edges of the ring. To attempt control, punch lots and lots of holes eight to ten inches deep inside the circle and half the distance to the outside. Now apply the powdered laundry soap program on page 8.

Fusarium blight: This nasty, tenacious little tyke is a new troublemaker on the block and can, within a short time and with little effort, wipe out the best of the bluegrass lawns. Prevention is to feed well, and keep the lawn from drying out. At the first sign of enlarged brown spots, which go deep into the soil, shampoo with the mouthwash and soap solution. Repeat regularly.

In the case of lawn diseases, it is an absolute must to do everything possible to prevent their emergence, as the cure is costly and slow.

INSECT CONTROL

What's a body to do? You work hard to maintain a good-looking lawn, and just when it looks its best, wham! A brown spot appears here, a yellow patch there. It seems you can't win.

Hold on! Winners never quit and quitters never win. When you're fighting the insect armies you must keep this slogan in mind at all times. In order to better fight your enemies, the lawn insects, you must realize one thing: they appreciate you a lot more than you do them. As a matter of fact, they're probably your greatest admirers and praise your abilities to all of their friends. After all, good, strong, healthy bugs wouldn't think of eating tough old diseased grass and roots when they can have the best at your expense—you grow healthy, tender foliage to provide them with gourmet delights. The healthier and better-looking your lawn is, in other words, the more inviting it is to all the bugs in the neighborhood.

By this time you're thinking, "To hell with a good-looking lawn. I think I'll tear the whole thing up, pour concrete, and paint it green." Many a home gardener has had this thought but soon passed it up when he discovered he could win the battle.

At the risk of repeating myself: good cultural

practices must be adhered to if you're to win. Dethatch, aerate, mow, water, and shampoo.

Remember when parents used to wash a child's mouth out with soap? Well, try that on garden bugs. Believe me, it's just as effective. Pests and people both like things that taste good and neither likes the taste of soap in any way, shape or form. Therefore, it is absolutely necessary that you use mild shampoo on a regular basis to discourage the return of the insects. See page 8 for the routine.

By applying lawn and garden gypsum, which I have described as being the "Hadacol" of the garden kingdom, you deal those unwanted visitors even more discomfort. Gypsum has a considerable amount of natural sulphur, which acts as a preventive insecticide in the soil in spring and fall.

Soon the word will go out throughout the insect kingdom that you're a mean host who grows bitter foliage. It doesn't matter where you live or what kind of lawn you have, gypsum and soap will act to safely keep insects away without harming the environment.

"Stop trying to solve fly-swatter problems with an atom-bomb control."

From time to time it will be necessary to use some chemical control. Before you use any chemical control, be sure it's really necessary: isolate your problem and really dig into it. Dig up some affected turf and soil and really look at the bug. Don't just take someone else's word for what's causing your problem simply because he once had a spot or brown patch he thought was like yours and that turned out to be insect damage. It could be one of the other problems that I've already acquainted you with. If you don't know for sure, you could treat for the wrong thing with the wrong chemical, destroying all your hard work. Why endanger your health or that of your pets or the birds by using a chemical control when you don't need one?

Now, treat your problem! Go to your local nurseryman with the intruder in a jar and confirm your identification if there's the least bit of doubt in your mind. Ask him for a recommendation as to what chemical will be necessary to treat the problem. Then read every single word on the label, including the copyright symbol. Buy only enough of any chemical for the present application. Don't buy for the future. When applying a chemical control, use it only at the strength described. You see? We don't treat the plant world any differently from the way we would treat ourselves—and we'd be foolish to self-prescribe an overdose.

After I've identified an insect infestation on a lawn, I follow these steps:

1. I remove the thatch in the infected area and for the same distance beyond.
2. I aerate the area with golf shoes and a pointed stick or other sharp object.
3. I water lightly.
4. I shampoo the area.
5. I apply the chemical control prescribed exactly as recommended.
6. I cover the treated area with a weighted down thin mesh cloth, like cheesecloth, to discourage pets and birds from entering the area.
7. I keep adults and children from the area.

I follow these steps to protect the plant area—it's weak and ill and needs rest just like any other patient—and to protect any visitors that wander by.

Because I haven't come out against hard pesticides, I'll probably get many letters and cards from would-be conservationists and self-styled do-gooders who don't practice what they preach but live by the adage, "Do as I say, not as I do." I have received so many preprinted cards berating the hard pesticides, some signed and some not, that I could probably give next year's supply free to all the sending organizations by returning what I've got.

We use—and abuse—medicines on ourselves and our loved ones, day in and day out, in the form of both patented and prescribed medicine. We bally-hoo their benefits through advertisements in the press, on TV and over the radio. Take "Aspirin A," or drink "Solution B," or take "Zap" and sleep better. Any one of these, I am sure, can be misused and dangerous. Why isolate DDT for attack when it's increased the yield per acre over the years so that we now feed millions more than we did formerly? The so-called hard pesticides have provided us with many benefits over time. Banning them outright is like throwing the baby out with the bathwater. But I'll leave this subject to you to decide.

When you have an insect problem and must use a chemical control, you'll be dealing with one of two types. The first is a *contact* killer, which paralyzes the insect on contact. The second is a *stomach poison*, and this the insect must eat. Both are sold under the category of soil insect controls; some will be recommended for lawns, some for food gardens, and some for nonfood gardens. They are available in dry form or liquid.

When it becomes necessary to use a soil insect control, make sure you first treat your lawn with the bar laundry soap solution with tobacco juice added (see page 7). If these fail, move on to the flea and tick shampoo. Always add any chemical spray to one of the soap solutions when you do use it.

In the last few years, the wisdom of Grandma Putt, Sid Trueheart, and the other wise old garden-ers I trained under has been heralded as a scientific breakthrough, not just a crazy old witches' brew.

Using predator insects, parasites, and other natural organisms instead of chemical controls has come to be an everyday practice, recommended even by its former critics. Bacillus thuringiensis is the best and safest caterpillar killer. Bacillus popilliae, known as milky spore, controls grubs for up to five years. If biological controls like Grub Attack are available, try them first. Only if they can't cure the disease should you go to chemical controls.

BE AN ALERT GARDENER

If you're alert when you're working on your lawn, you can detect trouble when it first begins and treat a small problem with as small an amount of chemical as is necessary. If you wait and hope, or expect it to go away by itself, you're asking for a much larger problem that will need much more expensive and time-consuming control over a larger area.

I'm reminded of the story my Grandma Putnam told me of the Indian brave who would not stamp out a small fire for fear of burning his new moccasins. He ran for help from a brave with old, worn moccasins. When they returned the little fire had grown into a big one that neither could stamp out. His moccasins did not burn, but his tepee burned to the ground with all his blankets and skins for clothes. Grandma Putnam reckons he was the first American to go south for the winter—without furs.

Fire is a good thing when used properly. Medicine is a lifesaver when used properly. Both are killers when abused. In the same way, when properly used, pesticides account for our agricultural abundance and our good health through the control of disease-spreading insects.

Remember, any of the dry or liquid insect controls will more effectively control insect damage if you use the liquid dish detergent, flea and tick shampoo, or bar laundry soap plus tobacco juice spray first, mix the chemical into the spray mixture, or wash it in with the soap solution.

CONTROLLING SURFACE INSECTS

INSECTS	DAMAGE	AREA TO TREAT
Ants	May sting or bite. Attracted to food served outdoors.	Treat soil surface or individual mounds. Wash into soil after application.
Armyworms	Feed on blades of grass near soil surface.	Treat lawn surface with garden soil.
Box elder bugs	Do not damage grass but travel over lawns to enter homes and garages where bugs congregate.	Spray or dust basement and living areas as well as box elder tree trunks and plants.
Centipedes	Live in lawns, but do not damage grass. Some species have a painful bite.	Treat lawn surface.
Chiggers	Bite causes severe itching and raises a welt.	Treat lawn surface.
Chinch bugs	Feed on grass blades.	Treat lawn surface.
Cutworms	Feed on blades of grass, cutting them off at soil surface.	Treat lawn surface.
Earwigs	Travel over lawns to enter homes. Annoying pests.	Treat lawn surface and trash areas, along foundations, and around compost heaps.

INSECTS	DAMAGE	AREA TO TREAT
Grasshoppers	Eat blades of grass.	Treat lawn surface.
Lawn moths (Sod webworms)	Fly over lawn depositing eggs, which later hatch into damaging larvae.	Treat lawn surface.
Millipedes	Live in lawns, but do not damage grass. Annoying pests.	Treat lawn surface.
Mosquitoes	Hide and may breed in lawns that collect water or trash areas.	Treat lawn surface, shrubs and other foliage, low spots.
Slugs	Annoying pests. Do not damage grass but may damage garden plants.	Treat lawn surface.
Snails	Same as slugs.	Treat lawn surface.
Spiders	May hide in or travel over lawn. Some species have painful or poisonous bites.	Treat lawn surface and other areas in which spiders are observed.
Ticks	Live in lawns and attach themselves to passing humans and animals. Some species carry disease.	Treat lawn surface.

CONTROLLING SOIL INSECTS

INSECTS	DAMAGE	CONTROL
Ants	Make unsightly mounds and bare spots.	For overall treatment, apply on soil surface and along runways for most varieties of small ants. For carpenter ants and other nest-forming ants, locate the nest and saturate the nest area with a Dursban formulation.
Asiatic garden beetle larvae	Stunt or kill grass in patches by feeding on roots.	Apply to surface of soil. Water-in thoroughly.
European chafer larvae	Feed on roots of grass, causing patches of stunted or dead grass to appear in lawn.	Apply to soil surface and water-in to the upper two inches of soil. Heavier applications are necessary if the soil is compact and/or infestations are extremely heavy. Refer to additional information under the heading "Soil Insects."
Japanese beetle larvae	Same as European chafer larvae.	Same as European chafer larvae.
Mole crickets	Feed on underground portions of plants. Tunnel through the ground, leaving raised burrows on surface of the soil.	Water lawn before application to make mole crickets move around in soil. Then apply to soil surface.
Sod webworm	Feed on grass blades. May cut grass and pull it down into their burrows in the soil. Damage results in uneven grass, dying back of new shoots, and irregular brown spots.	Water lawn thoroughly before treatment. Apply to soil surface. Do not water again for several days.
White fringed beetle larvae	Feed on grass roots. Result in brown, dead patches of grass.	Apply to soil and water-in thoroughly.

SEED SELECTION— PICK A WINNER!

For some people, picking the right kind of grass seed for a lawn is just like picking a horse at the race track. If they like the name, that's what they plant. The result is usually the same in both cases—they run last. Or, you can always find a "tout" handy to give you a little free advice. Sometimes it's very costly advice, because this horse usually finishes out of the money. If the tout was so sure, he would bet on the horse himself.

The lawn tout is the vendor of the super-duper seed blend that he's selling at rock-bottom prices. He implies it's so powerful that it'll soon burst the seams of the bag it's in, it wants to grow so bad. But when you let it out to "run," it only lies there or runs down the sewer with the first rain, because it won't sprout in the soil.

Be a grass seed handicapper. Study the performance record and the breeding. Stick with thoroughbreds; they win more often. No matter where you live or move to, you'll find that a certain strain is a real standout, the growing champion of that area. That's the one for you.

When you've decided what variety will grow best in your area and your soil (for this you will need to know the drainage of your soil and how much sun and shade the lawn gets), look for the action. Avoid buying grass seed or blends where they would not be likely to be found: drug stores, gas stations, liquor stores, and so on. (I've even had a barber try to hustle me on a special buy he got.) I'm not saying that these people are not honest; it's just that in most cases, they don't know that much about what they're selling. It could be old, or suffer from poor germination, high weed count or some other lame leg.

I suggest that you go to a garden center or the garden section of a reputable merchant who has a specialist buying for him. Read the labels. The germination label is attached to the individually packaged seed and is (or should be) hanging on the bulk seed bin or bag. This special label will tell you the whole breeding record of the seed, much as the pony players' scratch sheet does for horses.

Germination: The percentage figure indicates what percentage of the seeds in the bag will sprout. You want as close to 100 percent as possible.

Purity: This number tells you what percentage of the seed is true to its name. Again, get as close to 100 percent as possible.

Other grasses: This can be a real problem if you get the wrong grasses, especially tall fescue. Here you want as close to 0 percent as possible.

Weed count: This is really a big, bad wolf. Be careful and again get as close to 0 percent as possible. And lastly, inert material: this is chaff and shells.

Not all lawns are started from seed. Some begin as plugs of grass, sprigs, or runners. Bermuda grass, some of the bents, St. Augustine grass, and zoysia are planted from small plants and sprigs.

Dichondra, which is used as a lawn in California, is not a grass but a ground cover, akin to the morning glory. It can be grown from seed or plugs. Dichondra is reasonably easy to take care of but can keep you hopping if cutworms get a foothold.

When seeding a new lawn, I highly recommend

that you use seed with as high a percentage as possible of the permanent variety you've selected. I do not recommend that you buy a premixed blend: I would rather you do the mixing yourself. The same holds true when reseeding an old lawn. In the case of overseeding an established lawn, it's important that you use only the variety you're trying to match up: Kentucky blue to Kentucky blue, for instance. When overseeding in the Southwest, some of the South, and southern California, you will use an annual grass and not a blend, since it's going to die come the hot weather.

No matter what you do, though, it's a sad fact of life that you can bury the purest seed, one with the highest germination and lowest weed count, with no other grasses and not an ounce of inert matter. You can sow it into the richest soil and still not get a single blade of grass. Grass, as you will discover, has a mind of its own, just like some horses that tolerate the jockey on their backs but run their own races. They know when it's time to run, and they know how. Grass knows when it's time to grow and how, and if you rush it, it'll balk. August 15 to September 20, give or take a few days, is the best time to sow seed in most every location of this big, beautiful land of ours, as this is the beginning of the harvest moon. You can go up to October 15 in the West, South, and Southwest. The stars are in the right places and Mother Nature is calm and happy. The evenings are beginning to cool and more moisture is in the air. Now your new lawn will get up and grow!

But grass, like horses and people, can be fooled and made to do something out of the ordinary. You can put blinders on a horse and lead him almost anywhere. People? Well, they put blinders on themselves and walk anywhere. Grass seed is no different. If you want to patch a dead spot or speed up germination of a slow seed type like Merion, you must fool it into thinking it's fall!

To fool grass—and get the garage floor or basement swept—add one cup of water with two tablespoons of brewed tea (not leaves) to each pound of seed, mix well, place in a covered container, and let stand in the refrigerator for five days. Remove from the refrigerator and spread out on the garage or basement floor and allow to dry partially. Sweep up the seed, getting into all the corners and underneath cabinets and chests, being careful to discard glass, nails, or seeds that have soaked up grease. You're now ready to spread this combination of seeds and dirt on your lawn.

You've accomplished two tricks at the same time. First, you've fooled the grass into believing that it woke up late from a cold damp winter and will have to rush out now to take root and grow. Secondly, you've fooled whoever you got to sweep out your garage or basement. He could have dried the damp seed some easier way!

Grandma Putnam used to call these her honey-dew jobs: honey do this and honey do that. She was a sweet soul, and smart, too, eh?

STARTING FROM SCRATCH: BUILDING A NEW LAWN

As the moving van pulls away and you stand on the porch surveying your very own piece of property, you're suddenly struck with a thought. . . . "What am I going to do with this sand patch surrounding me?"

In many cases, as the moving van pulls away it's taking your last buck. When most of us move into a new home, we've used up just about all our savings. Plus, by the time you make the down payment, the closing costs (which no one can figure out), and pay for the gas, water, phone, electric hook-up, and the mower, you're lucky if you can buy a loaf of bread and a quart of milk let alone think about a lawn, trees, shrubs, or flowers. But since you want to build a good reputation in your new neighborhood, you decide to build a lawn. Where do you start and what do you do?

You usually begin by swearing at the builder (whom you don't like anyhow, because you expected the Taj Mahal and he built a house that you're sure isn't as well constructed as the clubhouse you built in the backyard when you were only twelve years old). And now, with your shovel in hand, you begin to dig and find that he must have contracted with the city sanitation department to dump all of the city's old trash in your yard to get what he called a "finished grade," which you figure is the movie location for the Battle of Anzio, because the ruts are so deep. Nonetheless, it is yours, all yours, to do with as you please. But you want to have a beautiful lawn, so simmer down and let's all get at it— you, me, and Mother Nature. By the way, don't expect too much from either her or me. We'll just give a little advice here and there.

Contrary to the beliefs of many, you can have a good, healthy, lush green lawn, no matter what the soil content is—unless there's some chemical present. For instance, sometimes fill is brought from a construction site that had a heavy overflow of gasoline, oil, or a salt deposit. To make sure that

"Grass knows when and how to grow."

this is not the case, smell the soil from several places in your yard. If there are any strange smells you can't identify or that smell like petroleum, go to your local nurseryman and ask if he does soil tests or can get one done for you. If the soil turns out to be dead—by which I mean sterile, where nothing will grow as a result of the presence of a foreign chemical—contact your attorney. This advice has come in handy for many of my clients.

Assuming that all is well, let's proceed. Put down your shovel. You won't need it for a day or two. Begin by picking up every loose object that you can lay your eyes and hands on: stones, bricks, tar paper, lumber scraps, tree stumps, and glass. Don't pass over anything. If just a corner of something is in sight, work it out of the soil or it will haunt you later. (When you're sure you've picked up every rock, stone, and pebble, ask your wife and mother-in-law to look it over. You'll be amazed at what you missed.)

Now I want you to use a lawn spreader to apply fifty pounds of garden gypsum per one thousand square feet of soil to the surface for any soil—clay, sand or loam, it matters not. Next, in snow country, add one hundred pounds of peat moss per one thousand square feet. In the South, Southwest, and West you can use sawdust, leaf mold, or steer manure in the same proportions. Finally, add fifty pounds of any garden food with a low nitrogen content; 4:12:4 or 5:10:5 will do nicely. You don't want a big burst of growth; you want fat grass and healthy roots.

Here is where you'll have to stretch your budget. Rent a power tiller to thoroughly grind up the soil and the material you've spread on top. Work all this down to a depth of six to ten inches. Till back and forth, then crisscross the area. When that's done, go over the same area from corner to corner and crisscross that also. The secret is to get the soil ground as fine as possible—it will save you a lot of hand work.

Before you do anything else, take the rented machine back. I have received thank-you's galore for that simple suggestion. Remember, the rent goes on whether you use it or not, and you're done using it.

You may now pick up the shovel and begin to work on your grade. Work the soil up around the foundation of your home, garage, sidewalks, drives, flower beds, and trees. This is to force runoff away from foundations and hard surfaces and give you proper drainage. Look around. Any high mounds should be shaved, and any low pockets should be filled.

Getting the proper grade is going to take a little further effort on your part. I suggest that you see if you can find an old bedspring from a local junk dealer or, perhaps, a neighbor. It won't hurt to ask. Tie a rope to the springs as you would to the front of a sled; make it long enough so you can put the rope around your waist and walk with the bedsprings but it won't whack against your heels. Now walk in a large circle, overlapping the rows as you go. Continue to drag, stopping only to fill in or shave off spots. When you're perfectly satisfied that the grade is level and runs away from trees, beds, buildings, and drives, take up your rake. Begin from the house and other buildings, trees, beds, and walks, raking to the lowest point of the property all the stones and clods of earth that have not been broken up.

You're now ready to seed. If it's late August or early September (even a bit later in the South or Southwest), you don't need to soak and refrigerate your seed but I always do, however, to give myself an advantage in germination. Just plan the seed venture a week ahead, and if the seed has to stay in the refrigerator a day or so longer, it won't hurt. Make sure that you dry the seed only enough so it will separate. (See pages 46–47 for all the details.) The quantity of seed can be determined from the grass seed table (see pages 56–57).

I've always found that hand broadcasting does the best job spreading grass seed. First, check the wind direction by throwing a few small scraps of paper into the air. Then walk back across the property with your back to the wind, throwing the seed out ahead of you. When you've covered the area, then go back and rebroadcast cross-wind. You've then crisscrossed and laid down a heavy cover.

Seed has been spread, so then use the back of a bow rake to cover the seed just enough to discourage the birds from taking it and the wind from blowing it away. Next, with an empty roller, roll the area to make the seed come in contact with the soil. Do not use a full, heavy roller or you'll compact the soil; if you do that you can kiss your lawn good-bye before it even gets a start. Watering is the only thing left to do in order to get your lawn started. Keep the newly seeded soil moist at all times, watering in the early morning. During warm, windy weather, you may have to sprinkle several times a day. Moisten, do not soak or drench the area, or the seed will wash away.

Cutting will begin as soon as the new grass is one and a half to two inches in height. Mow with a sharp blade to a height of one and one-half inches.

Feed the new lawn as soon as it has been cut four times. Use a lightweight, nonburning, balanced lawn food, and then continue on a normal lawn program as outlined in this chapter.

When planting stolons, sprigs, or small plants, I find that I get a better start and hold if I dip the

"If you wonder whether a gardener's work is ever done, the answer is no. But my gardening is a labor of love, not a boring burden."

roots into water before I place them in the ground. When planting the warm grasses, I do not plant in straight lines; I make odd, uneven patterns and plant extremely heavily. When you purchase grass stolons, buy about 25 percent more than is recommended. Water, mow, and feed just like a seeded lawn.

FACELIFTING: REBUILDING AN OLD LAWN

For one reason or another, a lawn can get old. We won't even bother to ask why, but, like a plastic surgeon, we can take the sag out of an old face and make it look as good as new.

If you've just moved into a home and the lawn has been neglected, or if you suddenly get interested in a little home gardening, here's a good way to get started.

The best time to rebuild is in the fall, around September, just after the children have returned to school. This will give the lawn even odds for survival—without the pounding of little feet. Refrigerate your seed at this time (see page 47).

Begin by either renting a power renovator or purchasing a roto-rake bar that converts your rotary lawn mower into a dethatching machine. Go over your entire lawn using the crisscross method. Then rake up all of the debris that the machine brings to the surface, power rake it again, and remove the balance of the thatch.

Apply fifty pounds of gypsum per two thousand square feet, and follow with an application of low-nitrogen lawn food. Some of these foods are called Winter Green or Winter Survival, but any will do. Apply at the recommended rate.

Overseed the rebuilt lawn at the same rate as a new lawn, referring to the chart for seed and rate recommendations (see pages 56–57). Remember, your seed has been, or should be, germinated first for a week in the refrigerator.

After you've overseeded, apply a thin top dressing of half soil, half peat to the lawn area and roll with an empty roller just to make contact.

Water lightly with a solution of an ounce liquid dish detergent to ten gallons of water over two thousand square feet to insure penetration and prevent compaction of the top dressing.

When new grass is two inches tall, mow and remove the clippings. Continue to mow until the grass stops growing.

Crabgrass control can begin in early March in the North and in February in the West and South. Use any of the locally recommended pre-emergent chemicals and apply as recommended.

Begin a normal and well-planned lawn program in the spring and continue to follow it to a successful lawn.

NEW BLOOD SEEDING

• •

There have been many discussions among gramonologists (grass specialists) as to the advisability of introducing strangers to an existing lawn.

Some say you're asking for trouble because the new seed can carry diseases to the healthy grasses already there. Others argue that if you don't add new seed, the old will become weak from inbreeding.

I believe that plants communicate with each other—that they discuss the events of the day. And I believe that after so many years of living with each other in the same spot, they run out of conversation and get bored with the same old faces day in and day out. Consequently, they become short-tempered with each other, like children who've been cooped up all winter, and they begin to squabble over little things.

When you overseed, you bring a stranger into the neighborhood from another part of the country with tales of new places: Oregon, Washington, or any of a number of places where grass seed is grown. The old grasses soon make new friends, learn some new ideas, and, perhaps, change fashions.

And then there's romance. There might just be a tall, dark, and handsome stranger in the crowd. After all, grass doesn't just happen, although I will admit that some of the grass babies do arrive by stork. Also by pigeon, sparrow, crow, and most other birds. But while the babies arrive this way, so do hoboes like crabgrass, quack grass, and other unwelcome visitors. When you pick your lawn's friends, there is a much better chance that they will be compatible. For this reason alone I recommend overseeding.

Overseeding is best done in the fall when you'd do new seeding: August 15 to September 20 in snow country, and August 15 to October 15 in the West, South, and Southwest. Prepare the seed as you would for new seeding (see page 47).

Before overseeding the cool grasses, you should follow these few rules:

1. Mow the lawn before you start this project.
2. Dethatch. Remove all old grass clippings and

accumulated debris with the use of a lawn groom rake for the small lawn. The roto-rake bar, the conversion unit for your rotary lawn mower, or a power rake (which you can rent) should be used on larger lawns. Work the whole lawn back and forth in one direction and collect the debris.

3. Sow the seed by hand at half the rate recommended in the seed chart. Overseed with the same variety you're trying to build up. Don't use a blend or mix but the purest seed with the best germination rate you can possibly buy. Do not buy any bargains, even though you may be turning down a real steal.

If you have an all-American lawn, a little of everything, then you can buy a blend, but make sure the germination factor is the highest you can get. After all, even if we buy weed seed, we want to know how much of it is going to grow.

If you're overseeding Bermuda or any of the warm grasses for winter color, germinate the seed by refrigerating it as on page 47. Use the best rye grass seed you can buy.

Dichondra lawns, more than any other, need an annual filling in to keep a nice, bright color and replace the plants that die out.

4. Top dress the turf area if it's sparse. Use a mixture of half garden soil and half peat moss. Spread the top dressing over the area at a rate of about one-eighth of an inch; I know that's pretty thin, but that's all that will be needed.

5. Feed the lawn and new seed with a low-nitrogen fertilizer, one of the Winter Green or Winter Guard types will do nicely.

6. Water well, but not heavily. As a matter of fact, until the new grass sprouts, which should be in a week or less, only dampen the lawn in the early morning. After the grass has sprouted, water three to four inches a week.

SEED TABLE

	RATE PER 1000 SQUARE FEET	APPEARANCE	LOCATION AND USE
Bluegrass species			
Kentucky bluegrass (Poa pratensis)	2 pounds	Medium green; medium texture.	Full sun, will tolerate light shade.
Merion bluegrass (Poa pratensis)	1 pound	Dark green; medium texture.	Full sun, will tolerate light shade.
Rough stalk meadow (Poa trivialis)	2 pounds	Light green; shiny leaf.	Shade; wet.
Fescue species			
Chewings fescue (Festuca rubra, var. fallax)	3 pounds	Medium green; fine texture.	Shade, poor or dry sandy soil.
Creeping red fescue (Festuca rubra)	3 pounds	Medium green; fine texture.	Sandy soil.
Tall Fescue (Festuca elatior)	6–10 pounds	Light green; coarse, striated leaf.	Athletic fields, very heavily used areas; coarse, striated leaf.
Bent grass species			
Astoria bent (Agrostis tenuis)	½–1 pound	Bright green; fine texture.	Sun and light shade.
Highland bent (Agrostis tenuis)	½–1 pound	Dark green; fine texture.	Sun and light shade.

	RATE PER 1000 SQUARE FEET	APPEARANCE	LOCATION AND USE
Seaside creep-ing bent (*Agrostis maritima*)	1/2–1 pound	Medium green; fine texture.	Sun and light shade.
Penncross creeping bent (*Agrostis palustris*)	1/2–1 pound	Medium green; fine texture.	Sun and light shade.
Redtop (*Agrostis alba*)	1–1 1/2 pounds	Medium green; medium texture.	Used in mixtures.
Rye grass species			
Annual rye grass (*Lolium multiflorum*)	3–4 pounds	Medium green; coarse texture.	Temporary lawns and in mixtures.
Perennial rye grass (*Lolium perenne*)	3–4 pounds	Dark green; coarse, shiny leaf.	Temporary lawns and in mixtures.
Nonseed species			
Bermuda (*Cynodon dactylon*)	1 sprig	Medium green; coarse texture.	Sun; dry.
St. Augustine (*Stenatophrum secundatum*)	2 plugs	Medium green; coarse texture.	Sun; dry.
Zoysia varie-ties (*Zoisia*)	1 plug	Medium green; coarse texture.	Sun; dry.

7. Do not mow for at least seven days. Be sure to pick up the clippings.

Some of you who've heard that a lawn can get too thick, but there isn't a golf superintendent who wouldn't like to have that problem. If you dethatch and aerate each fall as I recommend, your lawn will be fat and sassy.

INSTANT LAWN: SODDING

· ·

In the last few years, the pregrown lawn trade has become a billion-dollar business. This affluent generation, seeming to want instant results in everything, rushes out and buys sod because it seems like the answer to an instant, trouble-free lawn. I am by no means criticizing this attitude if you can afford it, but I do find fault with a great number of new homeowners who go to the expense of having a full-grown, mature landscape job done on their new homes. They begin with sod and end by planting fifteen- to twenty-foot trees. Then they let the whole works become diseased or die because they don't know how or want to take care of their "instant landscape" after they get it.

If you truly want to get involved with the good earth, preserve what we have, and repair or replenish what we've abused and neglected in the past, then I'll go along with anything you want to do in gardening. But to think that something like sod comes to you as a full-grown adult and can take care of itself—that grinds me no end.

Sod is the flesh of the earth; putting in sod is comparable to doing a skin graft. Before the surgeon applies a skin graft to the human body, he removes the old and dead flesh. He repairs any other damage and makes any structural changes that are needed. Then he takes patches of flesh from another part of the body that are as similar as possible to the area that needs repairs and grafts them. You'll need to do much the same in laying sod.

If you're planning to lay sod instead of sow seed, first you must make up your mind what kind of grass you want. Find what grass works best in your area.

There are many kinds of sod available, and the prices will vary for various reasons. And, yes, you can be had, just as you can with seed. Here are a couple of ways they can get you. In a new subdivision, a truck will pull up, or a man dressed in work clothes will knock on your door and say that they're just finishing up a big apartment complex and have some good sod left over. He'll sod your lot for only sixty-five cents a roll, including labor. Now let me tell you, McGee, that ain't a bad deal in anybody's book, but you don't have the lot graded.

Well, the man has his equipment there, so for twenty-five dollars he'll grade it for you. Oh, what a deal! For whom? Here's what you get. Ten minutes later, the tractor arrives, drops the grading blade and levels off the lawn. They don't pick up the builder's debris or stones, they just push it around until it falls into a rut somewhere or just gets hidden. They don't build up your grade away from the house, trees, buildings, and drives. They don't add compost, feed, or sod containers to the weak soil for good rotting action.

Next the truck arrives with about four helpers and the driver, and they begin to unroll and unload the sod so fast that you get dizzy just watching; but you can't smell a rat yet, eh?

What they are or could be laying in your yard

is a "buy out." This is a stand of sod that may, for instance, have been grown on a peat or muck bog where a weed infestation occurred. To control that kind of infestation, the grower would have had to destroy or remove the sod. So the grower offered it for sale at some ridiculous price, from a nickel to fifteen cents a roll, and the buyer had to cut and load it himself. The grower also stays close by when it's being cut to make sure that the buyer doesn't cut too much topsoil with the sod. So you could get thinly cut, weed-infected turf that isn't worth the powder to blow it to hell. The men end up by sweeping the walk, turning on your sprinklers, and telling you to keep it wet. You pay the dough by cash or check and feel great. In the meantime, the operator goes to your bank to cash your check.

Here is what you end up with. Because of the poor grade job, water runs into your basement; the buried treasure that they didn't remove will rot or work through the turf; the ruts will settle, and you'll have an uneven lawn with waterpockets. They didn't roll the sod, so it separates and dries out and dies on the ends. So, all in all, what deal?

If you're going to buy sod, buy from a reputable dealer. Next, prepare the lawn exactly the way you would for seeding a new lawn—including rolling, watering for the first week, mowing when the grass is one and a half inches tall, feeding when the lawn's been cut four times, and continuing a regular lawn program. (See pages 25–26 for all the details.)

To determine how many rolls of sod you'll need for your yard, multiply the length of your lot by its width. Subtract the area of buildings and walks and divide by nine. The result is how many rolls to buy.

FIRST-AID

In the last twenty years I have been asked thousands upon thousands of questions on lawn care and problems all over the world. What it all boils down to is that I want you to learn to face lawn and garden problems as an everyday occurrence and realize that Murphy's law is always in effect. But don't panic. And don't rush to weed, feed, prune, mow, or douse. Instead look for the obvious reasons a plant might be in trouble:

1. Recent sprays of weed killer or other chemicals on your or neighboring property.
2. Physical damage to limbs, trunk, roots, or foliage.
3. Overfeeding.
4. Bug bites on foliage or holes in trunk.
5. Unusual discoloration of foliage.

Before you call or write me or take any other action:

1. Give the plant a bath with children's shampoo; use a tablespoonful in a gallon of water.
2. Sprinkle a mixture of 25 percent Epsom salts and 75 percent bone meal on the soil beneath the affected plant or tree.
3. In the quart jar of your hose-end sprayer, mix together:

1 capful of liquid fish fertilizer
1 can of beer
¼ teaspoon of instant tea granules
¼ cup flea and tick shampoo
1 ounce of hydrogen peroxide

Fill the jar with household ammonia and a capful of whiskey. Spray the soil beneath the affected plant, tree, shrub, or over lawn that is in trouble and all its friends as well.

4. Relax. Now you've done everything humanly possible.

STEP-BY-STEP LAWN CARE ....

SPRING
....

Step 1. Clean up the lawn and the area under trees, shrubs, and evergreens. Remove this lawn and garden material to the unspaded garden areas for spading in as soon as weather permits.

Step 2. Lower your mower blade to a height just above new grass growth. Mow and collect the clippings, which go on the soil as a mulch for perennials, shrubs, and evergreens.

Step 3. If thatch buildup is extremely heavy, either rent a dethatching machine or have your local landscaper do the job. There are several roto-rake blade attachments available that cut, dethatch, and bag all at the same time. They're good; I have one and love it. But they don't fit all mowers.

Step 4. Always wear *golf shoes* when walking on the lawn to penetrate the invisible barrier called surface tension, which kills more lawns and gardens than any bug or disease infestation by preventing necessary food, moisture, fresh air, and chemicals from getting to the roots. Use *aerating lawn sandals* when deep penetration is needed.

Step 5. If you want a truly attractive and comfortable lawn area, have your lawn power plugged every other spring. Plugs two and a half to three inches long and half an inch wide are removed.

Step 6. If your lawn was plugged, mow over the soil cores on the surface to break them up.

Step 7. If you're as into gardening as I am, you'll test the soil of your lawn area (not just of gardens and beds) to better understand their overall health condition. Use a 1601 Rapid Test kit to measure pH and amounts of nitrogen, phosphorus, and potash. Any home gardener can use this simple but professional soil-testing kit, understand the results, and make any necessary adjustments.

Step 8. If your test results call for lime, add it now and wait three weeks to feed. (Lime counters acidity in the soil.)

Step 9. If the soil is heavy or if insects were a problem last year, apply gypsum now. Add three cups of diatomaceous earth to fifty pounds of garden gypsum. Broadcast at a medium open setting on your hand-held lawn spreader.

Step 10. If crabgrass or other annual weeds were a problem last year, now is the time to attack them with a pre-emergent weed control, either dry or liquid. If a granular material is used, add a cup of powdered laundry soap to each bag, mix well, and spread. If you use a liquid, add one-half cup of liquid dish detergent to the jar of your hand-held sprayer per twenty gallons of mix.

Step 11. Now overseed bare or thin areas, unless you used the preceding step. You can't seed now if you've used a pre-emergent weed control; you must wait until fall to do any seeding.

Step 12. Purchase seed at least a week before planting and germinate it in your refrigerator according to the directions on page 47. The low temperature speeds up germination.

Step 13. Apply the seed with a hand-held spreader and water it in to force it into contact with the soil.

Step 14. Spring lawn feeding is the most important meal your lawn needs; do it with a dry food. Any lawn food formula will do, but you must add four pounds of Epsom salts to each bag that covers five thousand square feet and then apply it at the medium opening of the hand-held spreader. Epsom salts contain magnesium sulphate and sulphur, which deepen the color, thicken the foliage, increase root growth, and triggers nitrogen.

Step 15. Apply spring tonic over the dry food and Epsom salts. In the quart jar of your twenty-gallon hand-held sprayer—with a white golf ball inside as an agitator—mix:

1 can of beer
1 cup of children's shampoo
or liquid dish detergent

Fill the jar to the top with any household ammonia. (If your lawn has soil insects, use a cup of flea and tick shampoo containing pyrethrum instead of soap or shampoo.) Fill the jar to the top with any household ammonia.

Step 16. Mow after 7 P.M. for your comfort and the lawn's health.

Step 17. Pick up the grass clippings and use them as mulch to keep down weeds and control moisture and temperature in garden and shrub beds.

Step 18. Keep the mower blade sharpened, clean under deck areas, and keep all plastic and rubber surfaces clean.

Step 19. Always wear your golf shoes when walking on your summer lawn.

Step 20. Continue to raise the mower blade as the summer gets warmer, keeping the blade sharp and the mower clean (a soap bath for the mower after you're done keeps it in top working order).

Step 21. Feed your lawn every three weeks with an all-purpose tonic within two days of mowing and before noon. To the quart jar of your twenty-gallon hand-held sprayer with a golf ball inside add:

1 can of beer
1 cup of children's shampoo or liquid dish detergent
½ cup of molasses
1 ounce of liquid seaweed
1 cup of liquid lawn food

Fill to the top with household ammonia. Twenty gallons covers 2500 square feet.

Step 22. Wash your lawn down every two weeks right after you mow in the evening. Mix in the quart jar of your twenty-gallon hand-held sprayer (with a golf ball),

1 cup bar laundry soap solution
1 cup of chewing tobacco juice
1 cup of brown mouthwash (see page 8 for directions)

In twenty gallons of water this solution covers 2500 square feet.

Step 23. Water between 5 and 9 in the morning, preferably with an impulse sprinkler.

FALL

· ·

Step 24. Kill weeds between September 1 and October 1 on a day when the temperature is between 70 and 80 degrees from 1 to 3 in the afternoon. Prewash your lawn with a cup of liquid dish detergent in the quart jar of your twenty-gallon hand-held sprayer (with a golf ball) per twenty gallons of water per 2500 square feet. Mix only the amount of weed killer you will need to kill the weeds. Use a twenty-gallon sprayer that's only used for weed killer; put in an orange golf ball to aid mixing and make it distinctive. Add a tablespoon of dish detergent to the weed killer solution. If liquid weed-and-feed is used, follow all of the same steps. If dry weed-and-feed is your choice, wash the lawn first and apply the weed-and-feed while the lawn is still damp.

Step 25. Overseeding or starting a new lawn is best done from September 1 to October 1. Don't use weed killers if you'll be seeding in the fall.

Step 26. Continue to feed with the all-purpose tonic of step 21 until September 1. Between October 15 and 31 reapply the feeding program in step 14, continuing to mow until the lawn stops growing.

QUESTIONS AND ANSWERS

Q. *What can I do about the damage the neighborhood dogs do to my lawn?*

A. Dog damage or urine burn can be repaired by applying a handful of gypsum to the affected area after scratching up the soil, then reseeding. To prevent this damage, apply gypsum in early spring at a rate of fifty pounds over one thousand square yards where the animals run. You can also add a yeast tablet to your pet's diet once a month.

Q. *What can I do to prevent the lawn damage caused by the salt that the city puts on pavements in the winter?*

A. To prevent salt damage, apply a five-foot-wide band of gypsum around all affected walks and drives. This will preserve the lawn against melting rock salt.

Q. *My lawn has some soggy spots caused by winter damage. What can I do?*

A. Repair soggy spots by cutting through them on three sides of the sod, gently rolling the sod back and filling them with topsoil. Press the soil down firmly, then roll back the sod and press it firmly to the new soil.

Q. *The soil in my yard is extremely sandy. What can I do?*

A. For sandy soil, add gypsum at fifty pounds per one thousand square feet, along with one yard of clay loam per one thousand square feet and all the leaves and grass clippings you can get your hands on. Fill it up.

Q. *It seems as though my yard is only good for making clay pots. Is there anything I can do about it?*
A. For clay soil, add gypsum at fifty pounds per one thousand square feet and one yard of sand per one thousand square feet and all the leaves and grass clippings you can find. Use a cup of children's shampoo per twenty gallons of water and spray the lawn monthly.

Q. *How can I get rid of moles?*
A. Moles are nearly blind, but they have a super-sensitive sense of hearing. You can control them by creating a noise that is offensive to them. To do this, bury wine bottles in the mole runs with the necks sticking out at angles. The wind passing over these sends the noise through the runs. The moles are after grubs that are in your soil. Apply Dursban according to directions to kill the insects. You can also place Pine Sol cleaner, soapy water, hair, rotten onions, Juicy Fruit gum, cottonballs, or moth crystals in their runs to aggravate them.

Q. *How can I correct green moss? Is it a disease?*
A. Green moss is a plant that likes it cool, dark, and damp, so it's usually found in lawns on the north side of trees and buildings where it's the result of lack of sunlight or poor drainage. Punch holes in the area to improve drainage and apply gypsum at fifty pounds per five hundred square feet. Let the sun shine in if possible by thinning a few limbs. It may be necessary to correct the grade or to tile the area if the water problem is too bad. Or you can buy moss killer in the garden shop.

Q. *Parts of my lawn turn dusty white. What causes this and what can I do about it?*
A. Mildew or white dust will appear on the grass blades in a shaded area. Wash this area often and apply turf fungicide—or move the house, tree, or garage!

Q. *I apply large amounts of insecticides to my grub-infested lawn, but nothing seems to work. What am I doing wrong?*
A. Insecticides can be made more effective. First poke holes in the infested area and spray a cup of liquid dish detergent per twenty gallons of water to the area. Add a tablespoon of liquid dish detergent to the chemical mix.

Q. *I have used weed killer in my sprayer. How do I clean it so that it's fit for other uses?*
A. You can't. You can clean out a lawn sprayer, wash it out with lukewarm soapy water, allowing some to spray through the tip. Follow this wash with two tablespoons of baking soda in the quart jar filled with water. Back flush and spray. Paint red stripes on top of the jar with nail polish as a warning that it's a weed killer sprayer, and add an orange golf ball as an agitator. Tape your weed killer bottle to this sprayer, and don't use it for anything else: you can never clean it well enough.

Q. *Is there any way to conquer devil grass?*
A. I have found that the best way to beat it is to join it and make a whole lawn out of it. However, it can also be controlled with 'most any of the spot grass and weed killers plus soap.

Q. *When is the best time to destroy crabgrass?*
A. For some reason, folks seem to think they should destroy the plant, which is a waste of time

and effort. To beat crabgrass, kill the seed before it germinates. In most parts of the country this should be done in February or March. Use a pre-emergent killer, dry or liquid, like Preen.

Q. *Can clover be killed without hurting good grass?*
A. Sure. You can use any one of the chickweed and clover killers on the shelf of your local garden center.

Q. *When is the best time to kill general lawn weeds?*
A. At the time when weeds are growing their best—spring and fall—not when it's hot and dry.

Q. *How long are weed killers good?*
A. As with any garden chemical you use, you should never purchase more than you can use soon. The vapors of 2,4-D weed killer can kill flowers and evergreens without your even opening the bag. There is a whole new family of weed killers that are now environmentally safe *and* effective.

Q. *Should quack grass be dug out, or can I use a spray of some sort?*
A. Dig, dig, dig used to be about the only way, if it's growing in your yard. There are weed killers that can be used for quack grass control in special crops. Check with your nurseryman.

Q. *Can I use the same weed killer to control weeds just offshore at a cottage?*
A. No, no, a thousand times no! Your neighbors might even tar and feather you. Fish can be destroyed by ordinary weed killers. For aquatic weeds use a diquat weed killer, or ask a garden center

operator near a lake, or make a call to the county extension agent.

Q. *I absolutely refuse to use any weed killers on my lawn. They kill birds and our furry friends. What can I use in place of them?*
A. You can feed the lawn extra specially, dethatch, and dig out what few weeds you do have. You can also spot kill with an ounce of vinegar in twenty-six ounces of water.

Q. *Can all weeds be destroyed with one kind of weed killer?*
A. The 2,4-D's in combination can control most broadleaf weeds.

Q. *I just can't afford these expensive fertilizers, but I want a pretty lawn. What can I do?*
A. If you will follow good commonsense cultural practices, like removing grass clippings, shampooing, mowing often, aerating, and feeding a minimum of twice a season, a cheap lawn food will give you passable results. But it does take a well-balanced diet to have a fat and sassy lawn.

Q. *How good is expensive lawn food?*
A. Very good! The more types of nitrogen combined in a lawn food to spread the meal over a long period of time, the longer your lawn will stay a deep green.

Q. *Is liquid lawn food, applied by these lawn companies, worth the money?*
A. A call to the Better Business Bureau will tell you if a particular company is reputable. Of course, having someone else do the work makes it easier. As to the results, I've had just as good luck with

liquid fertilizers as with the dry ones, but the cost is a little higher.

Q. *Is there a good way to spread fertilizer?*
A. You bet your lawn there is. Always use the crisscross method. Apply the dry fertilizers and weed killers in dry form at half the rate recommended, back and forth in one direction, and then the other half back and forth in the other direction.

Q. *What is meant by dormant feeding?*
A. In snow country, you can and should feed as early as possible in the spring. The best time is when there is still a little snow on the ground and more to follow. Feeding then is called dormant feeding.

Q. *Is there any one good formula in a lawn food?*
A. Not really, because different grasses and different soils require different quantities of the basic and special trace elements to grow good grass. I find that the ads in your local paper will soon tell you what formula is needed in your neighborhood.

Q. *How much lime should I feed my grass?*
A. None. Lime is not a food. Lime is merely used to change the acidity of the soil and should only be used if a soil test indicates that your soil is sour.

Q. *How good is good old-fashioned manure for lawn?*
A. Raw, unaged manure is so harsh that it'll burn an established lawn out, and it's full of weeds. Driconure, a commercial product that's a blend of many manures, has been dried and the damaging salts and fertile weed seeds have been destroyed, making it a gentle and effective product. However, raw manure can be used when building a new lawn

because the heat it creates helps the new seed to germinate.

Q. *Can I feed my lawn with a liquid fish fertilizer?*
A. You can, but I'm sure your neighbors would rather you didn't, and I think you'll find it a little too expensive.

Q. *What good is iron, and how often should you use it on the lawn?*
A. Iron builds blood, in humans and in plants. I've found that at least one application a season, just before the hottest part of the summer, keeps the color dark and fresh and eliminates the possibility of chlorisis.

Q. *Do you recommend a sprinkler system?*
A. I sure do if you can afford it and use it properly. A built-in sprinkler system, however, cannot just be left to look out for itself. You must still water early and deep.

Q. *Is irrigation bad for a lawn?*
A. In many of the southwestern states, lawns are irrigated at night. It's a bad way to water, as it causes compaction and carries diseases and weed seed from one lawn to another. I prefer controlled watering with a sprinkler.

Q. *Would it do any good to mix rainwater with my regular tap water for watering my lawn?*
A. I would say so if you didn't cut it down more than fifty-fifty. This can be done with an inexpensive attachment called a hose end.

Q. *How effective is underground watering?*
A. I have seen several systems, and I wouldn't

give you a dime for them. The roots usually end up plugging up the system, or the soil remains soggy.

Q. *How efficient are automatic feeding systems?*
A. Not very. These pieces of equipment are designed for the use of professionals, not that of homeowners.

Q. *I've heard that riding lawn mowers are bad for lawns.*
A. The only person who would say this would be someone who couldn't afford a rider. However, any mower must have a sharp blade.

Q. *How effective and practical would it be to lay drain tile in a lawn area?*
A. If drainage were a real problem, I would say that it would be extremely practical, but I've never found an average home lot that I couldn't improve for a lot less money and work just by altering the grade.

Q. *I have a siphon hose that hooks onto the faucet and meters liquids into my water stream. Can I use a weed killer through this attachment?*
A. Not if you cherish your other plants and your own health. When using any kind of attachment that hooks into your drinking water, be careful. Stop at a plumbing supply shop and purchase a backflow valve, which will keep anything from flowing back into your drinking water. Do not use chemicals through a hose that something or someone might ever drink from.

Q. *I have no one who can turn the water off for me during the day, so I must water at night. What should I use to prevent lawn disease?*
A. Some expensive and strong chemicals. But I

have another suggestion. You can buy an automatic water timer that you can set to start when the sun comes up and then you can shut it off on the way to work. It's a lot less expensive than fighting a sick lawn.

Q. *All professionals have a preference in equipment: baseball players, hockey players, football players, racing drivers, etc. And since their livelihood depends on that piece of equipment, you can be sure that it's the best. Now, what is the best constructed, most efficient, least expensive lawn mower available?*
A. Eight sheep to the acre. The average homeowner or sportsman wouldn't pay what we pay for our equipment because it isn't his livelihood.

Q. *I've been told that it's a good idea to lower the blade of your lawn mower in the fall. Is this true?*
A. As long as the grass is growing, don't change your cutting height. I do, however, recommend that you cut your lawn to a height of one inch in the early spring to cut off the dead, brown grass and to let the new rhizomes through.

Q. *Zoysia grass is called a southern grass, but we receive advertisements saying that it's good for northern zones. Can I use it at my cottage in northern Wisconsin?*
A. It will grow in the North but it'll turn straw brown at the first hint of frost and stay that way until the temperature hits 75 to 80 degrees and stays there. I have a friend who sprays it green. He lives next to you in Wisconsin.

Q. *Will turf dye hurt grass?*
A. Not at all. Turf dye is used more than you can imagine. In the fall of the year, when a pro football

team is sharing the same stadium with a baseball team that is still in action, the turf superintendent uses plenty of grass dye on Monday morning. In most cases it's food coloring. You can also buy a professional product called Links Turf Dye.

Q. *What is Kentucky 31 and where do I use it?*
A. On someone else's lawn. Thirty-one is known in weed circles as tall fescue, and it's a real tough customer to destroy. However, if you live the summer on a lake with lots of child traffic or a play area and want the world's toughest grass, plant Kentucky 31.

Q. *I've heard that it's a good idea to burn off a bad lawn in the fall so that a good one will return. True or false?*
A. Smokey the Bear will haunt you the rest of your days if you miss. I have on occasion used fire, but then, I am very careful. And I only use it where I'm not concerned with the texture of the grass. For this reason it is best used on field grasses only.

Q. *What harm can earthworms do to my lawn?*
A. None, unless you have a bent lawn. Then the nightcrawlers push up little mounds on the turf. I find that when I use a surfactant of shampoo, worms go away but don't die. A tablespoon of lime added to the shampoo also helps.

Q. *Is it true that weeds and lawn diseases are brought to my yard by my landscaper?*
A. A good, well-trained landscaper and maintenance man doesn't have any sick lawns in his care, and if he does, it will usually be the last one tended of the day. And his machines are cleaned that

night. If he isn't well trained and his equipment is dirty, I would change men, because he can transport trouble on his machines.

Q. *If I have a landscape company take care of my yard, what questions can I ask to make sure that I'm not being taken?*
A. None. You wouldn't know if the man was giving you fact or fiction. Enjoy your yard and garden and learn something about your permanent visitors; they know a lot about you. If you make friends with your garden, it'll tell you what ails it.

Q. *Is it true that no one should walk on a lawn when there's snow on the ground?*
A. That's right; when the snow thaws, you can see the footprints where compaction occurred for weeks. This applies to a wet lawn in the East, South, or West.

Q. *Is there any one fungicide that will cure most lawn diseases?*
A. There are so many that I won't even begin the list. I'd only advise you to look on the shelves of your local garden center and ask your nurseryman when you have a problem.

Q. *Can I make my own fertilizer cheaper than I can buy it?*
A. I daresay that you could, but it would be more work than it was worth, unless you were a bull, horse, sheep, or chicken.

Q. *How much eggshell would it take to put calcium into my lawn?*
A. More than the eggshells collected each day for a week in three of the suburbs of any one of our large cities.

Q. *Where is the best place to get information when you have a lawn problem?*
A. This book first, then your local nurseryman, and, third, your county extension agent (check the Yellow Pages).

Q. *How can I keep the water from my swimming pool from killing my grass?*
A. Put a three-foot-wide band of cement where the wet little feet run.

Q. *Can chemicals be used with the same effect in any part of the country?*
A. Yep! They are all the same.

Q. *Should you burn weeds when you cut them down or pull them?*
A. No! Add them to your compost pile along with the grass clippings and leaves.

Q. *Dichondra gets weeds in it just like any other grass. What do we use to get them out?*
A. Dichondra is not a grass but a plant. So to control the weeds, pull them, or look on the shelves for a weed killer for use on dichondra.

Q. *We're having problems with a large bank washing away. Can we plant grass on it to hold it?*
A. There are some ground covers that will hold it better, but I would refrigerate field timothy and clover for germination, and then I would seed during dry weather. Just sprinkle it with water for a few days until it is damp, not wet.

Q. *We have a flying ant problem in our yard every year. What can we use?*
A. Soap and water. If this fails, try flea and tick shampoo.

Q *Is there any difference between cheap grass seed and expensive?*

A. The price, to begin with. Grass seed is a commodity bought, sold, and traded like any other grain and seed. Futures are bought and sold with prices being decided on the basis of availability, which is determined by weather. Good weather produces a good quality, large crop, which generally results in lower prices; bad weather produces smaller quantities for which there is big demand, which forces prices up. If anyone asks you whether you deal in commodities and you own a lawn, you can seriously say yes—grass seed.

Q. *I have seed left over from last year. Is it still good?*

A. As a rule, yes, but to find out for sure, fill a paper, plastic, or Styrofoam cup three-quarters full of water and add a used tea bag for a minute or two. Then sprinkle a teaspoonful of seed on top of the water; set it in a window that gets a lot of light. In a couple of weeks you should see grass. The tea-and-refrigeration method—detailed on page 47—will improve marginal seed performance.

Q. *What can you do to keep the birds off new grass seed until it sprouts?*

A. Adopt six or seven cats. Seriously, though, cover the seed with one quarter inch of topsoil, pat down or roll gently. The faster it sprouts, the more you keep and the less the birds eat. You can also slit an old tennis ball and force it over the end of a six- to seven-foot piece of old garden hose. Draw two mean eyes and a nasty mouth, and place yellow strips of tape like Xs down the hose. Let this lie on the seeded area until the seed sprouts. Why? The birds think it's a snake. Eagles and hawks won't be fooled, but then, they don't eat seed.

Q. *Which blend of grass seed is best for a play area?*
A. Plastic, concrete, and iron, none of which is available yet. In the South you can count on U-3 Bermuda grass, and in the North, Kentucky 31 tall fescue. I want to caution anyone who is planting a play area not to be tempted to add clover seed to these areas to fill in spots as it can cause injuries. Clover is slippery, and when running feet try to stop quickly, clover won't cooperate.

Q. *Which grass seed is best for a shady spot?*
A. None, really. That's not exactly true, but then they haven't developed an Astroturf seed yet. There is no true shade grass; all grasses like some sun. However, the best of the bunch that can get along with less sun than the rest is *Poa trivialis*. Kentucky 31 tall fescue, Zoysia, Japonica, Zoysia matrella, Astoria bent, Highland and Penncross bents, as well as creeping red, Illahee, and Chewings fescue, all will tolerate light shade.

Q. *Which grass seed do you recommend for a really steep embankment?*
A. As a rule, none. It's not that many grasses won't grow and hold on hillsides; it's your safety I'm concerned with. More accidents occur from falls and severe cuts from mowers on hillside maintenance than anywhere else. For your own safety, I would prefer that you plant any of the low- or no-maintenance ground covers.

Q. *What's the toughest grass seed you can think of for a family of five boys and three dogs?*
A. Inverted wire brushes set in concrete and painted green. For something softer, you can depend on Kentucky 31 or Alta, coarse, or Meadow coarse fescue.

Q. *Can I grow a bent grass lawn from seed or must I use plugs?*
A. Positively and without a doubt you can grow it from seed. Be my guest. Astoria, Highland, Penncrooo, or Seaside bents all can be grown from sown seed. Before tackling a bent lawn, though, make sure you understand that they take a ton of work and a special mower.

Q. *What's the difference between all the different rye grasses?*
A. What do you mean all? There's perennial or annual. If you're talking about brand names, they're improved varieties of the same two.

Q. *It may sound funny, but can I have a different type lawn—backyard, retreat area, and putting green all at one home?*
A. Sure, why not? Just remember—sex knows no barrier, and if clippings or seed are transferred from location to location, there's going to be some hanky-panky, with the possibility of a strange lawn born out of wedlock.

Q. *How often do you water new seed?*
A. Enough to keep it damp (moist), so that depends on where you live and when you plant. Remember, I said damp, not soggy wet.

Q. *When do you feed a new lawn?*
A. Before you plant. With a cheap lawn food, set on the lowest spreader setting and till into the soil when you prepare for seed. I feed with a weak liquid solution of lawn or plant food—just enough to change the color of the water in the container of the hand-held sprayer.

Q. *Can you sow grass seed in the winter?*
A. Why not? Remember, just before a snow, top dress with a light sprinkle of soil so the birds don't think you're a horticultural philanthropist.

Q. *Why do they dye grass seed with different colors?*
A. Some companies do it for the fun of it, as a sales gimmick; others coat the seed with an insecticide or fungicide. Read the bag. It'll tell you if they are kidding or serious.

Q. *Should you add grass seed to an old lawn every year?*
A. Only if you're too darn lazy the rest of the year to feed, dethatch, water, and mow it properly.

Q. *Can you plant grass seed where a dog killed the grass or grass died over the winter?*
A. Yep! Scratch up the dead grass, say a prayer, soak and refrigerate the new seed, scatter the seed and top dress lightly, pat or tamp down and—voilà! New grass!

Q. *If grass seed freezes in the garage over the winter, is it still good?*
A. Hell, yeah! If it goes to seed in the wild, do you think it builds a new house to keep warm in the winter? It just goes dormant (to sleep); it will wake up in time to give you a good lawn.

Q. *How many different kinds of grass seed are there?*
A. How many stars are there in the sky, raindrops in a cloud, grains of sand on a beach? Every time I turn around they have a new "strain." For all intents and purposes, there are thirty to thirty-five popular types of lawn grass seed.

Q. *We moved from the East Coast to the Southwest. Everyone gives us a different recommendation as to types of lawn. Who really knows?*

A. Your feet or a bicycle. Take a walk in your new neighborhood. Look at the lawns—different kinds, the ones that are well kept. Stop and introduce yourself and ask questions—how much time, effort, and money was spent—and then make up your own mind.

Q. *Some grass seed is for shade, some is for wet areas, some for sand, and so on. Give us a simple description of which is which.*

A. You have got to be kidding. I would be here from now till harvest. All grasses like sunny, well drained locations. The fescues will tolerate some shade, which means a little dampness. If you feed properly—water clay a shorter time but more often, and long and deep, and good soil three times a week—you can't miss.

Q. *We had some grass seed that had sprouted in the bag. My wife threw it out. She said it wouldn't grow. Was she right?*

A. She was sort of right. In most cases, it would have had marginal growth, but it would have rooted. It's best to start with fresh seed.

Q. *I have heard that grass seed in plastic bags is not as good as grass seed in cloth or paper bags. Is that true?*

A. It would depend on whether you are selling cloth or plastic bags. It doesn't make a bit of difference as far as I'm concerned.

Q. *Do the numbers and dates on bags of seed mean anything, or do they just make them up?*

A. Certainly they mean something. The purity

percentage indicates what percentage of the seed in the bag is the seed variety you're purchasing. Germination figures tell you the results of a sprout test the land grant college performed for the state in which the seed was grown. The weed content tells you what percentage of weeds you can expect.

Q. *What's the best type of grass seed to grow for animals' play area?*
A. Either of the tall fescues, Kentucky 31 or meadow.

Q. *Is it true that grass seed cannot be planted in hot, dry weather?*
A. No, it is not true. If you soak and refrigerate it, scratch up the soil, top dress it, pat the seed down, and keep it damp, it will sprout at any time.

Q. *Should we cover up our grass seed with straw?*
A. Your neighbors will hate you, but you can if you want. Why not just top dress with soil, roll with a nearly empty roller, and keep the neighbors happy?

Q. *Can you plant new seed if you've used a crab-grass killer?*
A. If you've used a crabgrass killer that kills the mature plant, you can go ahead and plant seed with no problem. But if you used a pre-emergent killer, which is used in early spring to kill dormant seed, forget it.

Q. *How old does new grass have to be before you can use weed and feed?*
A. I like it to have undergone at least three mowings and one good, normal feeding.

Q. *How tall should new grass be before you mow it.*

A. Tall enough to go through the mower set at one and a half inches for most cool grasses. But with bent grass, you should let it get its feet in the ground a couple of weeks before you mow.

Q. *What's the best type of lawn to grow on clay soil?*

A. If you can get that soil loose enough by using garden gypsum at the rate of fifty pounds per one thousand square feet, then any grass seed will grow.

Q. *Is there a right time of the day to plant seed?*

A. I always try to plant, drill, or broadcast seed after 5 P.M. Plants grow in the dark, so I give them a head start.

Q. *Should you spread seed by hand or can you use your lawn spreader?*

A. I find that you get better coverage by using a cyclone-type broadcast spreader. If you don't own one, borrow one. The next spreader you purchase should be this type.

Q. *How deep should you plant grass seed?*

A. Big seed like rye, one-half inch; medium like fescue, one-fourth inch; and fine like Merion, one-eighth to one-fourth inch.

Q. *Do you really have to hire those expensive companies to plow up and grind your dirt in order to have a nice lawn?*

A. Only if you're lazy or rich. Pick up all wood, stones, grass, brick, rocks, or other debris, and go rent a rototiller. It's a great way to lose weight and does a hell of a job.

Q. *How far apart do you plant plugs of grass?*

A. I guess it depends on how long you want to wait for your lawn to fill in and how much money you want to spend. For folks with patience, eight to ten inches will do, and for those with ants in their pants, three to five inches apart.

Q. *When is the best time to plant stolons of grass?*

A. In the spring, the first day of which is August 15: that's Mother Nature's spring. September 20 is probably the best, and you can go three days on either side.

Q. *What's the difference between stolons, plugs, and sprigs?*

A. Stolons are lengths of grass roots with some foliage attached; plugs are coin-sized and coin-shaped pieces of grass; and sprigs are pieces of root with a piece of foliage.

Q. *When do you feed new lawns planted by stolons?*

A. I wait five days and then lightly feed with any liquid plant, lawn, or garden food at 25 percent of the recommended rate.

Q. *How do I stop weeds from growing between my plugs of bent lawn before it fills in?*

A. Not for six to eight weeks, and then make darn sure the weed killer you use definitely says "safe near bent."

Q. *Is sod better than seed?*

A. Only if you're short on patience and long on money. No matter how you cut it, you have to wait for the seed to sprout, and sod is instant.

Q. *When is the best time to sod?*
A. Whenever you have the money and the man's got the sod. Early spring and midfall are probably the safest times to avoid the grass burning up from lack of watering.

Q. *How soon after you sod do you feed?*
A. I wait until the second time I cut it and then feed with a lightweight nonburning or liquid feed.

Q. *Can you water sod too much?*
A. Not as a rule the first week. I have found that if you pay extra attention around the edges (walks, drives, and curbs), a once-a-day soaking will do fine.

Q. *My new sod has what looks like eyes (brown) on the blades. I noticed it the day after it was laid. Is it sick?*
A. You bet your grass it's sick. The ailment is called leaf spot. The chemical cure is a lawn disease control, but you shouldn't have to pay for treatment. Call the crook that sold you that pig-in-a-poke and make him take care of it.

Q. *How long do I have to leave the wooden stakes in the sod on the side of a hill?*
A. Until you are sure the new roots have a good grip on the soil. Grab a handful of grass the same way your teacher grabbed your hair when you were a kid, and tug gently. If it holds, remove the stakes. Should any slide appear, replace the stakes; if you forget, your lawn mower will let you know.

Q. *How many different types of lawn can be planted by sod?*
A. All of the blues, bent, fescue, and Timothy rye.

I have honestly seen darn near every domestic type of lawn grass applied as sod.

Q. *Can I use weed killer to kill the weeds between my sod?*
A. You can, but I would caution you to wait until the third mowing and then a week after the first feeding. Let the grass recover from the shock of transplanting before you give it a dose of foul-tasting medicine.

Q. *Should I leave the grass clippings on new sod?*
A. How would you like the barber or hairdresser dousing your head with glue and then dropping all the hair clippings back on your head? No, pick them up.

Q. *Shouldn't you roll new sod?*
A. With a very light roller; just enough to let the roots make solid contact with the soil.

Q. *I cannot afford to sod my whole lawn. Can I seed the other half and ever have it look as good as the sodded half?*
A. Sure, you can. It all started from seed. If you seed in early fall you will see results sooner. Jack Barber, my next-door neighbor, did it your way. He made only one mistake; he didn't use the same variety and you can see the difference, though it doesn't look bad. If you have the same problem as Jack, overseed lightly with the same variety seed in the fall; top dress the mixed grass with a light sprinkle of soil, blending the two into each other.

Q. *Our Merion blue sod is two weeks old, and the blades next to the house and buildings are all covered with white dust. What's wrong?*
A. You bought your sod from the same crook the

guy with the brown spots did! (I'm just kidding.) The powder is mildew caused by lack of sunshine and grass that's too long. Cut more often, and feed less in those spots.

Q. *We had our lawn sodded three months ago, and I can still pull it up. It grew, but when we try to mow it, it lifts. How can we make roots?*
A. See if your garden center has a bag or two of 0-20-20 or a low-nitrogen garden food and apply it according to directions.

Q. *What's the best formula fertilizer for a bluegrass sod lawn?*
A. Whichever one you can afford. Your grass doesn't care, 'cause it can't read. I apply two normal feedings, one in the spring and one in the fall. Feed after two or three mowings, with any "cyclone" spreader set on number 2 setting. Wow, what a lawn!

Q. *How do you figure how many rolls of sod you need for any given area?*
A. Length of lot times width of lot divided by nine will tell you how many rolls of sod you will need for that lot. Make sure you deduct area of house, garage, and flower beds.

Q. *Why would anyone want to sow grass seed over newly laid sod?*
A. I don't know! You tell me. First, it's a waste of good money, and second, you're asking for trouble 'cause there are unwanted grasses and weed seed in the bag.

Q. *Should you apply a lawn fungicide to sod laid in the summer?*
A. Only if the sod gets sick. And then, as they say

in the military: Move it! Move it! Move it! Move what? It rhymes with grass.

Q. *What is Hydro seeding and is it recommended for the homeowners?*
A. It is a method of seeding by mixing the seed into a foamy plastic-type material and applying it with a high-pressure hose. Would I recommend it to homeowners? I guess not; I have yet to see a good full stand Hydro seed job.

Q. *My husband wants to sow grass seed himself, and then have our lot Hydro seeded on top of that. The seed underneath will be wasted, won't it?*
A. No, as a matter of fact, that's probably going to be the seed that will sprout, and the Hydro foam and a little seed would protect it. You can save some money, though, by just seeding.

Q. *Can any seed be used in Hydro seeding?*
A. Sure, it can; all with about the same degree of success.

Q. *Don't you have to water a lawn when it is Hydro seeded?*
A. Yep! Just like any other seed job. Keep it damp.

Q. *When do you feed a Hydro seeded lawn?*
A. After the first time you cut it.

Q. *We live in an area that has soil that looks like gravel. Water runs right through it. Can we possibly have a lawn?*
A. Sure, you can; you will just have to water a lot more often.

Q. *What can you add to sand to make it hold water?*
A. Clay, sawdust, or peat moss. Take a plastic gallon jug or two and poke holes in the bottom, fill it with sand, and pour water over it. See how long it takes from the time you pour until it comes out the bottom. Now, add the clay or other material until you lengthen the time to four times the plain sand rate.

Q. *Won't weed killers hurt birds and pets?*
A. Sure, if you feed it to them. Keep the pets off the lawn for at least a day after using weed killer. The birds don't like the smell and generally stay away for two or three days.

Q. *Is it better to use liquid weed killer or dry?*
A. When it's properly applied with a tank type compression sprayer, I'll go with liquid any time. But if you don't want to take the time, use dry.

Q. *When is the best time of the day to apply weed killer?*
A. Between 1 and 3 in the afternoon because when it is hot and dry the roots drink without thinking and *zap*.

Q. *Is it really necessary to use so many different kinds of weed killers?*
A. I'm afraid so, because, like people, weeds come in all different sizes, shapes, and forms.

Q. *Should you mow your lawn before applying a weed killer?*
A. I don't! I wait at least three days after. Remember, the good guys smell and taste the weed killer, too, and it gives them an upset stomach. So, wait a day or so to cut their hair.

Q. *When's the best time to kill crabgrass?*
A. Before it's crabgrass—that's when it's still seed. You might call it performing a horticultural abortion. In early spring (March or April), apply a pre-emergent crabgrass control, either dry or liquid.

Q. *Is it better to treat only the weed areas and not the whole lawn?*
A. I'll go along with that and add only that you give a 10 percent fringe factor—go 10 percent beyond the weed areas.

Q. *Should you water right after you apply weed killers?*
A. Please read the directions on the bag, bottle, or can. Do what you are told.

Q. *If all the weeds don't die, can I spray again?*
A. Take any weed that's lived through the battle to your garden center to make sure that the weed killer you have will do the job on this type of weed.

Q. *What do you use to clean out your sprayers?*
A. Soap, water, and baking soda. And never use it again for anything but weed killers.

Q. *What's the easiest way to tell if spots in your lawn are caused by insects, disease, animals, or fertilizer and chemicals?*
A. Take the spot to your neighborhood garden spot checker—your local garden center.

Q. *Is there a guaranteed way to spray lawn insects and be sure that they are killed?*
A. If you spray the right time, the right way, and with the right thing, you can be certain—but since neither you nor I can ever control all those variables, the answer is no!

Q. *What's the best nonpoisonous spray to use on a lawn?*
A. To do what? You try to use the mildest medication to control any illness and then work up to stronger medication if it doesn't work.

Q. *When's the best time of the day to spray your lawn for insects?*
A. Late in the afternoon or early evening, just before the dew comes.

Q. *Is there a sure cure for chinch bugs?*
A. I have found that a spring and fall application of lawn and garden gypsum really does the job. The chemicals most commonly used are Dursban or Sevin, added to a spray of a cup of flea and tick shampoo per twenty gallons of water.

Q. *Our baby is being eaten alive by chiggers. What can we use to kill the bugs but be safe with the baby?*
A. Safety first! Keep the baby out of the sprayed area for at least twenty-four hours to ease the minds of the environmentalists and then spray the room with Pyrithine, which I consider mild, safe, and effective around people, pets, and plants.

Q. *How do you get rid of slugs in your lawn?*
A. For those of you who are surprised to see this question in the lawn area, don't be. Slugs and their shelled cousins from France do feed on grass. A medication called Slug Bait does the job on turf areas.

Q. *Where do earwigs come from?*
A. From heaven, like the rest of God's creations. The earwig is both in the good and the bad bug families, but his bads outdo his goods, so we must

remove his presence. The good is that he eats some smaller insects; the bad is that he eats everything else in sight—foodstuffs, houseplants, and flowers. He sleeps all day and eats all night, hides indoors in dark places and outside in dark, dry places. To keep him outside, spray or dust around your house foundation with Dursban or Sevin and spray plants with Malathion. Use flea and tick shampoo in spray.

Q. *Sod webworms are carrying off our lawn. How do we stop them?*
A. Punch many holes in the soil area where the damage has occurred and 10 percent beyond. Now water the lawn with one ounce of your liquid dish detergent per gallon and then spray Diazinon, Sevin, or Dursban. Use the bar laundry soap spray with them.

Q. *Do mosquitoes live in grass? And how do you get rid of them?*
A. They sure do live in the grass, and in all other cool damp places. Mosquitoes can be controlled in your own area by spraying shrubs, grass, gutters, under lawn furniture, and wet spots with Methoxochlor, Diazinon, and flea and tick shampoo.

Q. *We have sprayed the lawn with everything to get rid of clover mites. They come into the house and cover the walls. What kills them?*
A. Clover mites won't bite you or your kids, so that worry is gone. In the house, vacuum, then spray with a house bomb or use a pest strip. Outside use Malathion, Diazinon, and flea and tick shampoo.

Q. *We have small dogs that are being driven nuts by ticks. What's safe to use around the dogs?*
A. To begin with, dust the dog with the proper

medication recommended by your vet. If the dog runs near shrubs and small tree areas spray those areas with Sevin, Diazinon, or Malathion.

Q. *I would sure like to get rid of the ants that fly, crawl, and march around my yard and garden, but if I stop them in one place they show up in another. Is there a way?*
A. Rent a roller with an attachment that has small spikes for making holes. Now add only enough weight to just make the points go into the ground. After rolling the whole lawn, water the lawn with one ounce of liquid dish detergent per gallon of water per 2500 square feet, and follow up with Diazinon.

Q. *My grass gets more diseases than my kids did. Where do they come from and how do you get rid of them?*
A. Plant diseases travel just like people diseases do by hand, air, foot, and dirty tools. To cure, use plant fungicides. I find that a lawn fungicide called Fore at eight ounces per one thousand square feet of lawn does the job. That's usually mixed in five to seven gallons of water.

Q. *If you have both insects and lawn diseases, can you treat both of them at once?*
A. Sure you can. That's like asking if you can treat athlete's foot and a sore throat at the same time. To make sure that both garden medications work, punch many little holes in the infected areas, water, then apply one ounce of liquid dish detergent to fifteen gallons of water over the same area. Then apply the insect control, next the disease control, or wait three to five days in between.

Q. *What can we do to stop the grass from dying where our dog does his duty?*

A. Apply garden gypsum at fifty pounds per 2500 square feet in the fall and early spring.

Q. *Is it true that moles come in your yard only if you have grubs in the lawn?*

A. And skunks, too. The animals are really doing you a favor, because they're alerting you to a problem. The two best garden chemicals to control lawn insects are in Dursban, Diazinon, and flea and tick shampoo.

Q. *My son and his friends wash their cars in our drive and use soap. Won't this kill our lawn and trees?*

A. Heck, no! This will make them grow better. I wash my garden and lawn once a month—whether they need it or not—with one ounce of liquid soap to fifteen gallons of water.

Q. *My husband changed the oil in our car and accidentally spilled almost all of it on the lawn. The grass is dead, and I was told nothing would ever grow there again. Could this be true?*

A. No, this could not be true. Try to remove eight to ten inches of soil and replace. Spread garden gypsum at fifty pounds per one thousand square feet of oil spillage and reseed.

Q. *I have a business office on a busy main street. All winter rock salt is scattered from county trucks. It kills my lawn and shrubs. Is there anything to take care of this?*

A. Gypsum wins again. Fifty pounds per one thousand square feet in the fall and fifty pounds per 2500 square feet in the spring.

Q. *Are Merion blue and Kentucky blue lawns fed the same way and with the same food?*
A. They sure are. After all, they're brothers. Feed in the spring and fall as recommended by the manufacturer, and then every third cutting. Set your lawn spreader on the lowest setting, and feed with any lawn food.

Q. *I have a mixed-seed back lawn—Kentucky blue, red fescue, rye, and tall fescue—while my front lawn is Merion blue. I feed the back just as often as the front, but it looks worse. What's wrong?*
A. Fescue grasses do not like a lot of food. One feeding in the spring should do fine.

Q. *How do you know how much lawn food you need for your lawn?*
A. Multiply the length of your property by the width (subtract the area of buildings, drives, walkways, and beds) and divide by ten. Then divide that answer by the nitrogen figure on any fertilizer bag or box. The end result will tell you exactly how many pounds you must buy of the stuff you're looking at.

$L \times W \div 10 \div N$ = your purchase in pounds

100 feet $\times$ 200 feet = 20,000 square feet

$$\frac{20,000}{10} = 2000$$

Lawn food is labeled 20-10-5, so divide by 20.

$$\frac{2000}{20} = 100 \text{ pounds of 20-10-5 lawn food.}$$

You would need to buy one hundred pounds of this lawn food and then apply it at one-half the recommended rate and Epsom salts and powdered sugar and double your money.

Q. *Is it good to use a different type of lawn food in the spring, summer, and fall?*
A. I do, and my golf course and sod growers do, regularly—lawn food in the spring, Milorganite summerizer for the summer, and garden food in the fall or winter, but always add the magnesium salts in Epsom salts.

Q. *Is there something you can put on your grass to keep it from growing?*
A. Yes, but you don't want to try it for a few more years. I have tested it and it's not worth the worry yet.

Q. *Is liquid lawn food as good as dry?*
A. If you can afford it, I think it's great. I use both from time to time so my lawn doesn't get bored, at 25 percent of the recommended rate. Plus a can of beer, a cup of children's shampoo, and one-half cup of molasses. Fill any room left over in the hand-held sprayer's quart jar with household ammonia.

Q. *How do you know when your lawn needs lime?*
A. Take a soil test with a piece of litmus paper. Get it in a drugstore or at your garden center.

Q. *Is there a thing called liquid lime?*
A. Yep, sure is. One gallon is equal to five hundred pounds of the dry, dusty, messy stuff. I use it, and I'm pleased with the results.

Q. *My sister says she uses liquid gypsum. I didn't know gypsum would dissolve. Does it?*
A. She probably uses a material called "liquidlike gypsum." It's not gypsum. It does break up clay soil but does not contain all the things gypsum does and will not repair salt damage. However, this material isn't bad; as a matter of fact, not bad at all.

Q. *How do you discourage dogs and squirrels from digging in your lawn?*
A. I've used paradichlorobenzene moth crystals on the soil to discourage animals. Crush them into a fine powder, add two tablespoons of chili powder per cup, and sprinkle lightly.

Q. *Is it true that not all dog urine burns up shrubs and grass, just bitches'?*
A. That's what they say, but, on occasion, when males are not given enough drinking water, they can cause the same damage.

Q. *Should you top dress an old lawn every year?*
A. I seldom recommend it unless you're overseeding it in spring or fall.

Q. *Will cat manure hurt my lawn?*
A. Not unless your dog catches the cat putting it there.

Q. *We have year-old Merion blue sod that is dying from fusarium blight. What will stop it and not cost me a fortune?*
A. About the best thing available right now is Benomyl and prayer.

Q. *What do skunks and moles have in common? They are both making a mess out of my yard and my social life.*
A. What they both have in common is your lawn and the bugs underneath it. Kill the insects, and your social life will return.

Q. *Can you get rid of weeds by burning them off on property on which you are going to plant grass seed?*
A. Burning off weeds only kills the tops and the

new seed, but the roots will return to haunt you again.

Q. *Can I mow weeds down and sod over them and not worry?*
A. That's like sweeping dirt under the rug; someday you've got to remove it. Weeds will find their way through the cracks and take over the whole lawn.

Q. *How do I get rid of slime molds?*
A. Use Benomyl according to package directions.

Q. *How short should you mow a lawn in the spring?*
A. If you are talking about the blues, I drop the blade to cut just above the green that can be seen underneath. This means that my blade is usually set for one to one and a half inches.

Q. *Isn't a built-in sprinkler better than lawn sprinklers?*
A. If you have the money, it is; if you don't, it isn't. It all depends on whether you feel the convenience is worth it.

Q. *When is the best time to water a lawn?*
A. Before 2 o'clock in the afternoon. Never let a lawn go to sleep with wet hair, or the tonic you will have to buy might cost more than your lawn.

Q. *What's the best kind of spreader for weed and feed?*
A. It's not the spreader we worry about, it's the spreadee. You are the "spreadee." Any spreader works fine, though I prefer a cyclone or broadcast type. What's more important is to go slow and watch what you're doing.

Q. *Are weeds killed faster with liquid or dry weed killer?*
A. Liquid will generally begin faster, but they both end up doing the same job.

Q. *Are grass clippings good for a compost pile?*
A. They sure are. Just make sure that you spread a thin layer of soil between each three-inch layer of clippings.

Q. *Can I spread dried manure on my lawn in the spring?*
A. If you don't mind being asked to leave the neighborhood by summer. Boy, oh, boy, that stinks—and it doesn't really help the lawn.

Q. *Who invented the lawn mower?*
A. A sadist! Isn't it funny that you should ask that question, because I asked my Grandma Putt the same thing thirty-eight years ago, and she knew the answer. She said, "Junior" (that's me), "Mr. Hills invented the lawn mower in 1868." So, now you know as much as I do.

EVERGREENS AND SHRUBS

. . . .

EVERGREENS ARE FOREVER

. . . .

Over the last few years, I've had the opportunity to travel all over the world, including Eastern Europe and Russia. No matter where I went, home gardeners were the same and had the same concerns. They look for a safe, simple, inexpensive, easy way to control insects and disease in their gardens. Vegetable gardens, lawns, evergreens, flowers, and shrubs were of interest only if the plants were native and the space was not needed for a food source. In most of North America, on the other hand, our lawns are first, evergreens second, and then the rest follows, based on income and age. Since evergreens are second in our interest, it's second after lawns in this edition, as it was in the original.

We discussed the lawn at length. With the proper tonics, tricks, and tips in place, and a little bit of pride mixed with a pinch of patience and blended with a dab or two of persistence, you can have a pretty good looking lawn. But you can't stop there. Just having a lawn, a green carpet from walk to walk, drive to drive, is like having wall-to-wall carpeting in your living room and no furniture. It just doesn't look lived in. A garden, to be truly appreciated, must have the warmth and lived-in look that can only be achieved through the use of evergreens. Evergreens frame your house, soften its lines, and tie your house into the earth.

The common term "evergreen" means what it implies—that the tree will keep its foliage year round, and in most cases the foliage is green. There are, however, many evergreens that have two faces—the summer face and the winter. Examples of this would be the conifers (the professional classification of evergreens) called Andora junipers, a spreading evergreen; and the hills Dundee, an upright grower. These two plants are both green in the summer months, but when frost comes they turn a beautiful burgundy color. When selecting plants for your landscape, you should take this into consideration and buy plants that are as attractive in the winter as they are in the summer.

Contrary to the belief of many a new gardener, not all evergreens have needles as do the pine, spruce, juniper and yew. Many have large or small leaves, like any flowering shrub. These are called broadleaf evergreens. Many in this group also have two faces, the difference being that they produce foliage in the winter and burst into flower in the spring, like rhododendrons and azaleas. You can make quite a masterpiece out of your property, be it large or small, with a little bit of planning and a lot of imagination. How can you choose the right evergreens for you? First, you need a plan.

PLAN
BEFORE YOU
PLANT

Using this phrase is like beating a dead horse, because it's constantly used by nurserymen, garden writers, and broadcasters, until hearing it makes you sick. But drawing a plan is one of the most important steps you can take in building a desirable and presentable landscape design to complement your home and surrounding property.

A good, workable plan doesn't have to be a sophisticated, complicated work of art by a landscape architect, though this type of plan is great if you can afford it. What you're making is a plan of your property showing where everything is. It'll be necessary to use some sort of scale on your plan; the larger the scale (and your paper), the clearer and more detailed your plan can be. So a piece of brown paper—even a grocery bag cut open—will do nicely.

Now survey your property. Pace off and write down the length and width of your lot if you do not already know these measurements. Next, pace off and write down the distance from your property lines of your house and other building locations and put these down. Then continue by adding the walks, drive, fences and existing flower beds or other gardens. Now indicate where the downspouts are, any low spots that can or do hold water, and existing shade trees. On the paper show the size of the shadow they cast and for what period of time

"Buy plants that are as attractive in winter as they are in summer."

each day. I have found that my children's crayons make identification much easier: I use green for trees, gray for walks, black for buildings, brown for gardens and beds, chartreuse for wet spots, blue for water, ponds, or streams. Be sure to code the colors in the margin for quick identification.

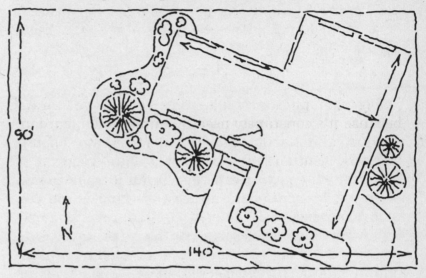

Put in all the windows and doors in your house. For windows, show their height from the ground and their width; for doors, their width and which room they belong to. Now indicate the direction north on the plan in the lower left-hand corner with a small red N and an arrow pointing to the north of your property. The end? Not by a long shot! What next?

"A garden, to be truly appreciated, must have the warmth and live-in look that can only be achieved through the use of evergreens."

As a rule, areas just happen because we tend to overlook them in the basic plan; by the time we discover our oversight, it's too late to work them in or screen them off without making it look obvious. Consequently, they stick out like a sore thumb. So put them in now. I have included a basic checklist and personal landscape survey that can be used to avoid some common oversights.

In the last few years, Home Planners, Inc., a

EVERGREENS AND SHRUBS 105

nationally recognized publisher of home plans published two super books for the home gardener and builder, *The Landscape Planner* and *The Deck Planner*. These include large-scale work plans, plant selections, and construction lists and how-to's. I suggest that you check your local bookstore or library for them, as they're terrifically helpful. The publisher is Home Planners, Inc., of Tucson, Arizona.

Now look at your plan, and look through nursery catalogs or walk through a large nursery and walk around your neighborhood. Do you want something low to cover a hill or follow the line of a walk or driveway? Maybe a tall, skinny shape would cover up that ugly downspout. A screen of not-too-tall evergreens will give you privacy from a major road that's too close to your house. You can plant evergreens for a purpose—to block out noise, or traffic, or a view. You can plant evergreens to provide color or color contrast—all dark as a background for what you'll plant later, or silvery blue or golden green to stand out. You can even plant them just for their shapes—spiky and dense or lacy. When you've got a list of evergreens you might like, check them against catalogs you get from the nurseries on pages 143–45 or the library's big plant reference books. You need to know what zone you're in, first. (Check that on pages 140–42.) See if the evergreen you want can live in your zone. Then see if what you want will fit what you've noted on the plan. Have you got a tree that needs full sun in the shade? Won't grow. Try another. People who work at nurseries are almost always helpful, patient, and kind. But don't go with a lot of questions at their busiest times. You should be able to find evergreens you want for any purpose.

LANDSCAPE PLANNING GUIDE

ESTIMATED BUDGET?_____

          Lawn $_____

          Evergreens   _____

          Shade Trees   _____

          Flowering Trees   _____

          Flowering Shrubs _____

          Flowers   _____

            (A) Annuals   _____

            (B) Perennials   _____

            (C) Bulbs   _____

          Vegetable Garden _____

          Total $_____

MEMBERS OF THE FAMILY   OUTDOOR HOBBIES

_____   _____

_____   _____

_____   _____

       PLAY AREA

       Pool?_____

       Swing Set?_____

       Tennis or Ball Court?_____

       Other Game Areas?_____

ANIMAL RUN/_____

GREENHOUSE and/or POTTING SHED/_____

SEND FOR CATALOGS_____

SHOULD YOU PLANT A POOL IN YOUR GARDEN?

Whether or not to have a swimming pool is a big question with lots of homeowners these days. Pools are highly recommended by most landscape architects and designers. But many people who love their gardens hesitate to install a pool because they are afraid that the pool and its associated chemicals will kill the lawn and shrubs.

From the horticultural aspect I have no objection to a swimming pool, as long as it is well designed, placed, constructed, maintained and landscaped.

Let's start with the design. The shape of any pool should complement the home. It should become part of the landscape and lend pleasure and beauty. It shouldn't be a big round or square hole in the ground or an oversized tin can in the middle of the lawn.

A good pool builder will take into consideration the style of building and design the pool to blend gracefully. For example, a ranch house can have a pool of any size or shape. To make it fit in, however, takes planning; place a coping of ledge rock around the edge, for instance, and the pool will take on a rustic appearance.

Above-the-ground pools present more of a challenge. On large lots, soil can be mounded up around the exposed sides and sandstone steps added, leading up to the deck. Pines and ground covers can be used at the base, so that the mound gives the illusion of being a natural hill. Pools on small lots are a bit more difficult, but I have used aborvitaes in random groups with spreading junipers in small beds between and have accomplished a very pleasant result.

The proper placement of the pool is very important. It's best to avoid shade as much as possible. However, this doesn't mean you should put the pool right in the middle of the lawn. For safety's sake it is recommended that you locate the pool where you can have a clear view from the house.

I need not linger on the aspect of construction quality. Common sense should tell you to be sure of a manufacturer's or a builder's reputation.

The true secret to success or failure in enjoying a swimming pool is proper maintenance. This never-ending job can be assigned to the teen-age members of the family, or can be done by hiring a professional pool service. Alternatively, you can always assume the responsibility yourself. Do not mix, or allow the mixing, of any pool-purifying chemicals on the grass areas or alongside evergreen and flower beds. Have a cement slab poured with at least a three-inch curb on which to place the pumps and filters. Do not store the chemicals out of doors on the ground where the containers can become damaged and leak on the turf areas.

The list of plant materials that can be used near and around the swimming pool is endless. The only restriction is your imagination. I only suggest to avoid planting deciduous trees and shrubs (the ones that lose their leaves) near the pool itself, or you will forever be skimming the leaves out of the water. I have found that using members of the juniper family (Hetzi, Armstrong, Greek, Andora, etc.) and combining them with a variation of ground covers can make your swimming pool a truly beautiful and scenic spot, summer or winter. Plants to avoid in and around your pool are the yew family and most of the aborvitaes. Neither can stand a great deal of water. When you combine the water with the acid-salt buildup from the splashing of pool water, the plants just don't have a chance.

When you talk to your pool builder or landscape designer, inform him that you would like the plant materials to have winter character as well as summer, and the joining link will be the selection of the right ground covers. You have over thirty of these to choose from.

Over the years I have found that a lawn of turf type perennial rye, overseeded in early March, June, and August, makes the most attractive and durable swimming-pool lawn. It will take the pitter-pat of tiny feet wet with chlorine and still look great.

Pool chemicals seem to be the primary concern of most home gardeners. They kill flowers, shrubs and evergreens. This need not be the case. Plain, old-fashioned garden gypsum should be spread on the lawn areas and in the flower beds and evergreen rows, at a rate of fifty pounds over one thousand square feet, two or three times a season. This will render the chemical reaction harmless to the plants.

To summarize this discussion I need only quote myself: "A garden is to be lived in and enjoyed, not just admired." Don't deprive your family or yourself of the pleasure of a swimming pool if you have the room, patience, and capital.

PERMANENTLY PLANTED

Most folks think that all there is to planting an evergreen is to dig a hole, drop the plant in, refill the hole with soil, and watch it grow. This attitude can lead to death, not life. Read through this whole section before buying anything, so you'll know what to do when. Makes no sense to buy plants only to have them die on the driveway as you realize how long digging a proper hole takes. When planting any living plant, be it a tiny petunia or a large pine, you must handle the plant as delicately as you would have the movers handle your antique or valuable furniture. The precise location as well as the permanent angle should be as well thought out as the placement of a mirror, plaque, or painting— even better thought out. *Tell* me you'll want to move that tree after it's planted. But that's what you'll have to do if you don't think ahead carefully enough.

"Before you make up your mind to move an evergreen of any size, make sure that moving it is absolutely necessary and not a whim."

The planting procedure begins before you ever bring the evergreen home. By this I mean that you must determine the soil conditions in which you are going to ask these plants to grow. Most evergreens, needled or broadleaf, grow best in light, loose soil, or growing mixes with good drainage. I therefore suggest that when you prepare evergreen beds or holes for individual plants you add liberal quantities of 60-40 gravel and sand to the existing soil if it's of a heavy consistency. That means digging out and breaking up all the soil in all the beds or holes you're going to plant, then mix the soil with gravel and sand. Sandy soil will need no preparation.

In heavy clay soil, it is of the utmost importance that you determine the direction of the water's surface flow. Many an unsuspecting gardener placed a plant in a spot that displayed it at its best, only to find that when it rained, the hole filled up with water, and the plant died, because the surface was badly graded, or the plant was under the downspout.

After you've put in your plants, you'll want to finish off with mulch two inches deep.

CHOOSING THE GUARDS

Evergreens come in three basic containers. The first is the traditional balled-in-burlap, the second is metal containers, and the third is plantable paper-pulp pots.

The type your purchase comes in doesn't make much difference. The plantable container is fast becoming the most popular, mostly because the average home gardener can plant it with the least amount of fuss and shock loss of plants. The metal container is rather cumbersome, and the plant must be removed from the container; that means cutting the sides of the can, which may result in a few minor cuts and scratches. Soil is often shaken loose from the roots in the process, exposing them to the air, which can cause damage to the plant. Also, the plant gets handled quite a bit as you take it out, with the result frequently being more damage.

The burlap ball is an excellent container but is fast becoming extinct because of automation, increased production, and a lack of ballers. Wrapping a plant's roots in burlap, my friends, is a true art, and a good baller has the skill and speed of any good journeyman. How he handles the plant when it is dug determines whether or not it lives in your yard.

When you go to purchase your plants, look at the container just as critically as you do the plant. If, for instance, you've picked out a tall and statuesque juniper and then you look down at the ball of soil covered with burlap and find that it's loose and sloppily done and that the soil is falling out, don't buy the plant. Odds are it will die in your yard from root shock. If paper-pulp containers are split, don't buy them. If the plants in the metal containers are loose and wobbly, don't buy them. Use as much care in the selection and purchase of an evergreen as you would a piece of furniture. There should be no flaws, and the plant should be shiny, bright, and healthy.

The size of the container has a lot to do with the future health of your plants. Make sure that you get as much soil as you can with the plants. I always pick the plants with the biggest ball or container.

THE RIDE HOME

You have now selected and paid for your plants. Next comes the ride home. Plants are just like some people and pets. They get carsick if some precautions are not taken. Whenever it can be avoided, plants in containers should not be laid on their sides in a trunk or back seat. Laying them down tends to crush the sides, loosen the soil and expose the roots. Balled-in-burlap plants should not be allowed to roll around and bang their sides for the same reasons. Set the plant containers upright and brace them. Block balled plants to keep them from rolling.

Don't bend tops to fit into car trunks or close the lids and tie them down on the limbs or foliage, or you can kiss your purchase good-bye. If your evergreen has a bad ride home, he may never adapt to the spot where you plant him, not to mention what he's going to tell the rest of the plants at home about you. If delivery from the nursery can't be arranged, and the plants won't be as comfortable riding home as you, rent a small trailer. Place all of the plants in an upright position—and fasten their safety belts. That's right, sudden stops and starts cause soil shifts and shocks. I tie the foliage gently, but snugly, with soft strips of cloth or old nylon hoisery to prevent the tops from blowing in the breeze and drying out or snapping off. When loading or unloading evergreens, do not let anyone rough handle them, drop or plunk them down, as this will separate the soil from the roots. Do not handle the plants by grabbing them by the trunk. Move them by picking up the container and not by dragging them around by the foliage or branches. Remember, plants have feelings. How would you or your pet feel if you were dragged around by the hair, tail, or legs? Your pet would bite or scratch, and you would yell! Evergreens can and do scream with pain, so be gentle.

DON'T
DELAY

● ●

"Plant all plants the day you purchase them. Be a good host and make them comfortable as quickly as possible."

More evergreens lose their lives on a driveway or in a garage than any place else. Once you have made a plan, selected the plants, and purchased the materials, take time! Take the time to plant your evergreens the day you bring them home. The worst thing I can think of is inviting someone to visit and then leaving him standing on the porch. It's rude and unkind. The plants you're putting in your yard are invited guests. They didn't ask to come to live with you; you asked them. So be a good host or hostess and make them comfortable as quickly as possible. They will soon show you their appreciation.

Plant all plants *the day* you purchase them. Don't buy more than you can plant immediately, but make additional trips and purchase them a few at a time. Ideally, you've prepared beds and dug holes before you make your purchases.

AFTER ALL,
A HOLE IS
JUST A HOLE

● ●

This statement is only true if you don't have to live in one! When you do it's home, and since "Home is where the heart is," let's make it enjoyable. No one likes to live in cramped quarters, and that's especially true of evergreens. If the planting hole is too small and cramped, the new visitor will be uncomfortable, its growth will be stunted, and it will soon become ill. I was always taught to dig a hole half again as wide as the width of the container. This is referred to as digging a five-dollar hole for a fifty-cent plant. The new evergreen visitor should be planted only one to one and a half inches deeper than it was in the nursery. If you plant it too deep you might smother the roots.

Once you've taken out the soil, lighten a heavy or clay soil with sand and gravel, equal amounts. Mix the sand and gravel mix half and half with your soil.

ONWARD AND UPWARD

A steel rigger would never be satisfied if one of his steel beams was not straight as an arrow. The reason is obvious. The rest of the building would be crooked. A home landscaper must not be satisfied with a slanted plant because his whole garden will look crooked and the plant will be terribly uncomfortable. After you have dug a wide hole, one and a half inches deeper than the plant was planted at the nursery, set your new friend in position. Be gentle! Don't drop him or her! Now stand way back and check the stance of the plant. Is it straight? Look from all angles, just as you size up a putt in golf. (This procedure is much easier if you have two adults do it—one to plant and one to view. Children tend to say, "It's okay, I guess," or wander off when you're making adjustments.) If the plant appears crooked, don't bend it or pull at it. Gently, carefully, remove it from the hole and alter the angle at the bottom of the hole to compensate for the crookedness of the plant. This same procedure goes for all of the evergreens, whether they are low spreaders or tall uprights. They should always appear straight and level.

FILL IT UP— FILTERED

I stated earlier that, almost without exception, all evergreens, broadleaf and needled, love loose, well-drained soil. If your evergreen friends do not have these first-class living conditions, they soon will not be living. The hole is now dug and you're reasonably certain that the plant will sit straight and level. Next you should determine if you have good drainage. Get out the garden hose and fill the hole with water, but don't wash away the sides or alter the angle at the base. Watch closely. If the water has not subsided in a very few minutes, you have a drainage problem. To correct this, dig a narrow trench the depth of the hole on an angle parallel to the downward grade of the property and fill it with gravel. If, on the other hand, the water runs through the hole like through a sieve, you can line the five-dollar hole with clay loam to hold some moisture.

It's now time to plant the evergreen permanently. One of my neighbors says, "Just throw the dirt back in." But that's not the way to make a friend of your evergreen. In the case of the balled-in-burlap plant, after you have half refilled the hole, you have to cut the twine at the top of the ball and where it's bound around the trunk before putting the plant in the hole.

The metal container is the toughest one. In most cases, the nurseryman will cut the sides of the can before you leave the nursery and bind the sides with cord. If not, you have to cut three sides all the way down with tin snips. Once this is done, place the can next to the hole and gently pull the cut can sides away from the root ball inside. Now gently lift out the evergreen and lower it into the hole. Do not touch the plant, only the ball. Don't drop it. By the way, I talk to the plants all the time while I'm planting them. It keeps them calm, and me, too. It also lets them know that they're welcome friends and not just decorations.

The paper pulp pot container should be placed in the hole with the plant and left to decompose. If the bottom can be removed without a struggle, it helps.

Once the plant is in place, begin to refill the hole with the mixture of half sandy gravel and half garden soil you've prepared. Fill in on all sides evenly until the hole is half full and pack the soil firmly around the ball with your foot to eliminate any air pockets or hollow spots that will later sink and cause exposure of roots or a tilt to the plant. After you have half filled and packed down, fill the hole up with water to further settle the soil. When the water's soaked in, continue to fill up the hole with the balance of the sandy gravel and soil mix. A mixture of 75 percent bonemeal and 25 percent magnesium or Epsom salts can be sprinkled in the hole as you fill and on top.

COVER UP
YOUR
DIRTY
WORK

"Never feed newly planted shrubs right away. Let them get used to the soil and their new neighbors for a couple of weeks first."

Your new friend is now almost comfortably situated in his or her new home, but not quite yet. *Do not,* I repeat, *do not* feed newly planted shrubs right away. Let them get used to the soil and their new neighbors for a couple of weeks and then give them a light snack of any one of the fish emulsion fertilizers. Then feed them again at the end of a month with a low-nitrogen, dry garden food, like 4-12-4 or 5-10-5, to stimulate root growth. In the meantime, cover up the roots with a mulch of wood chips about two inches deep all the way out to the ends of the bottom branches.

You'll notice that I didn't put any food in the planting hole. Nothing living wants food crammed down its throat—especially not a newly moved evergreen. The bonemeal and Epsom salts are just light helpers, like Jell-O would be to you and me after surgery.

SAY A FEW
KIND WORDS

After you have each of your guests well planted, take a few minutes out to stand back and look them over to see if they were damaged in the move or during planting. You might tell them how pleased you are to have them come stay with you and your family, and that you hope they will be comfortable.

You might also tell them how nice they look. No, I'm not crazy; I do talk to the plant. I find it both tranquilizing and rewarding. If a few of the skeptics of this world would walk out into Mother Nature's living room and communicate with the Almighty through plants, they wouldn't need uppers and downers to get happy. Happiness is all right here, right around us, all the time, and I can get high and happy just mowing the lawn or tending the roses. I get the troubles off my chest just by talking to the friends in my garden. Try it sometime; you might be surprised and enjoy it.

PERSONALIZE YOUR PLANTS

"Hey, you!" must be the rudest salutation anyone can use. At my house we take a small label maker and give all of the large permanent plants in the garden a name. Ours are mostly Indian names, but you can use any names you wish. I have a close friend looking over my shoulder most of the time I am writing this book. His name is Paul. He is a Paul's scarlet hawthorn. You'll be surprised at how much interest your entire family will have in your yard and garden when you make a few new friendships this way, especially if they all help choose names.

CHOW TIME!
FEEDING
EVERGREENS

Most folks who plant evergreens or move into a home with an existing landscape of evergreens just take them for granted. Soon the plants figure, "To hell with you. If you don't notice I'm around and don't care about me, I'm not going to try to look nice for you." And soon they don't. Then you notice them, but sometimes it's too late. If you want to get along with your garden but don't want to get personal, that's your business, but I suggest that you take a little time out and at least be friendly—feed them. They need food, and they aren't capable of foraging for themselves like their ancestors who grew free in the woods in a thick rich layer of natural organic mulch that fed them continuously. They must now rely on you. From some of the conversations I hear, a lot of you "green thumbers" are stingy and only feed a few favorites. That southern gentleman, Kentucky blue, and his girlfriend, Merion, get all the choice food and keep you broke. Well, food that's good for your lawn is good enough for the evergreens, except for those special blends with weed killers in them. Write this on your garden calendar: Feed the evergreens in February, April and June, coast to coast. But never after August 15, if you live in snow country. If you live in the warm areas, feed them in August and October, too.

You should feed all of your evergreens with the same lawn food you use for your lawn—except weed and feeds—at the rate of a half pound per foot of height. Sprinkle the food over the top of the mulch underneath the evergreens, then watch the difference.

You can also use any of the liquid fish emulsions. As a matter of fact, the evergreens appreciate a varied menu, just as your lawn does. Use the lawn food mix of fertilizer and Epsom salts found on page 25 at half rate, then use the beer and molasses tonic every three weeks, making sure the evergreens get their fair share. Prepare the tonic by putting into the quart jar of your hand-held sprayer a cup of beer, a cup of children's shampoo, a half cup of molasses, and fill to the top with household ammonia. Mix with twenty gallons of water.

"The best way to keep dogs away from evergreens is to get a big, mean cat."

KEEPING IN SHAPE

If you properly plant, feed, mulch, and care for evergreens, they're going to grow tall, wide, and full. Evergreens are just like people or pets; if they're allowed to get too fat, they tend to get sloppy, lazy, and weak from lack of exercise.

I'm not suggesting that you walk your evergreens, but I am suggesting that once in a while you gently shake them. This is like scratching your dog's back, and it will help to shake out some of the natural needle drop that occurs in most evergreens. It also lets them know that you're thinking about them.

Needle drop seems to upset many a home gardener when he isn't aware of what is happening. Most evergreens naturally shed the older needles toward the center of the tree in the fall of the year, and this is not cause for alarm. It's when the outside needles begin to fall that you should worry.

When evergreens begin to look thin haired, it's usually because of one or two causes: insects, or poor trimming procedure. First, check for insects. If you can't see them, get a sheet of clean white paper and place it under several different branches as you shake the foliage. Look closely at the paper. If bugs are the problem, you'll see them scooting around on the paper. Take insects in a closed jar to your local nursery for identification and to learn how to treat them. If there are no signs of insects, look over your tree carefully and ask these questions: Are all of the sides getting full sun? Did I use dull shears and injure the foliage? Did I cut too far back and expose coarse inner branches?

When trimming any plant, it's absolutely necessary that your tools be sharp. You can trim evergreens as often as you like and should do so periodically to contain them—in order not to have them growing over the sidewalk or covering windows or their nearest neighbor. When trimming the yews and junipers, you cannot invert your trim. I mean that your design can be a line perpendicular to the ground or flared, but not flared inward, because when you do this the upper branches cast a shadow and shut out the sun. When this occurs, the needles will begin to drop off on the ends.

Trimming can begin in the warm climates in March and as soon as the snow disappears in the rest of the country. As new growth appears, continue to trim to keep the evergreen looking neat and natural. I find that electric hedge trimmers work fine and save a lot of work.

When a large branch is broken or cut, it's necessary to sterilize the wound and seal it. A solution of two tablespoons household ammonia in a quart of water will do to sterilize the wound, then seal the wound with interior latex paint with a touch of liquid Sevin added.

For broken limbs, make a fresh, clean cut. Do not allow broken limbs to go untended for any period of time, or further damage will occur.

When it's necessary to cut into large wood, it's an excellent idea to cut just ahead of a young branch. This will then fill out and cover up the heavy stub. Pruning and trimming errors have to be lived with for a long time, so be sure before you cut.

MOVING DAY: TRANSPLANTING

There comes a time in every gardener's life when he finds that he must move a plant from one location to another. The reasons can be many, and they really make no difference. Before you make up your mind to move an evergreen of any size, be sure that it is absolutely necessary and not just a whim. Talk it over with the plant to be moved. If poor drainage is the reason and the plant is in danger of losing his life, you should tell him. Or if wind scald is giving him first-degree burns, or something like that, the plant will understand the necessity of the move. I don't recommend moving a plant just for the sake of looks, and believe me, he won't like it either.

If and when it becomes necessary to move any kind of evergreen, broadleaf, or tropical, it's mandatory that you take some presurgery steps. To begin with, tie the foliage up snugly but not tightly with old nylon hose so you can work beneath it without breaking any branches. Next, water the plant to be moved the night before. Do not soak the soil, just get it damp enough so that when you dig, the soil will hold firmly around the roots. The next step is to dig the new hole the same way as you would to plant a new evergreen. The quality of the tools you use can determine whether your plant will live or not, so be sure that your spade has a razor's edge. I always sharpen and resharpen the blade of my shovel with a file to insure that when I cut through the many feeder roots, the cuts will be clean and not ragged. I prepare a stretcher to move my friend as quickly and comfortably as possible. For this I use a large, heavy cardboard box broken down to resemble a flying carpet.

To dig up an established plant, one must take into consideration his age and the general condition of his health. The older the plant and the longer he's been in place will determine the amount of soil you must move with him, much like the older person who is forced to move and wants to take his cherished objects with him. As a rule, I take no less than half the soil beneath the lower branches, and more for older plants. On some plants, that can be a big, big ball and you will need help.

Take your spade and begin to dig a spade's depth straight down in a full circle around the plant at the drip line. When this circle is completed, move one spade's width back out from the plant and begin to remove the soil, forming a trench all the way around the plant. Once you've done this, turn your spade over and dig straight down again, but with the spade backward. (You'll be loosening the soil.) Then remove the loosened soil. You are now two spade depths deep. On the side of the plant closest to the new location, dig a slight ramp up and away from the soil ball. Continue to dig beneath the ball until it is free and the plant will rock a bit when gently pushed. Placing one end of the cardboard rug under the edge of the ball, pull the plant down toward and onto the cardboard. Now begin to pull the rug along the soil until you are opposite the new hole. Gently, ever so gently, work the plant into its new location. Don't drop, jerk, or bump the ball. Move as slowly as you can. Once the plant is seated well, make sure it's straight, and then begin to refill the hole in a normal planting procedure. Use the bonemeal and Epsom salts mix.

When the job is done, mulch with two inches of fresh clean mulch and water well. Feed two weeks later with a fish emulsion plant food.

The best time to transplant is in the early fall or very early spring when the evenings are cool—never during very hot weather.

There is now equipment that can dig up any size plant and reset it so that the plant never knows it was moved. I would suggest that you call a professional tree mover for bids, if you're going to move any large evergreen or tree.

R E L A N D- SCAPING

I guess I'm asked more questions about this subject than about any other phase of gardening. You will need to relandscape if you purchase a home that has a runaway garden or a neglected landscape that's overgrown, out of proportion, or insect-infested to the point where it contains too many dead plants to cover up the empty spots. The same rule applies to relandscaping as to a brand new plan, except you don't have to start from scratch.

Begin by drawing the paper bag plan described on pages 104–105. Put in your house, walks, buildings, trees, good shrubs, and any other plantings that exist. Be sure to show on your plan shadows cast, low spots, or any drainage problem. Next, check the catalogs for varieties of plants and their uses. Then, take your plan and catalogs to your local nursery and see if the pieces to the puzzle will fit. Since your existing plants are all full grown or larger, you're going to have to purchase plants of somewhat similar size, which will mean more money per plant. However, not as many plants will be needed. I would ask "the man" if he would stop by and guide you on which plants to cut back severely and which to remove. I find that most of these gentlemen are glad to assist anyone who is truly interested. At most they charge a nominal fee, which is waived if you buy from them. Your county agent is also available for no fee in most cases, though a cup of coffee and a piece of homemade cake or pie sure works wonders. Relandscaping is best done in the early fall when both the days and evenings are comfortable for you and the garden.

It's a lot of work, but the results are amazing. Some of your overgrown junipers, yews, and other shrubs need not come out but could be trimmed, even pruned into some pretty interesting and unusual shapes. A visit to your local library for a look at a book that has pictures of topiary designs can help make you the standout in the neighborhood.

IN SICKNESS AND IN HEALTH

With a little care and kindness shown toward our evergreens, we can expect some pretty, happy, and healthy results. But from time to time even the healthiest person succumbs to a minor illness. If it isn't immediately taken care of, it can become a very serious problem, even resulting in a fatality. Heaven forbid this should ever happen in your garden.

Let's review the needs of our fine green friends. Like the lawn, they need plenty of fresh air, sunshine, water (broadleaf evergreens don't need as much water), a balanced diet, and plenty of soap and water.

In the early spring, in the North and East and late winter in the West and South (see planting map page 105) begin your health cure program for evergreens and foliage plants. Give them a soap-and-water bath with a hose and sprayer. Use one ounce of liquid dish detergent per ten gallons of water in your hand-held sprayer. Wash inside and out, over and under. Don't miss a spot. Viruses and fungus diseases are insect-caused or are the result of poor hygiene and of airborne soot, dust, and various pollutants that settle on the foliage and needles. Soap and water are disinfectants of a sort that keep the plant clean and free of the viruses. It is therefore absolutely necessary that you bathe them once a month. In heavy smog or industrial areas, you should bathe your evergreens as often as needed. These frequent showers also keep the pores and cells open by eliminating surface tension and allowing photosynthesis to take place in a normal manner. If you're in close contact with your garden, you'll actually sense trouble before it really gets a start.

Fungicides are chemical materials used to control and cure the diseases that attack your evergreens, and every manufacturer of lawn and garden products has at least one broad-spectrum fungicide that will solve most problems. It's necessary that you understand that no chemical treatment will restore the appearance of your evergreens after they've been injured by a virus; they only prevent the spread of the diseases. You may have to trim away or just live with the damage. Isn't prevention easier? If you use the mouthwash, children's shampoo, or bar laundry soap solution sprays, odds are "there'll be no fungus among us." You'll find all these listed on page 7.

To keep your evergreens shipshape and free from the "foliage flu," I suggest that along with a good diet and frequent baths, you keep their home clean and free of weeds and debris, as these usually bear bad tidings. I have found that providing a two-inch layer of wood chips is the best preventive step you can take in protecting your evergreens. This mulch should be from a healthy tree, never a diseased one. A good layer of mulch will hold down weeds, act as a source of food, and retain moisture. A good-looking mulch enhances the appearance of the plant itself and lets it show off. There are many to choose from. The ones I like best are hardwood chips, redwood and pine bark. Next best is chunky peat. The ones that I do not prefer are the cocoa bean shells, buckwheat hulls, and straw, because these attract insects and mice.

Stone chips are an attractive mulch and do hold down weeds and retain moisture. The assortment of stone materials is limitless, from hard coal chips to pea gravel. There is on the market now a type of coated stone in bright colors that is extremely attractive. With some imagination, you can use these stones to create the most unusual effects. If you're going to put a mulch under your evergreens, place weed blocker fabric from Easy Gardener down first, not ordinary plastic, then the mulch. If stone is used, place that on top of the mulch to absorb the heat. A clean, neat well-trimmed and mulched garden will display healthy evergreens at their best. And remember, a clean garden is a happy one.

PARDON THE PESTS

I can't help but feel sorry for the poor bugs. There they are, going about their business, doing their thing, helping to balance nature, and what thanks do they get? They get slapped, swatted, flicked, gassed, burned, sprayed, dusted, and sworn at, when all they're doing is what they were meant to do.

If you will just think for a minute about how we prevent ticks, fleas, and lice from bothering our pets, you'll discover the simplest method by which you can encourage the insects to pass your garden by.

That's right, we are right back to the bath routine. Bugs have eyes, a mouth, a nose, and a very delicate stomach. When you wash down the garden, the bugs that are around get soap in their eyes, up their noses, and in their mouths. They soon move on. New bugs flying by stop for a snack or begin to set up housekeeping and soon discover the food in "dis here plaze" is not very tasty and their stomach is constantly upset. So they move out.

Insects have a great communication network, and they will soon pass the word along about your place. Not all bugs fly, as you know, nor do they all like the taste of foliage. Some prefer the tender young roots, just as we like bean sprouts. To discourage these underground visitors, poke a series of holes into the soil beneath the branches and water down this area with the soap solution. If you're wondering what happens to all the insects that you chase away, they run into one of their natural enemies along the way. Not all of the bugs will give up quite this easily, and it may be necessary to turn to the garden chemicals. When this step becomes necessary, then use only the strength of the chemical to do the job that is recommended by the manufacturer. I have found that methoxychlor will take pretty good care of the chewing and sucking insects and Dursban ends the problem under the ground.

I will make a brief comment at this point about using combinations, i.e., two or more chemicals mixed together to form a stronger wallop. I don't find it necessary to do this, or very safe. The softer chemicals are effective, and when it becomes necessary to use any of them, I use the most effective recommended. Tomato vegetable dust made into a spray or an all-purpose fruit tree spray with shampoo is best.

There's been a big push on the use of systemic garden chemicals. These products are applied to the soil and then accepted by the roots and transmitted throughout the plant's vascular system, making the plant and its products totally insecticidal. I'm opposed to them because these chemical groups are far stronger than the so-called hard pesticides and are applied to the ground, where they can easily be caught up in the movement of surface waters and deposited in the soil near vegetable gardens, fruit trees, or other food crops, thus making the fruits and vegetables very dangerous to eat. For this reason alone I avoid them like the plague.

I use safer materials for minor infestations, like the inexpensive flea and tick shampoo tonic with pyrethrum, and other mild chemicals for roses and food plants alike. Details are on page 8.

"Remember: Chemicals are medicine to your plants, and they don't like taking medicine any better than you do."

Just remember, chemicals are medicine to your plants, and they don't like taking medicine any better than you do, because it smells bad and tastes worse.

Winds, cold or hot, kill evergreens. That's why I recommend a spray called Cloud Cover in spring, early summer, and late fall in all parts of the country.

SHRUBS ....

With the cost of living at its peak in recent years, many young homebuyers are too strapped to finance any kind of landscaping. Flowering shrubs offer gardeners in even the most limited income brackets an opportunity for beauty, color, and fragrance at a very low cost. I by no means am implying that flowering shrubs make a second-class landscape. On the contrary, I personally prefer them to the evergreens because they have so much more to offer, not only from a cost factor, but from a beauty standpoint. Flowering shrubs are fast growers and spread out rapidly to cover a much larger area in a shorter time than evergreens. These versatile plants can be used to deaden noise, or hide a work or play area or dog runs. The flowering shrubs can be used as living fences or as formal plantings, or they can be planted alone as specimen plants. If you'll take a little time in selecting the right shrubs, you can have flowers of all colors of the rainbow, gorgeous foliage all summer, edible fruits throughout the season, and colorful and interesting wood all winter when the foliage has dropped off. All in all, you get more for your money with flowering shrubs than with any other garden group in the plant kingdom.

"All in all, you get more money with flowering shrubs than with any other garden group."

NEVER TURN
YOUR BACK
ON A SHRUB

● ●

"Flowering shrubs are like playful children. Be firm, but affectionate with them."

I've cautioned you to plan before you plant and to know all there is to know about each plant in your garden. I will refer to some groups and varieties as males and others as females. I have said some are temperamental, and now I'm going to discuss the children. Flowering shrubs are like playful children: every time you turn around they've grown inches, or they're doing something they shouldn't be doing, or they're growing into someplace they shouldn't be. I find that I have very good luck with all of my shrubs when I treat them like children: I'm firm but affectionate. I scold them when I find them doing something they shouldn't be doing and praise them when they bloom extra heavily. I reward them with an extra ration of food when they're good. I baby them when they're ill, and I have to scold them when they get sagging posture and their foliage lies in the dirt, because I have to give them an extra bath. I give this group of plants children's names like Patty, Susie, Tommy, Bobby, and so on. I keep my eyes on them all the time, because if I don't, they will grow right out of their home and right into some other plant's—or into mine! So be sure to know all of the children in your garden and any you intend to plant. They'll need extra care.

ANY BED
WILL DO

· ·

"Nothing fancy." That's the word from shrubs when it comes to living requirements: they can live pretty comfortably in any soil if it's well drained and mulched, and if they don't have to compete with weeds. All of the foliage and flowering shrubs are at the nursery in the standard selections: bare root, balled-in-burlap, potted in tin cans, and the paper-pulp pots. They should all be planted in the same manner as deciduous and evergreen friends. One suggestion I have is to discard the soil you remove from the new hole and replace it with professional mix. It has a little added punch for the shrub kids and gets them off to a good start. I've never found it necessary to stake shrubs when I plant them; some of my colleagues do, however, for no real purpose that I can see. It's necessary to cut back the bare root shrubs at least a third of the way when they're newly planted, to encourage branching. I do the same with the potted and balled-in-burlap shrubs, just to let them know what I expect from them. The best time to plant shrubs is any time you can get a shovel into the ground. I add one pound of bonemeal to the hole, then add one pound of low-nitrogen garden food on top of the soil after planting.

The worst enemy a flowering shrub can have is a pair of pruning shears in the hands of a novice. You can destroy everything you and your shrub have worked for if you prune at the wrong time. Flowering shrubs make the following spring's flowers on this year's wood, so the best time to give them a haircut is when they're in full bloom or just after they finish blooming. The year I lived with Grandma Putt was the year I received my best grades in school. Not because of my academic ability alone, I'm sure, but partly because I would take a bouquet to class each day from March to May. The reason for the bouquet was two-fold—to share the fragrance and beauty with others, and to have bigger flowers and more of them the following year. You should never let the blooms die on the vine; a dying bloom takes too much from the rest of the plant. To improve your plants' production and your youngsters' grades, cut bouquets all spring. By the way, little girls can carry the bouquets out in the open. Little boys prefer them in plain brown paper bags.

"To improve your plants' production and your youngster's grades, cut bouquets all spring."

Since many shrubs resemble the '60s generation of hippies in their bedraggled appearance, they tend to talk that way, too. I was talking to a rather sad-looking spiraea bush not too long ago, and he was complaining about the aphids on his new growth. "Hey, man, can you help me out and flick the fleas from the flesh? They're bugging me." I suggested a good shower, which was not quite what he had in mind, but it did the job and we parted friends—I happy, he still looking sad, but healthy. As with most children, I don't mention the word "bath" until the last minute, but to keep these shrubs healthy and happy, they too must be clean. Showers should be given at least once every three weeks to control most of the insects that crawl or fly and chew or suck, and oak leaf mulch should be used on the soil. If after all this trouble still comes to the tops of the shrubs, spray with fruit tree spray. Soil insects can be eliminated with Dursban.

The roots of most of the shrubs are as unpredictable as their tops: they go every which way.

Root pruning in the spring will help build a stronger body for the wayward children of your garden. This is done by forcing a sharp spade straight into the ground in a circle at the drip line once a year. This root-pruning operation stimulates more feeder roots and gives the plant an appetite.

Like all children, flowering shrubs are always on the go; consequently, they're always hungry. I feed them 4-12-4 or 5-10-5 garden food from February to August. I give three-foot shrubs half a pound per month, three- to six-foot shrubs one and a half pounds per month. Spread the food on the soil or mulch beneath. What a difference a meal makes to your shrubs! Use the all-purpose tonic found on page 7 (beer, ammonia, soap, molasses) every three weeks.

YOU CAN HEDGE ON THIS ONE

Fifty feet of chain link fence can cost you somewhere in the neighborhood of $150. Fifty feet of privet hedge, a living fence, will run about $15. I've never seen a flower on a chain link fence—at least not one that the fence itself grew. You can use these suggestions for hedge fences: red spiraea, (short) boxwood, *Multiflora rosa*, forsythia, privet, burning bush, and spiraea. There are many others.

MONEY CAN GROW ON SHRUBS

It always fascinates my neighbors to watch me take hard- and softwood cuttings from my shrubs and pass them out at no cost. I can do this because they cost me nothing. You too can make new plants from your existing shrubs with just a little know-how. It's easy. There are two basic types of cuttings: the softwood and the hardwood.

Softwood cuttings are slips of plants taken from the adult plant's soft growth. Most all of your perennials and your flowering shrubs will yield these cuttings. Take cuttings in May and early June from new growth. Make them three to six inches long, and remove the bottom three layers of leaves. Dip first in water, then dip about a half inch of the slip into a product called Rootone that you get in nurseries. Shake off the excess and place the slip in a prepoked, pencil-sized hole in sharp sand, covering at least one or two of the nodes or leaf breaks. The best temperature for rooting is 60 to 70 degrees, while the soil should be 5 degrees warmer. Keep the soil shaded and always damp, but not soaked, the first few days. Sprinkle the foliage often to control humidity.

Move the cuttings into the light as they progress in rooting. When roots are well established, pot the plants and move them into the garden. I plant pots and all into soil to protect them.

PLANTS FROM WHICH TO TAKE
SOFTWOOD CUTTINGS

COMMON NAME	SCIENTIFIC NAME
Azalea	Rhododendron
Barberry	Berberis
Beautybush	Kolkwitzia
Bittersweet	Celastrus
Boxwood	Buxus
Broom	Cytisus
Bush arbutus	Abelia
Butterfly bush	Buddleia
Camellia	Camellia
Crape-myrtle	Lagerstroemia
Dogwood	Cornus
Firethorn	Pyracantha
Forsythia	Forsythia
Fringetree	Chionanthus
Heather	Erica
Hemlock	Tsuga
Holly	Ilex
Honeysuckle	Lonicera
Hydrangea	Hydrangea
Jasmine	Jasminum
Juniper	Juniperus
Leucothoe	Leucothoe
Lilac	Syringa
Mockorange	Philadelphus
Oleander	Nerium
Pachysandra	Pachysandra
Privet	Ligustrum
Rhododendron	Rhododendron
Rose	Rosa
Rose-of-sharon	Hibiscus syriacus
Senecio	Senecio
Sequoia	Sequoia

COMMON NAME	SCIENTIFIC NAME
Silver vine	*Actinidia*
Spiraca	*Spiraea*
Spruce	*Picea*
Viburnum	*Viburnum*
Weigela	*Weigela*
Wintercreeper	*Euonymus*
Yew	*Taxus*

Hardwood cuttings are collected in the late fall or winter. Take cuttings to eight inches long from the stems, tie in bundles, and store in a box of peat moss in the basement until spring. After the frost has gone, remove and untie them and dip one end of each slip in Rootone and then place the slip into the soil in your garden, leaving about half of the slip above the ground.

PLANTS FROM WHICH TO TAKE HARDWOOD CUTTINGS

COMMON NAME	SCIENTIFIC NAME
Barberry	*Berberis*
Burningbush	*Euonymus*
Catalpa	*Catalpa*
Chaenomeles	*Chaenomeles*
Crape-myrtle	*Lagerstroemia*
Deutzia	*Deutzia*
Dogwood	*Cornus*
Elder	*Sambucus*
Firethorn	*Pyracantha*
Flowering quince	*Cydonia*
Forsythia	*Forsythia*
Hazel	*Corylus*
Honeysuckle	*Lonicera*

COMMON NAME	SCIENTIFIC NAME
Ninebark	*Physocarpus*
Oleander	*Nerium*
Poplar	*Populus*
Privet	*Ligustrum*
Russian olive	*Elaeagnus*
Viburnum	*Viburnum*
Weigela	*Weigela*
Willow	*Salix*
Wisteria	*Wisteria*

FLOWERING SHRUBS FOR HOME USE

	ZONE	COLOR FLOWER	FRUIT OR BERRIES
Andromeda	5	white	no
Azalea	5	many	no
Barberry, standard and dwarf	3	yellow	yes
Beach plum	4	white	yes
Beautybush	5	pink	yes
Blueberry	4	white	yes
Blue-spiraea	5	blue	yes
Bottlebrush	5	white	no
Buckeye	3	yellow, white	yes
Broom	6	yellow, red, blue	no
Butterfly bush	6	lavender	no
California lilac	4-8	blue	no
Camellia	7	pink, red, white	no
Cherry laurel	6	white	no
Chinese redbud	6	lavender	no
Cotoneaster	4	pink	yes
Crape-myrtle	7	pink, red, lavender, white	no
Daphne	5	red, pink, lavender, white	yes
Deutzia	5	white, pink	no
Firethorn	6	white	yes

	ZONE	COLOR FLOWER	FRUIT OR BERRIES
Flowering almond	5	pink, white	no
Flowering plum	6	pink	no
Flowering quince	5	yellow	no
Forsythia	5	yellow	no
Gardenia	8	white	no
Genista	2	yellow	no
Glossy Abelia	5	pink	no
Hardy orange	6	white	yes
Heath	6	red, white, lavender	no
Heather	5	red, lavender, white	no
Holly olive	7	green	yes
Honeysuckle	3	pink	yes
Hydrangea	3	white, pink, blue	no
Japanese snowbell	6	white	no
Jetbead	6	white	no
Kerria	6	yellow	no
Konsa dogwood	5	white	no
Korean Abelia leaf	5	white	no
Leatherwood	6	white	no
Leucothoe	5	white	no
Lilac	3	pink, lavender, white, red	no
Mahonia	5	yellow	yes
Mockorange	4	white	no
Mountain laurel	4	pink, white	no
Ocean Spray	5	white	no
Parrotia	6	red	no
Pearl-bush	5	white	no
Photinia	7	white	yes
Privet	4	white	yes
Pussy willow	5	gray catkins	no
Rhododendron	5	red, lavender, pink, yellow, white	no
Rock rose	8	pink	no

	ZONE	COLOR FLOWER	FRUIT OR BERRIES
Rose	5	yellow, white, pink, red	no
Rose Acacia	6	pink	no
St. Johnswort	6	yellow	no
Sandmyrtle	6	white	no
Sapphireberry	6	white	yes
Shadblow	4	white	yes
Skimmia	7	yellow, white	yes
Smoke tree	5	green	no
Snow-wreath	6	white, green	no
Spicebush	4	yellow	yes
Spike-heath	6	pink, white	no
Spiraea	4	white, pink, red	no
Star magnolia	5	white	yes
Stewartia	7	white	no
Strawberry shrub	5	yellow	yes
Summersweet	4	white	no
Sun-rose	6	yellow, red, white	no
Sweet spire	6	white	no
Tamarisk	5	pink, red	no
Trailing arbutus	3	white, pink	no
Tree peony	5	white, pink, yellow	no
Viburnum	5	white, pink	yes
Vitex	5	lavender	no
Weigela	4	pink, red, white	no
Winter-hazel	6	yellow	no
Winter jasmine	6	yellow	no
Witch-hazel	4	yellow	no

Zone hardiness indicates the coldest climate in which a plant can survive. The zones are set out in a map compiled by the National Aboretum for the USDA. You can find it on page 407.

GET ON THE
LIST

● ●

If you're a real home gardener, you'll want to get on as many garden catalog lists as you can, no, not with the intention of buying from them all, but to get new and updated listings and pictures of plant materials.

The Banana Tree
715 Northampton Street,
Easton, PA 10842

Burgess Seed and Plant Company
Dept. 89,
905 Four Seasons Road,
Bloomington, IL 61701

W. Atlee Burpee Company
300 Park Avenue,
Warminster, PA 18991-0001

D. V. Burrell Seed Growers
Rocky Ford, CO 81067

Caprilands Herb Farm
534 Silver Street,
Coventry, CT 06238

Comstock, Ferre & Company
P.O. Box 125,
Wethersfield, CT 06109

The Cook's Garden
Box 65,
Londonderry, VT 05148

Farmer Seed and Nursery
Dept. 77,
Reservation Center
2207 East Oakland Avenue,
Bloomington, IL 61701

Henry Field's Seed & Nursery Company
Shenandoah, IA 51602

Gurney Seed and Nursery Company
Yankton, SD 57079

High Altitude Gardens
P.O. Box 4238,
Ketchum, ID 83340

J. L. Hudson, Seedman
P.O. Box 2058,
Redwood City, CA 94064

Ed Hume Seeds
P.O. Box 1450,
Kent, WA 98032

Johnny's Selected Seeds
305 Foss Hill Road,
Albion, ME 04910

Jung Seeds & Nursery
335 S. High Street,
Randolph, WI 53957-0001

The Meyer Seed Company
600 S. Caroline Street,
Baltimore, MD 21231

Harris Moran Seed Company
Eastern Operations,
3670 Buffalo Road,
Rochester, NY 14624

Park Seed Company
Cokesbury Road,
Greenwood, SC 29647-0001

Peter Pepper Seeds
H. W. Alfrey,
P.O. Box 415,
Knoxville, TN 37901

Pinetree Garden Seeds
New Gloucester, ME 04260

Ripley's Believe It or Not
10 Bay Street,
Westport, CT 06880

Stillridge Herb Farm
10370 Route 99,
Woodstock, MD 21163

Stokes Seeds, Inc.
Box 548,
Buffalo, NY 24240

Taylor's Herb Gardens, Inc.
1535 Lone Oak Road,
Vista, CA 92084

Texas Onion Plant Company
P.O. Box 871,
Farmersville, TX 75031

Thompson & Morgan
P.O. Box 1308,
Jackson, NY 08527

Tillingshast Seed Company
P.O. Box 738
La Conner, WA 98257

Vermont Bean Seed Company
Garden Lane,
Fair Haven, VT 05743-0250

Vesey's Seeds Ltd.
P.O. Box 9000,
Houlton, ME 04730-0814

Wyatt-Quarles Seed Company
P.O. Box 739,
Garner, NC 27529

REAL
COVER-UP
· ·

In this day and age we all seem to strive for privacy. To block out the action around us, we seem to be cultivating the "mind-our-own-business," "don't-get-involved" culture. This is wrong. We were created to mix and mingle, talk and listen, love and be loved and help one another. I am sure that Mother Nature did not intend the beautiful vines and ivies to shut others out or us in. She lives in hope that we will use them to enhance the beauty of our homes or gardens. These climbing beauties can cover up an object of work location that might detract from the overall beauty of our garden. The ground covers were created for the purpose of cooling the toes of our trees and shrubs, or to grow in a spot where other plants don't dare to wander.

The variety of both the climbing vines and creeping ground covers is virtually unlimited in color, texture and fragrance. Both vines and covers are nearly maintenance-free, with a few exceptions. Both tend to reproduce new plants without much effort.

If you find it necessary to screen a dog pen or children's play area, control dust, or muffle street noise, or if security is needed for children's safety, then by all means screen or cover up with these members of the Plant Kingdom. But never use them to block out the wonderful world around you. As the younger generation says, "Let the sun shine in" and "Let it all hang out!"

FE - FI - FO - FUM

· ·

I guess the first climbing vine any of us learn about as children is Jack's famous "beanstalk," which is still being used by some of the wiser and more imaginative home gardeners. Whenever anyone thinks of a climbing vine, he naturally thinks of a flowering vine, but since we are all concerned about space in today's day and age, we should first consider a plant that will return food and flowers. When I find it necessary to disguise an object or location, I always look at my fruit and vegetable list first. There are many vinelike crops like pole beans, peas, grape vines, etc. that can do the job, and pay their way at the same time. If it is a ground cover I need, I always check to see if strawberries will fill the bill, or cucumbers and squash. Don't waste space if you can fill your table and eye at the same time.

WHAT'S THE PURPOSE?

· ·

When you select a vine for flowers and/or foliage, it should serve some purpose. The plant in question can be used to detract from an objectionable surface, perhaps a crumbling or stained stone wall. In this case, the plant selected should be one trained to grow on wires to form a design.

To form an arbor you should use a dense foliage vine with delicate flowers. If you wish to divide your yard into recreational areas, you can use medium foliage vines with large flowers, etc. Entryways can be enhanced with the use of cascading vines like the wisteria, to give the effect of elegance and size. Before you select a vine, decide what its purpose in life is going to be.

NO MAN'S LAND

The ground covers are a different story altogether. In the garden, we consider them lifesavers, plant lifesavers. Anyone who attempts to grow grass under trees, or in heavily shaded areas, is taking on a losing battle for both himself and the grass. Ground covers are the answer to your grass's prayers and your problem. These hardy boys can manage almost any situation. In shade, partial shade, damp, wet or soggy soil, they forge ahead! The ground cover crowd lives up to the old popular saying, "When the going gets tough, the 'tough' get going!"

PERMANENT RESIDENCY

Both the vines and ground covers are tough customers, but only after they have established themselves in their new homes. Spade leaf mulch, peat moss, and garden food into the soil where you are going to plant your climber or crawler. Make sure that the soil is in the same shape as suggested for the vegetable garden, level and fine. I'm a little on the impatient side when it comes to ground covers, so I plant them rather close together, in staggered rows. Top-dress the soil with a regular lawn food at least twice a year.

KIN TO CRABGRASS

Most ground covers are virtually indestructible, just like quack grass and crabgrass, and since they seem to resemble these same weeds in growing habits, I plant my ground covers in May when the weeds are growing their best. This is a good time any place in the country.

KEEP MOTHS OUT OF THE CARPET

You will find that you are not the only one that appreciates a thick cover of green foliage. Almost every creepy, crawly bug in the garden will, at one time or another, stop by to rest beneath it. Mice and moles will occasionally take a breather or build a winter nest there. To discourage the insects, wash with soap once or twice a month. Bury a wine bottle or two to keep the moles moving, and rattle the brush to move the mice. To control the soil bugs, if they appear, use 6 percent chlordane. Fungus diseases will appear from time to time if you do not use a soap shower. If the itchy diseases do appear, use one of the rose dusts in liquid solution.

WEEDS ARE NO BOTHER

I will, very briefly, mention this subject because it is no longer a problem if you use the kneeless weeders early in the spring. I do not cultivate ground covers, but I do mulch after I have spread my garden weeder.

NEED SUPPORT

Vines are much heavier than one imagines. Primarily, because of their total mass, they hold back the winds, putting a strain on the wires, poles or arbors supporting them. Make sure that the supporting pole or post is well anchored and the wires are thick and tough. The vines can usually hold tightly to whatever you supply them to climb. Oh yes, some have fine roots like fingers, especially the ivies, while grapes wrap their fingers around anything in sight. Some twist their whole body around a wire or pole, like bittersweet. And others have sticky fingers to help them hold on. However, since there is nothing worse than trying to stand a vine back up that has tumbled down with a broken support, be sure your supports are strong enough to support the ultimate weight of a full-grown vine when you first put them in.

BEST OF THE BUNCH

•••

Here are the names of a few good climbers and ground creepers:

CLIMBERS
Wisteria
Clematis (Princess of the Garden)
Star Jasmine
Trumpet Vine
Boston Ivy
Winter Creeper (Scale's Delight)
Passion Flower
Fatshedera
English Ivy
Pyracantha (Living Barbed Wire)
Silver Lace Vine
Climbing Hydrangea
Waxy Bittersweet (looks great in a vase)
Flame Honeysuckle
Bougainvillea
Vine Lilac
Madeiravine
Dutchmanspipe (most for your money)

GROUND CREEPERS
Crown Vetch
Sedum
Winter Creeper (Colorata)
Hardy Baltic Ivy
Myrtle

Pachysandra
Dragon's Blood (Sedum)
Halls Honeysuckle
Creeping Phlox
Lily of the Valley (not my favorite)
Strawberries
Ajuga
English Ivy
Wildginger

QUESTIONS AND ANSWERS ....

Q. *Which evergreens can I use as a ground cover?*
A. Any of the low-growing junipers like Armstrong, and many of the compactas.

Q. *Which is the most fragrant of the ground covers?*
A. You might enjoy fragrant sumac or peppermint. It depends on your smeller!

Q. *Is there some special care for clematis vines?*
A. The only special care is to plant the roots in the shade and keep the top growing in the sun.

Q. *Is there a red clematis?*
A. Sure is, crimson star. Best-looking clematis I have ever seen.

Q. *They are going to build a new home next to us. What can I use as a temporary screen?*
A. How about sweet peas, morning glory, or bal-

sam-apple? These are annuals, and so you won't have a great deal of money tied up.

Q. *Can I plant ground covers through plastic for weed control?*
A. Sure you can, but I don't advise it. Plastic is a pain in the you-know-what when it begins to tear. Mulch and a garden weeder are just as good in the beginning and better in the long run

Q. *Will all ground covers grow in the shade?*
A. No! Most of them will tolerate some shade, some full shade, and some only full sun. Here are a few of the sun-only covers: basket-of-gold, lavender, moss pink, the sedums, snow-in-summer, ice plant and ivy geraniums.

Q. *What do you recommend for a bank that keeps washing away?*
A. I have had some great luck with the crown vetch called penngift, which has lovely pink flowers. Plant in the fall or spring, three feet apart.

Q. *When do you prune wisteria?*
A. Prune the top twice—in the spring and early summer. Feed well, after trimming, with a garden food.

Q. *What kind of wire do you use to train vines?*
A. I use a galvanized twist if possible. Otherwise aluminum will pass.

Q. *How do you put a vine back on the wall after the house has been painted?*
A. Most garden centers have vine supports that you can cement or screw into the wall. These will hold until the clingers catch hold.

Q. *How often do you trim ground covers?*
A. Whenever they get out of hand. Use a sharp pair of trimmers.

Q. *Do you feed all vines and ground covers with the same food?*
A. If it flowers I use a garden food, and if it's all foliage, I use lawn food.

Q. *Does it hurt to plant bulbs in ground cover?*
A. On the contrary, it's a great idea and excellent for the bulbs.

Q. *When is the best time to transplant a clematis?*
A. In the early spring is about the best time in snow country and early fall in the South and West.

STEP-BY-STEP EVERGREEN AND SHRUB CARE................

SPRING

Step 1. The most important thing to remember when it comes to this landscape group, whether it's warm southern foliage and shrubs or the northern cold weather plant material, is that you must clean out beneath them at the beginning of the season. Use a bamboo or wire flexible rake only to remove leaves and trash, or mice, voles, shrews, and other varmints use this for nests.

Step 2. Every three years, remove the bark mulch very early in the season, while it's still cool. Apply Preen, a weed killer or pre-emergent weed killer, and sprinkle a light dose of Repel, along with two tablespoons of chili powder and one-half cup of crushed paradichlorobenzene moth crystals mixed in. Mix new mulch with old and replace.

Step 3. Wash down all shrubs, foliage, and evergreens with one-half cup of flea and tick shampoo and a half cup brown mouthwash in the quart jar of your ten-gallon hand-held sprayer with a blue golf ball inserted as an agitator.

Step 4. Remove old dead wood, wild suckers, and broken limbs, and seal large cuts with interior latex paint, thinned with a small amount of brown mouthwash. Use throwaway sponge brushes to seal.

Step 5. Shape early spring flowering shrubs as soon as they bloom, sealing cuts, and late flowering shrubs when new growth begins, just above and outside the foliage break.

Step 6. If shrubs have never been mulched, do it now. First sprinkle Preen on the soil according to the directions on the package, cover with Weed Block fabric, and mulch with shredded bark or mulch of your choice. The same holds true for beds of evergreens and foliage growth.

Step 7. Mix together ten pounds of gypsum, one cup of diatomaceous earth, one-half cup of paradichlorobenzene moth crystals (crushed with your foot is fine). Apply this mixture using a spreader setting of 1 on a hand-held spreader to enhance the foliage and needles and detour trouble.

Step 8. Feed all evergreens and shrubs in early

spring with a dry mix of a pound of sugar, a pound of Epsom salts, three cups of Scott's Summerizer (iron and sulphur) mixed into fifty pounds of any garden food and applied at a setting of 3 on a hand-held spreader.

Step 9. Water this feeding in with your ten-gallon blue sprayer with white golf ball, the jar filled with:

1 can of beer
½ cup of liquid dish soap
¼ cup of clear corn syrup
½ ounce of liquid seaweed
½ cup of hydrogen peroxide
to ten gallons of water

Step 10. If aphids, mites, scale, or other above-ground bugs have been a worry, then add any fruit tree spray (not just Diazinon) at one-half the recommended rate into the jar of your ten-gallon blue sprayer, mixing in:

½ cup laundry bar soap
½ cup chewing tobacco juice
½ cup antiseptic mouthwash
to ten gallons of water

(Details on making the solutions are on page 7.) Remember to apply all medicinal sprays after the sun starts down.

Step 11. Feed all evergreens and shrubs every three weeks, early in the morning, with this all-purpose tonic. Into the quart container of your twenty-gallon sprayer add:

1 can of beer
1 cup of children's shampoo
½ cup of molasses
1 ounce of liquid seaweed
1 cup of liquid lawn food
to twenty gallons of water

SUMMER

Step 12. Continue the spray in step 10 every couple of weeks, leaving out the fruit tree spray.

Step 13. If there is any indication of soil insect damage or activity, add Dursban to the step 10 tonic.

Step 14. Before hot weather sets in, spray foliage with Cloud Cover. This material is a lifesaver from both cold and hot weather.

FALL

Step 15. Never feed evergreens or shrubs in the snow belt after August 15.

Step 16. Tie all vertical growth with nylon pantyhose to prevent ice and snow weight damage in the North.

Step 17. Protect evergreens in both the North and South against unexpected freezes with Cloud Cover.

Step 18. Protect evergreens from an open southwest wind with a burlap screen.

Step 19. Root prune shrubs in early October, and lightly sprinkle a cup of Epsom salts over the cut; this will force new feeder roots. Use a very sharp spade, and force it into the ground at the tip of the farthest branch in a circle around the shrub.

Step 20. Place three rotting apples into the center of each early flowering shrub to help set buds for the fall.

QUESTIONS AND ANSWERS.............................

Q. *Is it better to plant evergreens balled-in-burlap or in containers?*

A. I just don't think you can beat the results of a well-balled evergreen, but then as a rule they're much larger plants and would be almost impractical to put into containers. Metal cans (the container that the plants are grown in, mostly in California and Oklahoma) are dangerous for the planter, not the planted. In most cases the can is cut open or split at the nursery before you leave. Some of the roots may dry out on the way home, or the soil may come loose. I really would prefer the plantable container—either burlap or paper pot—for small stock.

Q. *When is the best time to plant evergreens?*

A. Take a map of the United States and draw a line from the coast of Massachusetts to the top corner of the Kansas-Missouri border. Draw a line from there south to the middle of Texas and west to the middle of Arizona. Next, continue the line right up the middle of California, Oregon, and Washington. Plant evergreens south and west of that line all winter, north of this line in the early spring and early fall.

Q. *The leaves on our rhododendrons look terrible in the winter, they droop so badly. What causes it?*

A. At 10 degrees below zero your bones would droop, too. That's natural. You can help them by spraying late in the fall with Cloud Cover; that's like putting a snowsuit on them.

Q. *Won't bare-root evergreens die?*
A. Yes, if they aren't kept damp and haven't been planted properly, which means in a good, comfortable hole. Add a teaspoon of children's shampoo and an ounce of hydrogen peroxide per gallon of water to help them breathe easily until they get established.

Q. *How do I keep dogs away from my evergreens?*
A. Get a big, mean cat. You can dip pipe cleaners in tobacco juice and hang them on the plant, sniff high. Also spread parabenzene moth crystals on the soil underneath. This will also control some of the soil insects that try to move in. Hinder, a repellent, as well as Repel garbage can spray, work well.

Q. *How do you get rid of red spiders once and for all?*
A. Dig up all of your evergreens. Or you can spray with an ounce of liquid dish detergent in ten gallons of water; if that fails use methoxychlor according to package directions.

Q. *Will bag worms kill my evergreens, and how do I get rid of them?*
A. They sure do make your evergreens uncomfortable. They won't destroy them, just make them itch a lot. You can use tobacco juice, soap and water, and *Bacillus thuringiencis*.

Q. *What's the largest evergreen that can be planted? We would like a ten- to twelve-foot spruce.*
A. There's equipment now that will allow you to plant spruce twice that size or larger. Your only restriction is your bank account.

Q. *What evergreen can we plant in a wet spot to make a hedge?*
A. Got just the thing: Canadian hemlock. Makes a great hedge, looks rich, and it's thick. The American arborvitae will take some water, but not too much.

Q. *When is the best time to take cuttings from my cedar trees? And can I grow plants from them?*
A. I take them in the early spring and root them in sharp sand, then transfer them to peat pots to get a good start. You bet you can grow your own, and they turn out to be the best kind, because they're your babies.

Q. *Are ground covers considered as good as mulch under evergreens?*
A. You bet. They are really great and, when possible, I do use them. If you want to be the talk of the town, use strawberries as a ground cover beneath evergreens; foliage, flowers, and fruit . . . delicious. You can also use vinca, ajuga, and pachysandra, to name a few.

Q. *If you have a large number of evergreens to plant, when is the best time?*
A. It doesn't matter how many you have, the best time to plant evergreens is when the days are warm and evenings are cool. That goes for any part of the country.

Q. *Will all broadleaf evergreens grow in the North?*
A. With very few exceptions, yes. but in really cold, blowy areas you must remember to protect them from constant winds. This can be done with burlap screens or snow fence columns with burlap tacked to the front. I gently but firmly tie my azaleas and rhododendrons with old nylon pantyhose

to keep ice and snow from breaking them. Spray with Cloud Cover in spring, summer, and fall.

Q. *How many different types of evergreens are there and can I grow most of them in Southern California?*
A. Almost as many as there are stars in the sky and more on the way each season from the propagators. Yes, you could grow most of them in Southern California. If you would like to see most of them, take a Sunday ride up to Monrovia Nursery in Azusa, California. They are the largest nursery in the world.

Q. *Do you recommend mulching broadleaf evergreens?*
A. I do it myself and so do some of the most successful landscapers and gardeners. I use straw at the base of my rhododendrons and azaleas. I screen my holly and ilex.

Q. *I love rhododendrons, but I don't have a northern location in which to plant them. Am I out of luck?*
A. No, not really. They like shade but will tolerate some sun. An eastern exposure or any other will do if you can shade the rhododendrons, say with a large tree. Azaleas, mountain laurels and *Pieris japonica* are all great friends and like the same acid soil, moist and shady.

Q. *We've got the world's hardest clay. Evergreens just don't have a chance. What can I do?*
A. You can mound plant. For this I suggest you purchase evergreens that are balled-in-burlap. I have a landscape architect friend who brags that he's never lost an evergreen. The trouble with the brag is that he never plants them in the ground,

always above: he mounds plants. He places hills of good soil in strategic locations that blend into the contour of the building or setting and then plants the evergreens in the mound. You can do the same thing on your hard clay and not lose a plant, and you can create some pretty original and spectacular designs and effects. Mound planting can be carried out with all types of plants. When using this style of construction, you must remember to be constantly aware of your permanent grade and leave paths for the water to shed off and away.

Q. *If you were going to use evergreens as a wind barrier, which would you use—pine, fir or spruce?*
A. I would go with the pine because they're much faster growing and generally less expensive. Spruce is a rather stodgy guy—handsome, yes, but he can be hard to get along with from time to time; and fir only likes it where it's cool and damp. We usually use either of these last two as a point of view.

Q. *What's the willowy evergreen they use for hedges?*
A. Ah, heck, that's got to be Canadian or American hemlock. They're both great. They're terrific for shady and/or wet areas as well.

Q. *What's the showiest of the firs?*
A. I have to cast my vote for Concolor. His Latin name is *Abies concolor*.

Q. *Is poultry manure good for palm trees?*
A. Do you mean the one the birds deposit on top or the one you use at the bottom? Sure, it's great at the bottom. As a matter of fact, it's good for most any plant.

Q. *When and how do you trim a Scotch pine?*
A. In June and July. You can use a sharp knife or hedge trimmer, which should also be sharp. Cut the main leader the same height as the swirl below. That way each layer of branches will be the same distance apart.

Q. *We have a large upright yew on the corner of the house that never has been a dark green as the one in the backyard bought at the same time. We feed and water it. What's wrong?*
A. I'm just guessing from what you tell me, but I would say it's a little chlorotic, and a dose of iron will help. Four to six ounces of micronized iron in two gallons of water will do the trick. Or you can apply Scott's Summerizer in early spring at a half handful per foot of growth.

Q. *Is it true that it's better to cut a Christmas tree when the weather is warm than a few days before Christmas?*
A. It's true you should cut a tree when it still has its sap. I use Prolong tree extender for mine. It's an IV of glucose, just like you and I might get. Also spray the tree with Cloud Cover before you cut it.

Q. *Can ground-up Christmas trees, needles and all, be used as a mulch?*
A. It's a lifesaver, but remember it will tend to make the soil acid. If you use this material, add some lime in the spring.

Q. *Can you use sanitation-fill sludge to feed evergreens?*
A. I've been asked that same question about every area of the garden. Yes, you can use it and be glad—it's generally free.

Q. *How do you kill scale on evergreens?*
A. Spray with a dormant or scaleicide spray in the spring. Make sure you read and follow the directions. Malathion is the next step.

Q. *What kind of evergreens do you use in a rock garden?*
A. Low-growing junipers like Armstrong and many, many others. Check the nursery catalogs.

Q. *How much should it cost to have a set of plans drawn up for landscaping?*
A. How high is high or deep is deep? It depends on what you're having done. A registered architect will charge a reasonable fee; he's earned it. A landscaper might furnish you plans free if you buy from him. You might also look at the *Landscape Planner*, from Home Planners, in your bookstore.

Q. *Is plastic good to use as a mulch under evergreens?*
A. Now we use Weed Blocker, a material that looks like spandex from Easy Gardener.

Q. *Is limestone a good ground cover?*
A. If it's washed, it's okay, but I don't like it as well as mixed stone or marble chips. Make sure you put down Weed Blocker, covered with shredded bark there.

Q. *How do I keep the birds from eating the new shoots off the top of our spruce tree?*
A. Place a small plastic bag over the bud until it breaks open. This takes about three weeks. Repel will also help.

Q. *Can a live Christmas tree be kept alive?*
A. Why, certainly. Keep its foliage moist, keep the

ball wet, and after Christmas set the tree in the garage to let it go dormant gradually, letting the ball freeze. Then plant it in a predug hole. Make sure it is sprayed with Cloud Cover or Tree Saver, both from Easy Gardener.

Q. *What are the brown balls that appear on the ends of our spruce tree?*
A. This is a gall caused by an insect. First use an ounce of liquid dish detergent in ten gallons of water with Malathion or methoxychlor added. Or use fruit tree spray according to package directions.

Q. *The children want to grow Christmas trees from seed. Is this possible?*
A. That's what cones were put there for. Soak the cones, pierce the seeds, and plant them.

Q. *I have seen some of the most beautiful designs cut from evergreens. Does this hurt them, and can I do it?*
A. You can do it. It's called topiary—the shaping of evergreens into forms resembling animals, flowers, buildings, and so on. Rudolph Valentino, the movies' most famous lover, came to this country as a topiarian.

Q. *Can any of the spruces take salt air and still look good?*
A. I'd book odds on a green guy called Dragon spruce, even though he grows only about half as high as his cousins. Dragon will usually be sixty to seventy-five feet high and quite thick.

Q. *Which is the early pretty silver green spruce?*
A. Koster's blue, a fine gent you'll be glad you asked to stick around.

Q. *When I was in California I saw an evergreen, a cypress called golden coat. Can I grow it in Fort Wayne, Indiana?*

A. The real name is, get this, *Chamaecyparis pisifera filifera aurea*, or goldthread cypress, and yes, it will do fine. Most folks who are not familiar with this golden yellow evergreen and its brother, plume cypress, always think they look as if they're about to croak. I think this is as good a place as any to suggest you go to the library and check out a horticultural plate book (color pictures of most plants available for sale in this country). You can then see for yourself if you like the plant's looks.

Q. *What's the fastest-growing spruce?*

A. A burly guy from Norway grows like hell when he is young and handsome but goes to seed as he gets older. You're usually sorry you planted him when he gets old and scraggly.

Q. *How often do you water evergreens?*

A. In the warm, dry periods, three times a week. Let the hose run on the ground and water them deep, so that the roots stay down where it's cool. In the early spring when the drying winds are blowing, spray the foliage every day.

Q. *I have a space problem, and I want to grow tomatoes between my evergreens. Will it hurt the evergreens?*

A. No, but the tomatoes will be awfully strong tasting. I've seen all sorts of vegetables grown among evergreens, and they both do well. Go ahead.

Q. *Can you use weed killers under or around evergreens?*

A. The so-called garden weeders you can, but as for weed and feeds, I never get near or within the drip line of all trees, shrubs, and evergreens—that's the point the farthest branch reaches. As for liquid weed killers, be awfully careful. They'll ruin the foliage for life.

Q. *What flowering shrub would you suggest for long-lasting fragrance and a white flower?*
A. Double mockorange blooms almost all summer and smells great. I like them near a patio. This plant grows five to six feet.

Q. *Can I use raw fish for my hydrangea?*
A. The plant will love it, but so will all the cats in the neighborhood. Use liquid fish plant food instead.

Q. *When and how do you prune azaleas?*
A. You don't, if you can avoid it! If it's absolutely necessary, prune them when they're in bloom. Use a sharp pair of pruning shears, mulch beneath azaleas, and never cultivate.

Q. *Can I prune a rhododendron?*
A. Not in my garden! If you must, cut above a foliage branch, sterilize, and seal. Don't cultivate, but do mulch.

Q. *What kind of a shrub can we plant in wet soil?*
A. You can plant my favorite, the red twig dogwood, or the speckled alder.

Q. *How far north can we grow bottlebrush shrub?*
A. This can be used as a tree or shrub, and you can grow it as far north as zone 7.

Q. *Which flowering shrub is the first to bloom?*
A. Most folks say the forsythia, but the pussy willow beats it by a long shot.

Q. *Which of the flowering shrubs can you take wood from and force to bloom in water in the house?*
A. My grandma made just about all of them bloom inside.

Q. *What would keep a hydrangea from blooming?*
A. It could be any number of things: poor soil, too much shade, or too much nitrogen fertilizer. The most common reason is pruning at the wrong time. You only prune when the plant is through blooming.

Q. *We haven't had a bloom on our lilac in three years. What would make it stop?*
A. More likely than not, you have mostly sucker shoots. These are straight shafts from below the soil that will never flower. Cut them all back to the ground, and you should get flowers.

Q. *Can I take cuttings from my flowering shrubs? If so, when and how?*
A. You sure can—almost any of them. You can take cuttings in the fall and root them in sand. Or you can air layer some shrubs, like forsythia.

Q. *I have heard that sumac is a bad shrub for beekeepers to have around.*
A. If you are a beekeeper, you would not care to have this honey in the frames, for no other reason than the fact that it's a bright green. But it's still good, pure honey.

Q. *Can we use regular edible berry shrubs in our landscape plan?*
A. That's what it's all about; use the land to the best ends for you and the plants. I suggest blueberry, currant, or gooseberry.

TREES

● ●

SHADY TREES

As I sit in my comfortable corner of the basement, where I wrote the original manuscript for this book and reread the text, I get some of the most heart-warming flashbacks to my childhood and my days in the arms of Grandma Putt.

When I was a small boy, I spent a school year with my Grandmother Putnam. I learned more about love and tenderness in that year than any other time of my childhood. You see, my grandmother truly knew the language of the flowers. I'm convinced she could talk to Mother Nature and would be answered. She spent most of her days in her garden. When I would come home from school each afternoon, I would hustle into the house and head for the kitchen and the cookie jar and then on out into the garden. On nice days I'd find Grandma

169

sitting in her wicker chair, with her Bible in her hand, under the shade and protection of Great Grandpa Coolidge. She would tousle my hair and kiss my cheek and want to know about the important happenings of my day.

Of course a lot of things happen in the ordinary day of a six-year-old boy. Billy Annoble caught a frog in the ditch on the way to school and put it on Maxey Smith's seat, and he sat on it. I spilled water-color paint on the new linoleum, and so on. Grandma Putt would take the time right then to tell me a story about Mr. Frog and all the good he does and explain that Billy shouldn't hurt frogs. We would sit there in the garden and she would tell me a story from the Bible and then get up and pat Great-Grandpa Coolidge and would go inside and begin to make dinner, and I would do my chores and go to play. By the way, Great-Grandpa Coolidge was her favorite maple tree.

The way the story goes in our family, Great-Grandpa planted that maple tree himself as a living monument. And, to this day, whenever I pass that way, I can see Great Grandpa Coolidge still standing. Not too far from him stands my Grandpa Putt; his monument is a horse chestnut. Grandma Putt told me that that particular kind of tree was picked for him because he raised and raced horses. My grandmother said that every man should plant a tree on a spot where he would like to be forever, and I happen to believe that's one of the most important ideas that anyone ever told me.

Could you imagine what the world would be like with no trees? To me, there's no greater beauty than the tall elegance of these masterpieces of Mother Nature's craft. Shade trees give so much and ask so little. They shade and cool you when you're hot; the soft rustle of their leaves can calm you when you're uptight; and to lie on your back

"My grandmother taught me that every man should plant a tree on a spot where he would like to be forever—one of the most important ideas that anyone ever told me."

and look at the sunlight filtering down toward you can bring your mind and heart closer to happiness than most of us have a right to be. So why not plant a tree as your own living monument?

Most homeowners who have trees take them for granted until it looks like they're going to lose them, and then they begin to worry. Most of the time, their concern comes too late.

After a heavy rain or a hard wind, the first thing I do is walk under and around the shade trees on my property and survey them. I look them over very closely, much in the same way as I look over my children when they come to me crying after a spill or a fight. I check first to see that nothing is broken, and then I look for cuts and bruises. I don't take anything for granted with either my children or my trees. Trees are like humans; they suffer pain; they weep and bleed; they become arthritic and feeble, anemic, and even neurotic. Trees can go into shock and develop ulcers. There is really a human side to growing trees.

THE PERFECT MATCH

. . . .

Selecting a shade tree should be done with as much care as picking your spouse, but this is one time that I don't recommend love at first sight. Your home and your shade tree are probably going to be married for a lot longer than you or I, so it's important that they be compatible. The trees in your yard (since your home can have a harem) should complement your house and garden in the same way a woman complements her man. As the saying goes, for every man there's a woman; likewise, for every tree there is a garden. I've never met an ugly tree or one I couldn't like. But there are happy trees and sad ones, happy-go-lucky trees and selfish trees. There are trees to match every human personality, so pick the tree that matches yours and you'll fit your setting.

PLAN AHEAD

If you've completed your evergreen landscaping, you're ready to turn your attention to the shade trees for your property. You'll find that you can use trees to screen off objectionable views, deaden the sound of street traffic, to act as windbreakers, to help control poor drainage in some areas, and to fit almost any bill. But first you must plan.

Let's refer back to the paper bag plan you did (on page 105). Take a sharp pencil and draw lines representing telephone or electric wires and note their heights. Now, take a felt tip pen and indicate your sewer lines, underground pipes, or drain tiles and their depth, if you can find out. (Utility companies will mark all lines for free.) Get out your catalogs and begin to make a list of the trees you would like in the order of your preference. Do you want something very tall, or not so tall? You can get a tree with lacy, delicate foliage and light shade or one with a heavy canopy of leaves and dense shade. A shade tree can also have interesting bark or leaves that aren't green—silver, or purple, or red. Check the catalogs or reference books to find out how tall and broad the trees will grow. You don't want to plant too close to the house or garage and have to remove your tree in a few years because it raised the roof or tried to grow into the living room.

"Selecting a shade tree should be done with as much care as selecting your spouse."

Check to see if it's an explorer of sewers and tiles. If so, it may end up trying your patience when you have to call a plumber a couple of times a year to drill and clean out the roots from your sewage system. Will it make a mess, dropping flowers, seed pods, then leaves, that you don't want to clean up? If the mess isn't worth the beauty for you, try another tree. Then, and only then, take your plan back to the nurseryman.

When you finally decide on the variety of tree you want, one that's compatible to your home and garden, pick out the right spot to plant it. Never plant a tree under any wires or directly over drains. Never plant it too close to walks or driveways, or you may have to end up moving it when it or its roots encroach. And, above all, plant it on *your* property, not the neighbors' or city property. Remember, it's a lot easier to change a mistake made with a pencil than one made with a shovel!

SHADE TREES WITH ATTRACTIVE FOLIAGE

SCIENTIFIC NAME	COMMON NAME	ZONE
Acer ginnala	Amur maple	2
Acer palmatum	Japanese maple	5
Acer palmatum atropurpureum	Bloodleaf Japanese maple	5
Acer palmatum 'Bloodgood'	Bloodgood Japanese maple	5
Acer palmatum dissectum	Threadleaf Japanese maple	5
Acer pseudoplatanus	Sycamore maple	5
Acer saccharinum 'Pyramidale'	Pyramidal sugar maple	3
Acer saccharum	Sugar maple	3
Acer saccharum 'Columnare'	Columnar sugar maple	3

SCIENTIFIC NAME	COMMON NAME	ZONE
Acer saccharum 'Monumentale'	Sentry maple	3
Acer saccharum 'Green Mountain'	Green Mountain maple	3
Betula papyrifera	Canoe birch	2
Betula pendula	European birch	2
Betula pendula 'Liciniata'	Cutleaf European birch	2
Betula populifolia	Gray birch	4
Butea capitata	South American jelly palm (Pindo palm)	9
Cedrus atlantica	Atlas cedar	6
Cedrus atlantica 'Glauca'	Blue Atlas cedar	5
Cedrus deodara	Deodar cedar	7
Cercidiphyllum japonicum	Katsura-tree	4
Cercis canadensis	Eastern redbud	4
Cinnamomum camphora	Camphor-tree	9
Cocos nucifera	Coconut palm	10
Eucalyptus globulus	Tasmanian eucalyptus	9
Fagus sylvatica	European beech	4
Fagus sylvatica 'Atropunicea'	River's purple beech	4
Fagus sylvatica pendula	Weeping beech	4
Ficus retusa	Indian-laurel fig	10
Fraxinus americana	White ash	3
Fraxinus pennsyl-vanica lanceolata 'Marshall's seedless'	Marshall's seedless ash	2
Fraxinus velutina 'Modeste'	Modeste ash	5

SCIENTIFIC NAME	COMMON NAME	ZONE
Ginkgo biloba	Ginkgo	4
Ginkgo biloba fastigiata	Sentry ginkgo	4
Gleditsia triacanthos 'Inermis'	Thornless honeylocust	4
Gleditsia triacanthos 'Moraine'	Moraine locust	4
Gleditsia triacanthos 'Rubylace'	Rubylace locust	4
Gleditsia triacanthos 'Shademaster'	Shademaster locust	4
Gleditsia triacanthos 'Skyline'	Skyline locust	4
Gleditsia triacanthos 'Sunburst'	Sunburst locust	4
Gyminocladus dioica	Kentucky coffee-tree	4
Lagerstroemia indica	Crape-myrtle	7
Liquidambar styraciflua	Sweet-gum	4
Metasequoia glyptostroboides	Dawn redwood	5
Olea europaea	Common olive	9
Phellodendron amurense	Amur corktree	3
Phoenix canariensis	Canary Island date palm	10
Phoenix reclinata	Senegal date palm	10
Pistacia chinensis	Chinese pistachio	9
Platanus occidentalis	American sycamore	4
Platanus x acerifolia	London plane-tree	5
Populus nigra 'Italica'	Lombardy poplar	2
Prunus avium	Sweet cherry	3
Prunus cerasus	Sour cherry	3

SCIENTIFIC NAME	COMMON NAME	ZONE
Pseudotsuga men-ziestii 'Glauca'	Douglas fir (Rocky Mountain strain)	4
Quercus agrifolia	California live oak	9
Quercus alba	White oak	4
Quercus coccinea	Scarlet oak	4
Quercus palustris	Pin oak	4
Quercus phellos	Willow oak	5
Quercus rubra	Red oak	4
Quercus virginiana	Live oak	7
Reystonea regia	Royal palm	10
Salix alba 'Tristis'	Golden weeping willow	2
Salix babylonica	Babylon weeping willow	6
Salix x elegantissima	Thurlow weeping willow	4
Sophora japonica 'Regent'	Regent pagoda tree	4
Thuja occidentalis 'Nigra'	Dark green American arborvitae	2
Trachycarpus fortunei	Chinese windmill palm	8
Tsuga canadensis	Canada hemlock	3
Ulmus americana	American elm	2
Ulmus americana 'Princeton'	Princeton elm	2
Ulmus carpinifolia 'Christine Buisman'	Christine Buisman elm	4
Ulmus parvifolia	Chinese elm	5
Washingtonia filifera	Washington fan palm	10
Washingtonia robusta	Mexican fan palm	10
Zelkova serrata	Japanese zelkova	5
Zelkova serrata 'Village Green'	Village Green zelkova	5

FOREVER YOURS!

Shade trees, like evergreens, come in an assortment of containers: balled-in-burlap, paper pulp pots, and tin cans. You want all the soil with your tree that you can get. It's more difficult to transport shade trees because their trunks and limbs are more vulnerable than evergreens, so you must make sure that the trunk is wrapped with a large blanket or rags when it's put into your car or trailer. Also make sure that the limbs are securely tied with old nylon hose. I don't recommend that you move a shade tree in an automobile trunk. The ball or container weighs too much for one man to handle. I suggest that you pay the few dollars extra to have your tree delivered.

When the tree arrives, go through the same procedure I've suggested for planting your evergreens. Make sure that the hole is large enough and wide enough to plant without cramping—one and a half times as wide as the root ball and deep enough to cover it by several inches. Shade trees must be planted on the day they arrive, regardless if they've been grown in a container. All too often, they blow over or get upset in some way, and stand a chance of breaking the soil ball, which will damage the roots, It's absolutely necessary that the tree be planted straight and braced for the first six months. Too many times there's a soil shift or a prevailing wind that causes the poor tree to grow cockeyed the rest of its life. Shade trees are best braced by the use of a guy wire attached to a heavy band of nylon pantyhose. Nylon is extremely strong yet is soft and pliable enough so that it will not chafe the bark.

The tree of your choice is now in the ground, straight as an arrow. Now, mulch the ground around it and soak the soil. Do not feed for two weeks, then feed with fish emulsion and follow with any lawn food that does not have a weed killer in it.

Now it's time to wrap it up—I mean the trunk. For this job you'll need a roll of tree wrap, a strong paper with a tar center that keeps the dry winds from cooking your young trees in the summer and keeps them dormant in the winter. I wrap all new trees and leave the wrapping on until it rots off. Start at the lowest main branch and wrap it all the way to the ground.

The best time to plant shade trees is in the early spring or early fall. In snow country, you can plant or set trees in a hole and partly cover with soil and straw in the cold of winter when both the root ball and the soil are frozen.

Stand back and look over your new friend. Make sure he was not bruised or broken in the move to your home. If he was, sterilize the wound with a solution of two tablespoons household ammonia in a gallon of water and dress it with pruning paint to seal. A week after he's in the ground, give him a shower with an ounce of liquid dish detergent in ten gallons of water. Make sure you do this again before the winter freeze.

H E L P !
· ·

I stated earlier that all too often we tree owners are unaware of damage or disease until it is almost too late. And I find that in many cases it's because the trees are so big we can't see what's wrong with them, or we think that they're big enough to take care of themselves. None of us, man or tree, is ever quite that big. We all need attention and help once in a while. I had an elm tree where I once lived, and he moaned only when he was in trouble. Once I heard the noise and looked him over and found that the crook of the tree was split. I repaired it, and the noise stopped. Next time he moaned, I found a bees' nest in a large crevice that was hidden. As soon as I removed it, he stopped moaning. So you see, trees can talk. Just listen!

I'm sure you don't let your kids stop taking showers when they get big. Well, small trees and big trees need showers too! Now this can be a big undertaking for a big tree, but with a little imagination—or a community effort—you can have the large trees sprayed. My neighbors and I share the cost.

If you've had a problem with insects or disease, you'll have to use a dormant oil spray. This is a lime, sulphur, and Volk oil combination available at any garden center. You spray with dormant oils in the fall after the leaves have fallen and again in the spring before the buds swell. In the West and South, you continue to use the soap shower every month and add Malathion or methoxychlor to the spray if you have an insect problem. Trees fifteen to twenty feet tall can be sprayed with the standard hose and hose-end sprayer and should be showered once every three or four weeks with a children's shampoo and mouthwash solution. (See page 7 for the tonic.) FSS can be used in the shampoo.

THIS WON'T HURT

Pruning and trimming of shade trees should be approached with care and caution. An inexperienced, amateur tree surgeon can do more damage than good if he doesn't know what he's doing. If you think you've spotted a problem that requires surgery, stop right where you are, turn around three times, and then look at it again! Now ask yourself, if you can handle the saw, pruners, and branches yourself without damaging your safety or the tree's good health. If the answer is no, then ask yourself if you can do the job with the help of your neighbor. Still no? Can you do the job without leaving the ground? Also no? Then call a professional tree surgeon. You'll save time, money, and the tree. If you do decide that you're capable of doing the job, make sure you have the right tools. Makeshift surgical tools are as out of place in tree surgery as in an appendicitis operation. Make sure your saw and pruning tools are sharp and clean, not rusty. Purchase ratchet-type pruning tools; they're safer and easier on both you and the trees.

If a limb has been injured or broken and at least half of the bark is intact, the limb can be set

much like a broken arm. First, thoroughly sterilize the break with three tablespoons of ammonia per quart of water. Next, with a sharp pair of hand pruners, cut the splintered and ragged edges away so that the limb will come back into place and fit normally. Avoid lifting the limb more times than necessary, as it hurts. Cut two lengths of board the width of the limb. Wrap the ends with nylon pantyhose. These splints should be twice the length of the break. Now splint the break on top and bottom and tie with nylon pantyhose. The last step is to seal the wound and leave splinted until a heavy adhesion has occurred.

When it's necessary to amputate a branch or limb, make your first incision below and behind the break, just deep enough to penetrate the bark. This will prevent the bark from being torn all the way down the trunk. Now complete the operation by cutting from above. Talk to the patient. It's comforting to both of you, and, after all, nothing mixes better than trees and sympathy!

General trimming and shaping is best done when the tree is dormant, during the cold of winter. In warm weather you can do maintenance trimming at any time. However, fall still appears to be the safest time for minor surgery. Always sterilize and dress the wound. I have found that tree maintenance on a neighborhood level is much more economical for the care of large trees. Since any tree enhances the beauty and value of any neighborhood, it should be of vital interest for you and your neighbors to share the cost. Get more than one bid for work to be done and appoint a treasurer to pay and collect funds. By sharing the cost and having a professional do the job, you'll save yourself a lot of hard work and sore muscles, and you'll get much better results.

"There are trees to match every human personality, so pick the tree that matches yours."

FEED FOR
FOLIAGE

The toughest thing to convince a homeowner is that it's necessary to feed a great big old maple, oak, or elm, or any of the other big trees. He looks at you like you're out of your mind. But, as the old saying goes: "You ain't seen nothing yet!"

The first spring that you feed a large, mature tree, it will put on a foot or more of new growth, the foliage color will deepen, and the leaf canopy will be thicker. The second year, you won't recognize it as the same tree. The large, older trees need a meal early in the spring when the rains stop in the West and South. In the North, you'll have to wait until you can pound a stake into the ground. The old trees are fed in the spring and fall at a rate of one pound for every inch around the trunk. Drill or poke holes two feet apart in circles under the farthest branches or drip line, ten to twelve inches deep, and fill with any lawn food that contains no weed-killing chemicals. A perfect tree food mix is a pound of ordinary sugar mixed with forty to fifty pounds of any garden food.

SPARE THE ROD AND SPOIL THE TREE

• •

"I get my troubles off my chest by talking to my friends in the garden. Try it some-time—you might enjoy it!"

From time to time we find a lazybones sleeping in the sun in our garden. He can be an old fellow or a young guy. He can be large or small. He's a lazy tree, lying down on the job, not producing enough shade because his leaf cover is not thick enough. What he needs is a rude but effective awakening. To wake up a sleepy tree and get him back to work, you whip him. That's right, give him a good spanking with a stick on his trunk! "Wake up!" you shout, like my ma, who used to whip me and yell all at once. Believe me, he'll wake up and grow! Grandma Putt called her switch a "bearing" switch. Today, the nurseryman calls this whipping act "scoring." What happens when you hit the bark is that you jar the layer of tissue beneath the bark that carries the sap up to the foliage. It's the same effect as when you go to a steam bath and get a rubdown: they pound your flesh to improve your circulation.

Spank a tree and see. I use a four-foot soft switch, not a baseball bat: I want to wake him up, not break his back! Whip your tree from as high as you can reach all the way to the ground, all around the trunk. Not on the limbs—just the trunk. If you don't think this works, try it. I once had an old maple tree that just didn't have it anymore. Sleep, sleep, sleep. So one day I cut myself a four-foot sucker shoot off a lilac bush and as I passed ol'

"Sleeping Branch" (that's his Indian name), I gave him one hell of a crack. I'm sure I woke him up because he really paid me back later! He dropped his spinner seeds by the millions, leaves by the ton! Before, I was lucky if I got two bushels of spinners and some leaves. (What really made me mad was when he spit his sap all over my new car.) If your fruit and nut trees aren't delivering the kind of harvests that you'd like to see, just get out your trusty "bearing" switch!

DOCTOR, I HAVE THIS PAIN

From time to time, even the best-cared-for trees become ill for one reason or another. There are various and sundry diseases and insects that attach themselves to shade trees. When this happens, you'd better act at once, without delay! Call a doctor immediately. The best tree doctors are your local professional nurserymen or tree surgeons.

When you call for advice, it's necessary to give the tree doc the same information you would give if a loved one were ill. Your trees are loved ones; someone else would love to have them. Tell the nurseryman the name of the patient and its variety. Next tell him how old the tree is: this is done by telling him how big around the trunk is. Also, describe the care you have already taken. For example, tell him when you last sprayed with dormant oil, when you showered it, with what, and how often. Also tell him when you fed it, and what food you used. Now, describe the symptoms: color of foliage, shape of the leaves, color and description of the blight or insect, or the area where the disease appears. If at all possible, ask if he can make a house call. In most cases there will be no fee—but I would gladly pay a fee required to save my tree.

Most insect infestations of foliage can be stopped with Malathion, the safest of the chlorinated hydrocarbons. Soil bugs should be controlled with Dursban; it does its job and then is gone. Tree diseases can, generally, be controlled with a good washing with an ounce of liquid dish detergent in ten gallons of water, followed with a spraying of broad spectrum fruit tree spray according to package directions.

Dutch elm disease presents a different problem altogether. At this time we have no known cure, though there are some claims to partial control with various concoctions. The elm bark beetle carries the disease, and he will generally not stop strong healthy trees, only weak and injured ones.

If you'll just try to give your trees an ordinary bath, with either flea and tick shampoo or children's shampoo at one cup of shampoo per twenty gallons of water, using a hose-end sprayer, you can avoid most tree problems.

I'M NOT MOVING

Want to bet? Almost any tree can be moved nowadays, if you have the money. Modern-day equipment can safely move virtually any tree, with the exception, of course, of the big redwoods.

I do not recommend that you, the ambitious home gardener, try to transplant any tree larger than two inches in diameter. I say this for the tree's safety and yours! When transplanting a shade tree, I suggest that you stand underneath the tree and look up. Make the root ball half the size of the outer circle of the branches or the drip line. Follow the same procedure as in moving evergreens, on pages 124–26.

A large tree or a small, weak tree that's been moved should be braced to combat the wind damage that can be caused on a stormy day. Most braces should be placed by a competent tree surgeon or arborist as a poorly placed guy wire or loop can do more damage than good.

IRON - POOR BLOOD
. . . .

A shortage of natural iron in the soil can cause a condition called chlorosis, known as anemia in humans. The leaves turn a yellowish color, with the veins remaining a deep green.

When the tree has a bad case of chlorosis, the whole leaf turns yellow and drops off. The tree stops growing, the foliage becomes sparse, and in many cases, the plant dies. This chlorotic condition can be corrected with an iron chelate much like Geritol. Iron chelate places a storage supply of iron in the soil for the roots to absorb. I've found that the best method for feeding trees iron uses a Ross root feeder—a hose attachment with a long spike. At the top is a chamber where water-soluble cartridges of iron are placed. Two feedings are recommended, ten days apart. Chelated iron is applied any time the chlorotic condition is noticed.

Every tree in your yard is like money in your pocket when you go to sell your home—just ask the man who doesn't have any. If you will be firm, but friendly with your trees, you'll find that the shade trees in your garden will go out of their way to please you.

BEWARE OF BUILDERS

●●

I often feel that there should have been an eleventh commandment, and it should have said, "Thou shalt not deliberately kill a tree." I am sure this would have influenced an awful lot of real estate developers, bulldozer operators, and builders. I have never in my life seen such willful destruction of native trees as when a builder moves into an area for construction.

A friend of mine purchased a lot not too long ago to build a home. He selected the lot because it had some twenty-eight maple trees, sixteen hawthorns, three poplars, and a half-dozen other trees. When he described the lot he was so excited with his great luck in getting so many beautiful trees. I cautioned him to protect the trees closest to where the building was to be placed. "Oh," he replied, "the builder assured me that he will take special care." Construction began, and three weeks later I received a desperate call, "Come quick and look at my trees." When I got there it looked like the Battle of the Bulge had been fought on that spot. Limbs were broken, and bark was torn from the trunks. Some trees had been uprooted or bent, and many were buried in as much as twelve feet of earth. By the time construction had been finished, he had less than a third of the original trees. This can happen to you if you do not take precautions. Speak with your builder or contractor. Find out if he can save all the trees. If not, determine which he can save, or indicate clearly which you want saved. Do this *before* construction starts.

I'm aware that some trees must be removed for various and sundry reasons prior to or during construction. If at all possible, these trees should be moved by professionals. Trees that will remain in place and that are close to the actual construction should have boards fastened to three sides and held by banding of nylon stockings to prevent gouging. Very large trees or groups of trees close together should have a cinderblock wall put around them by the builder or contractor before construction begins. Excess soil should be removed from root surfaces as soon as possible. No more than eight inches of new soil should cover the roots. Holes should be bored or drilled through new soil out at the tops of the farthest branches so that the plant is able to breathe and eat. I always recommend feeding trees on your property before construction begins.

M O T H E R N A T U R E ' S F A N

● ●

When we talk about shade trees, we often forget that palm trees are shade trees, too. Palms are divided into two types: hand-shaped and those with featherlike leaves. The palms will grow up to the northern part of zone 8, and palms can be grown in pots indoors almost anywhere. The listing of patio palms gives palm species that are particularly well suited to living in pots. In cooler areas, you can move them outside in summer.

"If there were an eleventh commandment, it should be 'Thou shalt not deliberately kill a tree'—something that real estate developers, bulldozer operators, and builders should keep in mind."

PATIO PALMS

SCIENTIFIC NAME	COMMON NAME
Arecastrum romanzoffianum	Queen palm
Chamaedorea species	Feather palms
Chamaerops humilis	Mediterranean fan palm
Chrysalidocarpus lutesceus	Yellow butterfly palm
Hedyscepe	Umbrella palm
Howea species	Sentry palm, kentia palm
Livistona species	Australian fan palm, Chinese fan palm
Microcoelum weddellianum	Weddell palm
Phoenix species	Date palms

The most popular palms, in the table that follows, are available in most garden centers.

MOST POPULAR PALMS

SCIENTIFIC NAME	COMMON NAME
Brahea armata	Mexican blue palm
Brohea edulis	Guadalupe palm
Butela species	Pindo palm
Chamaedorea species	Neanthe bella palm
Chamaerops excelsa	Windmill palm
Chamaerops humilis	Mediterranean fan palm
Cocos species	Coconut palm
Cycas species	Sago palm
Phoenix canariensis	Ornamental date palm
Phoenix reclinata	Senegal date palm
Seaforthia	King palm
Trachycarpus fortunei	Takie windmill palm
Washingtonia robusta	Mexican fan palm

Most of the palms like light, sandy soil and need a great deal of water April through October. They are best fed with fish emulsion once a month.

To avoid drying the foliage, use an early summer spray with Wilt Pruf to contain the moisture. Insect control can be maintained by spraying the low growers every three weeks with a cup of liquid dish detergent in twenty gallons of water applied with your hand-held sprayer.

FLOWERING TREES

I think the reason I communicate so well with plants is because I can experience the same feelings they do at the same time, even if not always for the same reason! I get a ferocious appetite in the spring, and spring is the time of year when your whole garden gets hungry. This is especially true of your flowering plants, including the small flowering shade trees. They're hungry because of the long sleep they've just had, and because of all the early chores they are called on to perform almost before their eyes are open. My appetite increases with their efforts. When I was a small boy, I went to Washington, D.C., in the spring when the Kwanzan cherries were in full bloom. The more I looked at them and admired their beauty, the hungrier I got: they looked like cotton candy to me. They were so bright, pink, fluffy and mouthwatering that my father had to take me a mile away to a carnival to satisfy my appetite.

In spring when the small flowering trees are beginning to bloom, our grocery bill soars sky high!

"Flowering trees are lovely ladies—they worry about their figures, so trim them carefully each winter while they sleep."

You'd be surprised at some of the unusual foods that my appetite associates with those trees and their blooms. We have a Paul's scarlet hawthorn that gives me a yen for pumpkin pie, and an ornamental purple leaf plum that turns me on for plum pudding, and so on.

I've found that most flowering trees are extremely conceited, self-centered, and selfish, and they'll do best if you set them away from most of the other plants. I guess I'm suggesting that you flatter and spoil your flowering trees for best results.

Here's an idea for you, ladies. If you have a lovely flowering tree in your yard, have a name tag with your first name made for it and watch all of the special attention your husband will suddenly give it.

The ornamental flowering tree, because of its early elegant blooms and fine, delicate foliage, makes an extremely versatile addition to any landscape. An exception to this rule is the dogwood tree. I feel the dogwood should be showcased as a specimen tree, one that stands alone.

Flowering trees can be made to fit into many situations. Many of them, not just dogwoods, are great to use as specimen trees. But they can also be used to divide lot lines, shade the patio, frame a gate or other opening, accent a corner, or add privacy from the street. So when their spectacular beauty of bloom has gone, they're still pretty and functional too. You can also use them as shubbery borders. You must learn a great deal about the trees you wish to plant, because they have many different likes and dislikes. You can learn all of these idiosyncrasies by reading the nursery catalog that we talked about earlier. And talk to nurserymen in your area to learn which varieties are doing best in your area—or worst.

There is a colorful flowering tree to fit everyone's taste. There are trees that offer color and beauty over several seasons. Red and white dogwoods have spring flowers and fall colors and bright fall berries. The purple leaf plum has lovely pink flowers followed by purple leaves that make a colorful mark until fall. The Redbud tree, Golden chain and the Goldenrain can stand alone or blend in to a larger canvas of color. Magnolia is very widely used; Paul's scarlet hawthorn is a favorite of some of the older folks because of its long blooming season. The flowering cherries are always in demand—the Kwanzan and the Hisakura. Right behind the flowering cherries come the flowering crabs—Hopga, Almey, the pink Semcoe, Van Essentine, Sisipuk, Dolgo, and Amisk, Geneva, and on and on.

HANDLE WITH KID GLOVES

The flowering trees are available balled-in-burlap, in paper pulp containers, and in tin cans. However, more flowering trees are sold bare rooted than any other stock, with the exception of the rose. These small and colorful trees are planted in the same way as any shade tree.

Make sure the plant you buy is alive. Since it's dormant when you purchase it, it's going to take a little detective work on your part to find out if it is alive. First, look for definite signs of new growth, like small bud breaks. If none of these are visible, then gently peel a *small* piece of bark back in two or three places up the trunk to see if it is moist and green underneath. If it passes these tests, you

"Most flowering trees are extremely conceited, self-centered, and selfish. I suggest you flatter and spoil them for the best results."

can go ahead and purchase it. It is now your responsibility to keep it alive. When you arrive home, fill a bucket with two gallons of tepid water and throw in a tea bag. Next, carefully remove the packaging from the roots. You will notice, in most cases, that wood shavings have been used to protect the roots and retain moisture. This packing should also be removed. When the roots are free and loose, look them over to make sure that none of them is broken. If you find any, cut them off above the break, and also cut any real long, straggly roots. Now, soak the roots in the bucket of tea water overnight. When you're digging a hole for a bare root plant, you must make sure that the hole is wide enough to allow the tree's roots to spread out—but don't make it more than an inch deeper than it was in the nursery. To help you determine the depth, you will find a telltale "bathtub ring" around the trunk—that mark should not be underground. Mix heavy soil half and half with a half gravel, half sand mix to lighten it. Sandy or light soil needs no help.

It is now time to plant your very young flowering tree. Remove the plant from the bucket and bring it to the hole site. Laying it aside for just a moment, put enough soil back into the hole to make a pointed mound in the center, high enough that when the roots straddle it they will be comfortable, but not cramped. Cut off any that want to wind around. Now begin to recover the roots, packing the soil down as you go with your foot. Leave no air pockets. When you've returned half the soil, fill the rest of the hole with water and wait until it settles down. Then continue to replace the rest of the soil. Make sure that the tree is straight and true. When you've completed the job of planting, just sprinkle a half a pound of any garden food and three pounds of garden gypsum on the soil beneath your trees.

Bare root plants have no root support to keep the wind from blowing them over, so you'll have to drive a stake into the ground alongside and tie the young tree to the stake with a couple of ties made from old pantyhose. These will stretch but not cut into the bark. When you've finished planting and bracing the new tree, cut the new growth back by a third to control the excess evaporation that results from the short root supply.

S P O I L E D
R O T T E N

You can't plant a flowering tree and just forget it, or it will stubbornly pout and refuse to bloom. These pretty little ladies insist on special and undivided attention—much as any other beautiful woman does. Flowering trees must be fed on a regular basis in early spring with any good garden food, and then once a month until September. To feed, cast the food beneath the tree from just beyond the drip line halfway back to the trunk. Vary the amount of food at each meal with the size of the tree: five pounds is enough for a full-grown tree, two and a half pounds will do for a seven- or eight-foot-tall tree, and a pound is good for the younger trees. The average flowering shade tree will not exceed fifteen feet in height. I've found it much easier to use a hand-held whirling spreader set on setting 3 than to hand spread. Apply a dose of Epsom salts, using the hand-held spreader on setting 2 in both spring and fall.

KEEPING IN
SHAPE

• •

Nothing looks worse than a flowering tree that's
out of proportion, fat and sloppy, or one that's ill.
Like most women, the flowering trees worry about
their figures, so it is essential that you trim them
each winter when they're asleep. Only trim the
branches that are out of proportion to the tree's
natural shape. When you trim these lovely ladies,
be sure to sterilize the wounds or cuts and seal
them. Remember to shower these trees at least
twice a month with a cup of liquid dish detergent
to twenty gallons of water. All of the deciduous
flowering trees must be sprayed with dormant oil
in colder climates to destroy overwintering insects
before they can interrupt the flowering process in
the spring. A cupful of crushed paradichlorobenzene moth crystals spread beneath the trees in the
fall, and again in the early spring, will keep the
trees free from boring insects. Apply Dursban granules in early spring beneath any tree that had insect problems the season before. Many folks who
own these trees love the flower colorama but find
the fruit a nuisance. To cut down on fruiting and
end this nuisance, you can spray a chemical called
Amid-Thin when the flowers appear. Sometimes a
tomato-vegetable dust containing Sevin made into
a spray will eliminate the fruit. I found that most
flowering trees grow better when they have a little
company to talk to, so I always plant a flowering
friend beneath each of my flowering trees. Petunias
in contrasting colors seem to satisfy both the tree
and me. If you don't want to use flowers, then let

your tree be lonely and surround the base with wood chip mulch.

BEWARE OF THE UNDERGROUND

Since these flowering beauties are so gracious and tender, they're fair game for the grubs. A light spray of any recommended soil insect control at half strength mixed with a cup of children's shampoo per twenty gallons of water and applied to the soil at the first hint of irritation can curb a catastrophe. When it's necessary to spray the foliage for insects, I use a regular fruit tree spray as recommended. If you poke holes beneath the trees from time to time through the season with a sharp stick, you'll find that you can cut down on your trees' problems with these bugs.

TREES WITH FLOWERS

SCIENTIFIC NAME	COMMON NAME	FLOWER COLOR	ZONE
Acacia baileyana	Cootamundra wattle	yellow	10
Acacia decurrens dealbata	Silver wattle	yellow	9
Acer platanoides 'Columnare'	Columnar Norway maple	yellow	3
Acer platanoides 'Crimson King'	Crimson king Norway maple	yellow	4
Acer platanoides 'Emerald queen'	Emerald queen Norway maple	yellow	3

SCIENTIFIC NAME	COMMON NAME	FLOWER COLOR	ZONE
Acer platanoides 'Schwedleri'	Schwedler Norway maple	yellow	3
Acer platanoides 'Summershade'	Summershade Norway maple	yellow	3
Albizia julibrissin	Silk tree	pink	6
Albizia julibrissin 'Charlotte'	Charlotte silk tree	purple	6
Albizia julibrissin 'Ernest Wilson'	Hardy silk tree	purple	5
Albizia julibrissin 'Tryon'	Tryon silk tree	purple	6
Amelanchier canadensis	Shadblow serviceberry	white	4
Amelanchier grandiflora	Apple serviceberry	white	4
Arbutus unedo	Strawberry-tree	white	8
Bauhinia variegata	Purple orchid-tree	lavender	10
Bauhinia variegata 'Candida'	White orchid-tree	white	10
Castanea mollissima	Chinese chestnut	white	5
Ceratonia siliqua	Carob	red	10
Cercis canadensis alba	Whitebud	white	5
Cercis canadensis 'Withers Pink Charm'	Withers pink redbud	pink	5
Citrus species	Citrus fruits	white	9
Cladrastris lutea	Yellowwood	white	4
Cornus florida	Flowering dogwood	white	4
Cornus kousa	Japanese dogwood	white	5
Cornus nuttalli	Pacific dogwood	white	7
Crataegus mollis	Downy hawthorn	white	4

SCIENTIFIC NAME	COMMON NAME	FLOWER COLOR	ZONE
Crataegus phaenopyrum	Washington hawthorn	white	4
Eucalyptus ficifolia	Crimson eucalyptus	red	9
Halesia carolina	Carolina silverbell	white	4
Heteromeles arbutifolia	Toyon	white	7
Jacaranda acutifolia	Sharpleaf jacaranda	lavender	10
Koelreuteria paniculata	Golden-rain-tree	yellow	5
Laburnum anagyr-oides 'Vossi'	Golden chain tree	yellow	5
Lagerstroemia in-dica 'Ingleside Pink'	Ingleside crape-myrtle	purple	7
Lagerstroemia in-dica 'William Toovey'	Red crape-myrtle	red	7
Ligustrum lucidum	Glossy privet	white	7
Liriodendron tulipifera	Tulip-tree	yellow	4
Magnolia heptapeta	Yulan magnolia	white	5
Magnolia grandiflora	Southern magnolia	white	7
Magnolia stellata	Star magnolia	white	5
Magnolia virginiana	Sweet bay magnolia	white	5
Malus 'Almey'	Almey crab apple	red	4
Malusx arnoldiana	Arnold crab apple	white	4
Malus atrosanguinea	Carmine crab apple	red	4
Malus baccata	Siberian crab apple	white	2

SCIENTIFIC NAME	COMMON NAME	FLOWER COLOR	ZONE
Malus floribunda	Japanese flowering crab apple	white	4
Malus 'Hopa'	Hopa crab apple	red	4
Malus hupehensis	Tea crab apple	white	4
Malus 'Katherine'	Katherine crab apple	purple	4
Malus 'Prince Georges'	Prince Georges crab apple	purple	4
Malus pumila	Common crab apple	white	3
Malus sargentii	Sargent crab apple	white	5
Oxydendrum arboreum	Sorrel-tree	white	4
Photinia serrulata	Chinese photinia	white	7
Poncirus trifoliata	Hardy-orange	white	5
Prunus cerasifera 'Nigra'	Black Myrobalan plum	pink	3
Prunus cerafisera 'Thundercloud'	Thundercloud plum	white	4
Prunus persica	Peach	purple	5
Prunus sargentii	Sargent cherry	purple	4
Prunus serrulata 'Amanogawa'	Amanogawa cherry	pink	6
Prunus serrulata 'Kwanzan'	Kwanzan cherry	purple	5
Prunus serrulata 'Shiro-fugen'	Shiro-fugen cherry	white	6
Prunus serrulata 'Shirotae'	Mount Fuji cherry	white	6
Prunus subhirtella 'Autumnalis'	Autumn cherry	pink	5
Prunus subhirtella 'Pendula'	Weeping Higan cherry	pink	5
Prunus yedoensis	Yoshino cherry	white	5
Pyrus calleryana 'Bradford'	Bradford Callery pear	white	5

SCIENTIFIC NAME	COMMON NAME	FLOWER COLOR	ZONE
Pyrus communis	Common pear	white	5
Sophora japonica	Japanese pagoda tree	white	4
Sorbus alnifolia	Korean mountain-ash	white	5
Sorbus americana	American mountain-ash	white	2
Sorbus aucuparia	European mountain-ash	white	3
Sorbus decora	Showy mountain-ash	white	2
Stewartia pseudocamellia	Japanese stewartia	white	5
Styrax japonicus	Japanese snowbell	white	5
Syringa amurensis japonica	Japanese tree lilac	white	4
Tilia cordata	Littleleaf linden	yellow	3
Tilia cordata 'Greenspire'	Greenspire linden	yellow	3
Tilia tomentosa	Silver linden	yellow	4
Tilia tomentosa 'Princeton'	Princeton silver linden	yellow	4
Tilia x euchlora	Crimean linden	yellow	5

FRUIT TREES..........................

Every garden should have at least one fruit tree, if for no other reason than that the gardener should experience the joy of biting into a shiny red, delicious apple, and know that he and Mother Nature worked together, against all odds, to produce this object of man's heritage. Remember, all gardening began in an orchard. Most nutritionists say that fresh, home-grown fruit is the most health-giving food that we can possibly eat. With fruit being the basic diet food, I'd like to begin by suggesting that all people who are or think they are overweight plant a fruit tree or two, that all people with children plant a fruit tree, and that all the nation's beer drinkers plant a nut tree. By this point we've included about 90 percent of the nation's homeowners. When you stop and think about it, the fruit tree, with just a little care, returns more for the time and effort expended than any other friend in the plant kingdom. Along with the fruit they produce, consider the enjoyment we get from branches we bring inside in the winter that bloom and fill the room with the fragrance of spring weeks away from spring outside. Also, consider the splendid variety of pinks, reds, whites, and lavenders of the fruit tree's blossoms. Then, when the flowers are gone, we become fascinated watching the day-by-day formation of the fruit. And then comes the harvest . . . what a delight! After harvest time, we have those cider and doughnut times in the fall that create warm and happy memories of our youth. You can even use a cherry tree to remind yourself always to tell the truth, or use an apple tree switch to teach obedience. So fruit trees can mean a great deal to each of us and should be included in any master plan of gardening. Go back to your paper bag plan and see where a fruit tree's requirements of sun and good air circulation will fit.

When a home gardener decides to buy a fruit tree or two, the first thing he does is shop for the lowest price. This almost always turns out to be his first mistake. The difference between the top-grade tree and the bargain seller is usually a few cents, but their vigor and quality are miles apart—you get what you pay for. When you buy a fruit tree, buy it from a nurseryman who can answer your questions and who knows what he's talking about.

"Every garden should have at least one fruit tree—remember, all gardening began in an orchard."

Many gardeners purchase new fruit and nut trees from catalogs. That's fine if you stick to the old-line, reputable nurseries. The ones listed in this book have been in business for a good number of years and are proud of their reputation: they'll stand behind the vigor and quality of their stock, they know how and when to ship, and they usually include lots of information on care and feeding.

"Don't put off 'til tomorrow what you should do today" was never more true than when it comes to purchasing trees in the spring. Keep your eyes on your favorite garden shop for the early delivery of fruit trees, so you can make your selection before everyone else starts pushing and pulling the trees around and breaking limbs.

All nursery stock is graded by how tall it is and how thick or dense its foliage is. Fruit trees are no exception. Fruit trees are usually graded as number 1, 2, or 3. The taller and thicker the tree, the more expensive. They are also called one- and two-year-old trees. As a rule of thumb we suggest that you buy apples, peaches, cherries as one-year-old trees and plums and pears as two-year-old trees. Whichever you select, make sure you buy the first or top grade.

Fruit and nut trees can be planted in either the fall or spring, as long as you plant the day you buy. If there is a possibility the location you've selected will be too wet to plant next spring, then by all means plant this fall and mulch. If it isn't necessary to fall plant, then I suggest that you wait until spring for several reasons. The first is that field mice and rabbits are elated when you serve them such a tender and delicious meal to tide them over the winter. The new plant could make too much new soft growth and be frozen out by severe winter weather. Soil is generally healthier and more fertile after the winter snows. So, all in all, it is best to plan your orchard for spring if you live in snow country and for the first of February in the warmer climates.

Fruit trees are planted like any other normal tree, with one exception. I highly recommend that you discard the soil you remove to make the hole and replace it with a commercial mix. I've found the Hyponex professional mix to be about the best. When planting bare root trees, dig the hole thirty inches wide and eighteen inches deep, then build a soil mound in the center and follow general planting rules given on page 115. I always recommend that you stake new fruit trees to keep them from getting a crooked start, mulch the soil beneath, and wrap their trunks. After you've watered your fruit or nut tree, give it a shower with an ounce of baby shampoo in ten gallons of water.

When planting more than one fruit tree, plant them fifteen feet apart and keep them separated, or else they'll fight and break each other's limbs.

FEEDING

* *

"A hungry fruit tree will never be happy, healthy, or productive. Feed early in the growing season."

A hungry fruit tree will never be happy, healthy, or productive. Feed as early in the growing season as the buds begin to open, using any garden food with a pound of ordinary sugar added. Drill holes eight inches deep, twelve inches apart at the drip line—the outermost tip of the largest branch. Put in two tablespoons of mix per hole. Every three weeks, make sure the fruit trees get their share of the all-around tonic you use on the rest of the yarden. The recipe's given on page 65.

HELP THE BIRDS AND BEES

Fruit trees need to be cross-pollinated to bear fruit; and the failure of a tree to set blossoms is usually caused by a light-pollinating variety grown nearby. The birds and bees do their best, but it just isn't enough, so we must help. Cut a great big bunch of flowers with lots of pollen from a similar variety of fruit tree. Hang flowers up in the top of the non-blossoming tree in a bucket of water to make them last. Now, if there are lots of bees and other bugs flying around, you'll get fruit.

TREES TO FIT ANY YARD

Dwarf fruit trees have become America's favorite fruit trees because they seldom grow taller than eight feet, and you can grow several varieties in the same space that it takes to grow a tree of regular size. I've found the following varieties to be the most rewarding bearers for beginners—dwarf apples: 'Red Delicious,' yellow transparent, red 'McIntosh,' and 'Golden Delicious.' Dwarf peaches: 'Elberta,' 'Redhaven,' 'Halehaven,' and 'Champion.'

The best-bearing pear tree is the dwarf 'Bartlett,' and the best-bearing plum is the dwarf 'Stanley.' Dwarf 'North-Star Cherry' is the best pie cherry, and, last but not least, dwarf 'Hungary' is the best apricot.

For a real experience, order one of the five-in-one dwarf apple trees. This superbloomer produces five different varieties from one tree. It is a great gift tree for a house warming present.

If you have the room, then by all means plant regular-sized fruit trees. Here are my favorites: for a quick-bearing apple you can't beat 'Anoka,' or "old folks apple"; next in order come 'Yellow Transparent,' 'Double Red Delicious,' 'Golden Delicious,' McIntosh, 'Grimes Golden,' 'Jonathan,' and 'Double Red Staymen Winesap.' In a pear, I'm old-fashioned and enjoy the 'Bartlett,' while a 'Stanley' plum pleases my children. Peaches are good no matter which variety you choose: 'Halehaven,' 'Elberta,' 'Golden Jubilee,' 'Redhaven,' 'Burbank early Elberta,' and 'Champion Improved.' The largest peach you can grow is 'Rio-Oso-Gem,' and you'll be delighted with the new freestone called 'Reliance.' It's hardy all the way up to zone 3. 'Black Tartarian' and the 'Royal Ann' cherry complete your home orchard.

My wife, Ilene, has suggested an addition to my list, and that is the 'Dolgo' crab apple. The reason is because this is my favorite breakfast jelly. 'Dolgo' crab is about the heaviest producer of the crab apples and these, in my opinion, make the best jelly ever.

If you fancy a nut tree, let me make a few suggestions. Remember, the nut trees are as beautiful for their foliage as they are for their fruit. Let's begin with the American hazelnut and hardy mission almond. Check your map. They will grow in zone 5 and southern zone 4, if protected. Thin-shelled hardy pecans will grow in lower zone 4 and south. For more northerly regions, we go to the

American butternut, mammoth hickory, and black walnut. I like the hardy Carpathian walnut. Another one of my favorites is the Chinese chestnut. The foliage is superb, and the roasted nuts are a true delight.

To grow a nut tree, you need the same type of soil as you need in your vegetable garden. Nut trees need very little care; however, they need to be fed in the same manner and as frequently as fruit trees.

BEWARE OF INTRUDERS

You aren't the only admirer of the beauty and tastefulness of your orchard. The bugs of the world have their eye on it, too. But don't be disturbed; a little foresight will ward off the intruders. Grandma Putt would mulch each of her fruit trees with oak leaves and would plant nasturtiums beneath each one. That was biodynamic gardening long before it was named that or made popular.

In the days of Grandma Putt, the only thing gardeners had with which to control insect onslaught was the insects' natural enemies. For instance, those old-timers knew that the grubs did not, as a rule, bother the oak, so they would use oak leaves against grubs. The red spider mite would run from sour milk on a table, so they fought him with sour milk, which has since been adopted as a control. Use two cups of wheat flour and one cup of buttermilk to five gallons of water. Coddling moths on pears can be controlled by planting spearmint plants beneath pear trees. The only chemical control that these gardeners used was nicotine sulphate and Fels-Naphtha soap, which is still used to

"I never met an ugly tree or one I couldn't like."

"A clean garden is a healthy one."

this day. Look on page 7 for my tonics using tobacco juice and bar laundry soap—they're the same thing.

I have found that a dormant spray with lime sulphur solution and Volk oil combined, used in the late fall when the foliage has dropped and again in the spring before the buds swell, followed with regular soap-and-water sprays at three- to four-week intervals, take care of almost all problems. When I spot a new problem, I use a home orchard spray and apply it at fourteen-day intervals up to two weeks before harvest. However, I've seldom needed it.

PUCKER UP FOR PLEASURE

For some unknown reason, most garden writers seem to forget about the citrus trees when they write about the home orchard, maybe because they think citrus trees grow in such limited zones. I find that most of my southern and western acquaintances grow a lot of citrus trees, and I suggest that one or more be made a regular part of your warm climate landscape.

Lemons, limes, oranges, mandarins, and avocados should be planted in the early spring or fall. I find that the container-grown citrus trees are easiest to plant.

Insect control should not be too difficult if these trees are given a soap and water shower from time to time, following the instructions on page 8.

They should be fed lightly each month from February through September with a low-nitrogen fertilizer.

COMMONLY AVAILABLE CITRUS VARIETIES

SCIENTIFIC NAME	COMMON NAMES
Citrus Chimotto orange	Chimotto orange
Citrus Frost nucellar navel orange	Navel orange
Citrus Frost nucellar valencia orange	Valencia orange
Citrus kumquat nagami fortunella margarita	Kumquat
Citrus limequat	Common lime
Citrus limonia Eureka lemon	Eureka lemon
Citrus limonia dwarf Meyer lemon	Dwarf Meyer lemon
Citrus limonia rough lemon	Rough lemon
Citrus reticulata calamondin nobilis deliciosa	Calamondin lemon
Citrus sinensis 'Kara-Kara'	Mandarin orange
Citrus tangerine Dancy	Tangerine

SCIENTIFIC NAME	VARIETIES	COMMON NAME
Citrus sinensis	'Chimotto'	Sweet orange
	'Frost Nucellar Navel'	Navel orange
	'Frost Nucellar Valencia'	Valencia orange

Avocado has become a very popular salad fruit and is becoming a highly desired hobby tree by many home gardeners, including my friend actor Ed Nelson, who has more avocado trees than children. Or is it the other way around? There are two varieties that Ed prefers over most others because one is a late and one is an early bearer. We both recommend that two compatible varieties be planted together to avoid sex reversal of the flower, which would result in nonsetting.

'Avocado-bacon' is a medium-size tree. It has wide branches with heavy foliage. This variety has

TREES WITH FRUIT OR BERRIES

SCIENTIFIC NAME	COMMON NAME	ZONE
Amelanchler x grandiflora	Apple serviceberry	4
Arbutus unedo	Strawberry-tree	8
Citrus species	Citrus fruits	9
Cornus florida	Flowering dogwood	4
Cornus kousa	Japanese dogwood	5
Cornus nuttalli	Pacific dogwood	7
Crataegus mollis	Downy hawthorn	4
Crataegus 'Toba'	Toba hawthorn	3
Crataegus phaenopyrum	Washington hawthorn	4
Eriobotrya japonica	Loquat	7
Heteromeles arbutifolia	Toyon	7
Ilex aquifolium	English holly	6
Ilex opaca	American holly	5
Juniperus scopulorum	Western red-cedar	4
Juniperus virginiana	Eastern red-cedar	2
Malus 'Almey'	Almey crab apple	4
Malus pumila	Common crab apple	3
Malus sargentii	Sargent crab apple	5
Nyssa sylvatica	Black tupelo	4
Photinia serrulata	Chinese photinia	7
Poncirus trifoliata	Hardy-orange	5
Schinus terebinthifolius	Brazilian peppertree	9
Sophora japonica	Japanese pagoda tree	4
Sorbus alnifolia	Korean mountain-ash	5
Sorbus americana	American mountain-ash	2
Sorbus aucuparia	European mountain-ash	3
Sorbus decora	Showy mountain-ash	2

medium-size green fruit in the winter. 'Avocado-Haas,' a large tree with spreading branches, bears black fruit that ripen in the summer.

To grow avocados properly, mulch heavily with bark chips and feed with an organic food at the drip line. Wash with a mild soap for insect control.

STEP-BY-STEP TREE CARE......................

S P R I N G

Step 1. All trees deserve a bath, as early in the growing season as possible, and then another three or four throughout the season as weather permits. Use the ten-gallon sprayer with the blue golf ball and add to the container one-half cup of flea and tick shampoo, a half cup of brown mouthwash, and very warm water to fill.

Step 2. Dormant spray all deciduous trees (ones that lose their leaves in winter) as soon in early spring as the temperature will stay above freezing for at least twenty-four hours. This smothers egg masses.

Step 3. Fruit and nut trees are washed again as soon as the bud shows green. Into the ten-gallon sprayer with the blue golf ball put a half cup of children's shampoo, a half cup of tobacco juice, a half cup of brown mouthwash. If insects were a problem last season, add six teaspoons of tomato-vegetable dust per gallon of spray.

Step 4. Continue to spray every fourteen days up to fourteen days before harvest. You can switch to any all-purpose fruit tree spray: begin as flowers begin to drop.

Step 5. Wrap the trunks of all young trees. Dwarf fruit and flower trees should always be wrapped. Use tree skin or tree wrap.

Step 6. Decorate your fruit and nut tree with old Christmas tree ornaments of red and yellow, coated with sticky Tangle Trap: best bug catchers in the world.

Step 7. Spray the soil beneath birch trees and any other trees bothered by leaf miners, borers, green worms, and others with spray in step 1, and add Dursban.

Step 8. Flowering trees must be kept clean. Use the spray in step 3, without the tomato and vegetable dust, every two weeks in the evening all spring long.

Step 9. As silly as it may sound—and it looks worse—paddle your tree trunks in the early spring with a rolled up newspaper or a switch to get the sap flowing at peak performance. Try it late at night the first time (I'm serious). No singing and dancing, though; you get too much rain.

Step 10. Feed all trees with a dry application of any garden food, adding a pound of sugar and a pound of Epsom salts per fifty-pound bag of food. Out at the drip line drill holes that are eight to ten inches deep in two circles eighteen and twenty-four inches from the trunk, filling the holes with two tablespoons of mixture.

SUMMER

Step 11. Continue to bathe every two weeks with the spray in step 3, without the tomato and vegetable dust, all summer long. Do this in the evenings.

FALL

Step 12. Spray with dormant oil in late fall when the leaves have dropped and before the temperature drops below freezing.

Step 13. Wrap trunks of young trees with tree wrap for the winter in the North to protect from winter bark split.

Step 14. Root prune flowering trees. Using a sharpened spade, make a circle around the tree at the drip line by putting the spade straight down into the soil.

QUESTIONS AND ANSWERS

Q. *What's the best type of soil for trees?*
A. Most trees do well in a sandy loam to a good clay loam, but as a rule do not do well in heavy clay.

Q. *Is it okay to place stone chips underneath a weeping cherry tree?*

A. I love the appearance of large stone chips, either number 10 or number 12, beneath all of the small weeping trees. They just seem to go together. But make sure you put down Weed Blocker fabric and mulch first.

Q. *How do you stop borers in dogwood?*
A. Sprinkle a cup or two of crushed paradichlorobenzene moth crystals on the mulch soil beneath the tree in early spring and late fall.

Q. *Is it necessary to wrap the trunk of all newly planted trees?*
A. I do, and after a year or two I change the wrap and leave it on for a third year. Tree wrap keeps the moisture in and prevents bark split and sun scald.

Q. *Our flowering cherry gets about every tree disease that is in the neighborhood. What kind of spray should we use?*
A. The same spray that is used on fruiting cherry trees. Use any home orchard spray as recommended by the manufacturer.

Q. *When is the very best time to plant a tree, any tree?*
A. Today you can plant trees twelve months a year. Potted and balled-in-burlap trees can even be planted when you have to break the frozen ground with a pick. But for the most part, late fall or early winter is best for balled stock.

Q. *Can you plant bare root trees in fall with good results?*
A. Later October and early November are just fine. Brace the trees with wire, wrap the trunk,

mulch the base with leaves, and you got yourself some winners.

Q. *We have a fig tree that gets overrun with red spider mites. How can I stop them?*
A. Soap and water spray first. Malathion if that doesn't stop them.

Q. *What's the best way to water a tree?*
A. With a soaker base laid in a circle out at the drip line.

Q. *Should you wrap the trunk of a flowering tree for the winter?*
A. I wrap all trees, and I do it when I plant in summer, winter, spring or fall. I help my friends fight sun scald with tree wrap.

Q. *What's the biggest you suggest a tree be when planted?*
A. I can't say. The new power diggers can move thirty- to forty-foot-high trees the way you and I move a whip.

Q. *What is an espaliered tree really used for?*
A. According to an old story, some monks wanted to have fresh fruit in their monastery, but there was not enough room to plant the trees. These monks were sworn never to leave the monastery, so they could not grow trees outside the walls. Then one of the monks planted the fruit trees against the sides of all of the buildings and trained them to grow up wires but not out. I've heard other stories about the origin of espaliered trees, but I like this one best.

Q. *How much do you prune off a weeping cherry tree when you plant it bare root?*
A. About a third—as much as you would prune any other packaged shade tree or shrub.

Q. *Can trees make any real difference in reducing noise?*
A. Yes, sir-re-bobbie, they can. Trees and shrubs act as an acoustical sponge. If you place your trees properly, you can reduce noise by 25 to 35 percent.

Q. *How big does an orchid tree grow?*
A. I sure hope you didn't waste your money and buy one expecting it to grow in Sandusky, Ohio, where your letter is postmarked. The orchid tree, *Bauhinia variegata*, will only grow in zone 10 (see the hardiness zone map on page 407). It gets up to, and sometimes past, twenty feet.

Q. *What is the tree that has foliage that looks like mountain ash but has a flower like wisteria, only yellow?*
A. This is called a golden chain tree by us common folks, *Laburnum anagyroides 'Vassii'* by the professionals. It grows very well in zone 5, but will do pretty well in zone 4 if protected by other trees or in a protected location.

Q. *Do you have to brace all newly planted trees?*
A. I always do. Brace against the prevailing wind. Pad the bark area with sponge rubber, rags, old pantyhose, or some other soft material to keep the bark from being torn or rubbed off. I like to leave the stake on for at least one full season.

Q. *We have a magnolia tree that has never bloomed, but the foliage is thick, green, and healthy. What's wrong?*
A. Nothing. You have a seed tree, and I have known them to take ten years to produce flowers.

Q. *We have a tree wisteria that has very few clusters. What can I do to increase the blooms?*
A. Odds are the soil is too dry. The wisteria will grow in almost any kind of soil as long as you keep it damp. I always plant an evergreen ground cover under the wisteria to help keep the soil moist. I also cut off the new tangle growth that comes in early summer, and root prune in the fall.

Q. *Which of the flowering trees will grow in clay soil?*
A. I have found the purple leaf plum or thundercloud plum to be a great clay fighter, I guess because it was developed in clay country.

Q. *When is the best time to prune a purple leaf plum tree that is growing up into the overhang of our home?*
A. Ordinarily we don't recommend that you do much pruning of the stone fruit trees. In your case, when it's growing will do the trick.

Q. *Rabbits and mice eat the bark on my new trees. How do you stop them?*
A. Wrap the bark with tree wrap right down to the soil; then place medium-size stones around the base in a circle. If the problem is really bad, make a wire collar out of hardware cloth and place it around the trunk from the ground up.

Q. *Should weeping trees be braced at any time?*
A. I brace all of the main stems in the winter and

gently tie the streamers before snow so the heart won't break. You don't need to tie the streamers outside of snow country.

Q. *When I was a small girl in Germany, we had a tree called halesia. I saw one that resembled it in Pennsylvania; could this be it? If so, where can I get one?*
A. It can be. It's called a *Halesia carolina* or by the common American name of Carolina silverbell. I don't know why more designers don't use them. They are virtually insect and disease free as well as being one of the cleanest, neatest, and most beautiful trees I have seen. You can get one from Cottage Gardens, Inc., in Lansing, Michigan.

Q. *We have a Kentucky coffee tree in our backyard. Can we roast the beans and make the coffee?*
A. I was taught that in Revolutionary War days they did brew these beans; however, I've never tried it. This is another good-looking tree that is often overlooked.

Q. *What will grow in clay?*
A. Any tree you see growing in your community. The trick is to do what landscape contractors do in that kind of problem: build small hills in different locations where you want trees and then contour these hills. Plant your trees in the mounds, above the clay, and you'll never lose a tree. Plant groups of shrubs the same way.

Q. *When is the best time to prune a birch tree?*
A. In late June, as birch is a bleeder—the sap keeps running when you make a cut—and must be sterilized immediately with a solution of two table-spoons of household ammonia per quart of water,

sloshed onto the wound. Then seal with pruning paint. Maples and walnuts are also bleeders.

Q. *Is it necessary to prune trees every year?*
A. A well-manicured tree will be healthier and prettier than one that is left to go its own way. However, there may be seasons when they need no help.

Q. *Can you mulch trees with wood chips made from limbs you've taken from the same tree?*
A. You can if the limbs weren't removed because of sickness.

Q. *What do you think of iron plugs for trees?*
A. What this gardener is talking about are small capsules in a frame that looks like a flathead bullet. You drill holes in the trunk and tap in a capsule, which gradually breaks down and gives iron to the tree. I prefer any of the powder or liquid irons fed through the roots.

Q. *We had a colony of carpenter ants in a tree. We got rid of the ants but are left with an empty ant house in the run. What do we do?*
A. Because you have to look at it, I say fill the cavity with cement. First, clean out the cavity of all loose wood and chips. Sterilize with two table-spoons of household ammonia in a gallon of water and seal the inside with latex or priming paint. Then mix some ready mix cement and fill.

Q. *Why does my elm tree leak sap all the time?*
A. It's called "wetwood bleeding." The tree is sick inside and needs a tree doctor. Don't mess around: call the man.

Q. *Can a tree that was stuck by lightning be saved?*

A. Oh, I think so, but it depends on how it was damaged. You have to remove broken limbs, bark, and ruined foliage. Sterilize, seal, and pray. You'll have to bind together limbs that have been weakened. Make sure you used good-sized eyes and heavy enough cable for the job. Use a turnbuckle, not a straight cable, to adjust the tension. You may want to call in a professional to figure out the tree's survival odds.

Q. *How can you remove sap from tools?*

A. Wipe them off with alcohol and rub down with oil each time after using. Rust on tools doesn't do your trees or tools any good.

Q. *How do you repair bark split from the ground up to the first branch?*

A. That's called "southwest bark split," and it's caused by bark thawing out on the sunny side of the tree in winter and swelling up and splitting, when the cooler bark doesn't thaw. Remove loose bark, sterilize with two tablespoons of household ammonia in a gallon of water, and seal with latex or pruning paint. If it's a small tree, wrap with tree tape; if it's a large tree, protect it in winter by taping a strip of tar paper to the southwestern side of the tree.

Q. *My kids ran into a maple tree with the lawn mower. How do you stop this?*

A. Give your youngsters driving lessons on a mower. Better yet, remove a mower's width of grass from around the tree and put down mulch. To help the tree now, take a sharp knife and cut the rough edges of the bark back to undamaged bark, making the edges smooth. Sterilize with two tablespoons of household ammonia in a gallon of water and seal with latex or pruning paint.

Q. *Why do they call some trees wild trees?*
A. That's a terrible thing to say about any tree. The willows, soft wood maples, poplars, and soft wood elms have been tagged with this handle, I guess because they grow so fast and get into a lot of trouble. But then, boys will be boys. By the way, I like the whole bunch and recommend them for what they are—active growers. (I was one as a kid.)

Q. *What do you use to kill grubs under a tree?*
A. Poke holes in the soil under the tree and pour an ounce of liquid dish detergent per ten gallons of water into the holes. Then apply Diazinon according to package directions.

Q. *Give me the names of good, fast-growing trees that I can plant at our cottage.*
A. Every time I read a trade book or paper, they say don't plant weedy or fast-growing trees, but I'm all for them. I'm for any kind of tree I can get— and can afford. If you use one you don't like, you can remove it or not plant it again. Chinese elm (brace the crotch), mulberry (dry), corkscrew willow (I love it), weeping willow (its roots can grow into sewers), cottonwood, poplar, hedge apple (the fruit discourages roaches), hackberry (shallow rooted; good for mound planting on clay), and silver maple. That ought to keep you hopping.

Q. *Can you keep fruit from forming on ornamental crabs?*
A. Spray with plant birth control Amid-thin.

Q. *Is there a cure for Dutch elm disease?*
A. Not as far as I know, but they're working on it.

Feed your elms, spray and prune properly, and they should remain healthy because the elm bark beetle attacks mainly weak, sick trees.

Q. *Are systemic insecticides effective and safe?*
A. They're darn good, and used properly and on the right trees as recommended, they're safe. But it's very easy to use them improperly and affect groundwater or edible plants, so be very careful.

Q. *What's the name of the metallic bronze maple tree?*
A. It's called Schwedler's maple. It's a really regal tree for a front lawn.

Q. *What's the maple with the white edge?*
A. Variegated leaf maple, a real showpiece. It grows to about thirty feet—not really fast, but it's worth the wait.

Q. *Are any of the elms safe from the Dutch elm disease?*
A. Yep! Hybrid elm or *Ulmus americana* will fill the bill.

Q. *Why do my mountain ash limbs all bend over and look like hell all the time?*
A. Don't feed the tree so much with lawn food. Use a garden food and remember that this tree doesn't like wet or heavy soil.

Q. *Which is the best locust tree for shade?*
A. I have to cast my vote for the Moraine, hands down. That's *Gleditsia triacanthos* 'Moraine.'

Q. *Is the beech fast or slow growing?*
A. Slow, like its brother the hickory, and both have hard heads.

Q. *What's the name of the tree that grows cater-corner from your home?*
A. That's a basswood tree or, better yet, an American linden. Ilene wants one in our yard, but I've got no room for a sixty- to eighty-footer—that's what it's going to get to. Next door my neighbor has its little cousin, the littleleaf linden, which is as pretty, almost, and grows only to forty feet.

Q. *How do you get birch trees to produce white bark?*
A. You wait for them to reach puberty, when they're about five or six years old, and you buy the right variety.

Q. *How do you control birchleaf miners?*
A. Spray early with Malathion and keep it up three weeks. Then spray again in early July.

Q. *What's with the birch borer?*
A. He likes birches and sons of birches. Use a cup or two of paradichlorobenzene moth crystals sprinkled on the mulch beneath the tree in the late fall and early spring.

Q. *What's the best way to get rid of a stump without digging it up?*
A. Cut the stump at or below the level of the soil. Then drill a series of holes in it—the more the merrier. I would like them large and as deep as you can drill. Now fill them with a commercial stump remover that contains potassium nitrate and leave for one year, plugged. At the end of a year, remove the plugs, pour in kerosene, let it set for an hour or so, and then light. The stump will smolder away to ashes.

Q. *Is there an "animal-free" tree? One that the rabbits and mice won't bother?*

A. About the only one that comes to mind is a Paul's scarlet hawthorn. Use Repel on tree trunks of other trees.

Q. *Will wild morning-glory hurt a flowering crab apple tree? It grows up the trunk and all through the branches.*

A. Obviously it has not destroyed it yet, but you can be sure your crab apple is not happy with its piggyback rider. Pull the vines off and hoe them out of the soil below. Next, apply Preen following the package directions, then cover the soil with a good wood chip mulch. Spray any new growth with Round Up.

Q. *What makes the leaves of a dogwood turn red and fall off in the summer?*

A. Odds are your dogwood tree is calling for help for the third time—he's drowning! Check the drainage, quick!

Q. *Why can't I just use some black enamel to seal tree cuts?*

A. Because when the freeze comes, the paint will also freeze and crack, and then it won't act as a seal any more. Commercial tree paints are flexible and will expand and contract with weather changes. Or use equally flexible interior latex.

Q. *What can we do for a flowering crab tree that has sap oozing out of it?*

A. Inspect the tree to see if it is broken or damaged where it's bleeding. If it is, sterilize with two tablespoons of household ammonia in a gallon of water and seal with pruning or latex paint. Wash often with an ounce of liquid dish detergent in ten gallons of water.

Q. *Is it okay to buy mail-order fruit trees?*
A. It sure is. All my dwarf fruit trees come from Start Brothers Nursery, and I've never had bad luck yet. Mail-order houses have a much larger assortment of fruit trees than most nurseries. Up until the last six years, most home gardeners didn't have time for fruit trees, but that picture has changed.

Q. *Should fruit and nut trees be kept in a special area, or can you mix them up?*
A. You can mix and match any tree or group of trees. The whole idea is to make the trees and your landscape compatible—the size, height, shape, color, and commodity, be it fruit, nut, or berry. I try not to put fruit trees too close to patio or play areas, for the safety of both people and trees.

Q. *When is the best time to feed fruit trees?*
A. In light soil you should feed in March and April but not in the summer. In heavy soil, feed in November and December when the soil is frozen. Snow and rain will carry the food down through the cracks, and the food will be waiting when the tree wakes.

Q. *Cheez, have you ever seen the tap root on a pecan tree? Do you have to dig the hole that deep?*
A. Yep; I use a posthole digger. The pecan tree has a tap root about four feet long—longer than that of any other tree you can buy. They're certainly worth it.

Q. *Do I have to prune a newly planted fruit tree back? If so, how much?*

A. The grower and I suggest cutting newly planted fruit trees back by a third and generally just above a break to stimulate new growth and compensate for any root damage. And, by the way, this is true for large balled-in-burlap trees, as well.

Q. *We have a small Japanese maple that keeps turning green, not red. What's wrong?*

A. Its soil is not acid enough. Feed the tree in the spring with azalea food and mulch it with wood chips.

Q. *Why are dwarf fruit trees so weak?*

A. That's not a nice thing to say; after all, they carry the same load as their big sisters carry per branch but the branches are smaller. I make a point of bracing the limbs as the fruit grows bigger to prevent breakage.

Q. *How much room should you have between dwarf fruit trees?*

A. I like ten feet either way to give both the tree and me room to work.

Q. *Do you dormant-spray all fruit trees?*

A. I should say so. All woody caned trees should be sprayed in fall and winter, for sure. Recipe for dormant oil spray is on page 207.

Q. *What do nut trees eat?*

A. Girl food: low-nitrogen garden food. Feed them in the spring.

Q. *Should you cut off the big lumps on the side of a peach tree?*

A. No, just leave them alone. Odds are this kind

of lump is a scar from an old war wound that's callused over.

Q. *How do you keep borers out of peach trees, birches, and God knows what else?*
A. He does know what else. I apply paradichlorobenzene moth crystals on the mulch, about one or two cups per tree sprinkled on the mulch in early spring and late fall.

Q. *What's the best fruit tree spray?*
A. I use one that combines methoxychlor, Malathion, and captan, and I don't have a problem.

Q. *Do you have to have two fruit trees to get fruit?*
A. It helps, but it's not really necessary. The birds, bees, and wind and whatnot help. You can also put some blossoms from one tree into another to help (see page 204).

Q. *How can I keep grubs from killing all of my flowering peach trees?*
A. Poke holes beneath the tree and apply an ounce of soap in ten gallons of water to the holes. Then apply Dursban according to package directions.

Q. *We moved into an old house with an orchard of twelve trees. Some of the branches are dead, some have split bark, limbs are broken, and there are holes all up and down the trunks. Can we save any of them? There are four peach trees and eight apple trees, and no one knows the varieties.*
A. I would sure give it a go. To begin with, cut down and remove all of the weeds in the orchard and burn them. Remove all dead and broken limbs. Next, feed each tree with fifteen pounds of low-nitrogen garden food, apply half a pound of paradichlorobenzene moth crystals to the soil beneath

each tree within three feet of the trunk to control borers. Poke holes three feet apart and eight inches deep in a circle at the drip line, below the branches farthest out.

Q. *How do you protect peach trees from rabbit damage?*
A. First, feed the rabbits by putting out small feeders filled with pelletized alfalfa. Then get one of those plastic tubes that you can put into your golf bag to separate clubs. Split it and place it around the trunk, forcing it about an inch into the ground. Tape the cut shut to create a solid barrier.

Q. *Is it true that garden lighting will affect the health of fruit trees?*
A. Only if the heat of the lamp is coming in contact with the tree itself. I'm all for special lighting effects in any and all gardens. Using red lights will stop early fruit drop.

Q. *How much water does a young fruit tree require?*
A. I would suggest eight to ten gallons a week in dry periods and four to five in the average.

Q. *What would you suggest as the best cooking apple for sauce?*
A. You just can't beat Rhode Island greening. Some like them for eating out of hand, but I use them for applesauce.

Q. *How do you keep mice out of the mulch you put under the apple tree?*
A. I have always felt that if I could keep the mice from chewing at my trees, then I wouldn't need to bother them. In winter, I place small feeders on the

ground near each tree filled with mouse bait. This has worked for Grandma and me for years.

Q. *We're weekend farmers. How many fruit trees can we take care of by ourselves without a whole lot of work?*
A. I think four will keep you busy and give you and your friends all the fruit you can handle.

Q. *How heavily do you apply mulch to an old fruit tree? Or don't you advise mulching old fruit trees?*
A. Yes, I suggest you mulch old trees with a four- to six-inch layer of oak leaf mulch or other hardwood mulch in a band two to three feet wide around the tree to reach the drip line, the point where the branches are farthest out.

Q. *Is it true that the twigs of a cherry tree are poisonous?*
A. You can bet your life it's true! Never chew on any part of any plant unless you know it's nontoxic.

Q. *Can an adult apple tree be moved by mechanical means and still bear fruit?*
A. If the tree is moved in the winter, severely pruned, and mulched heavily right after it's moved, it should bear fruit. To protect its health, it should not bear apples the first year after moving, even if this means you have to pick off the blossoms.

Q. *Is it true that the colder the weather, the better the fruit?*
A. That's what they say. Cold weather is supposed to form stronger buds and firmer fruit for apples and pears in their southern varieties.

Q. *Is it true that if you plant an avocado seed up-side down it won't sprout and grow?*

A. That's nonsense! You should plant them pointed end up for speed. The shoots will find their way to the top any way you plant them, but the stem will be weak if the seed is planted upside down and the shoot has to grow around the seed to find its way to the surface.

Q. *We have a bee hive in our peach tree, and we can't go near it. What can we do?*

A. Clap your hands and shout with joy because you're going to have a bumper crop! The pollen should be so thick around your tree that the limbs will bend from the weight of fruit. Buy a hive and have a beekeeper move them for you, then learn how to take care of them. Honey is great, especially when it's free!

FLOWERS

· ·

There are four basic types of flowers: annuals, raised from seeds or plants, which last a single season; biennials, raised from seeds or plants, which generally take two years to grow and flower; perennials, grown from seeds or clumps, which grow year after year, and bulb types, which consist of tubers, tuberous roots, corms, and rhizomes. All four types can and should be interplanted to provide a full and balanced supply of beauty.

ANNUALS ·

An annual is a plant species that lives its full life span in one season. It has only one purpose in life: to give beauty and enjoyment to the world around it. These beauties are the elves of the flower world. Happy-go-lucky, carefree ramblers, they complement and help accent all the other plants in your garden. The annuals keep the rest of your garden in stitches most of the summer with their antics. They crawl under the pines and tickle the limbs, they snore beneath the maple and dance with the birch. They are truly the lovable jesters of the court and will try anything once: for instance, they'll try growing in the shade just because you want them to. You can grow annuals if you'll just relax and plan to have fun. There are only a few things that you need to know to have a beautiful and successful garden full of annuals, so pay close attention and follow me down the garden path. Call out to the little ones along the way—by name, of course: Rumpelstiltskin, Thumbelina, and any leprechaun name you can remember.

By this time, I shouldn't have to caution you, but I will. With annuals, as with anything else, you must stick with your brown paper bag master plan to make sure that you get the best possible results from the flowers you select. Make certain that you have a place for everyone before you buy. It's very easy to get carried away with annuals. Then you have the embarrassment of having invited a plant over to spend the summer only to find that you don't have a spare bed for him. And then you have to rush around and find a makeshift spot where he'd probably be uncomfortable all season. His discomfort will be reflected in his poor performance, and you'll have no one to blame but yourself. All it takes to have success is a little foresight, and that only costs a few minutes of your time.

Flowers are just part of the big picture you call your garden; they're not supposed to dominate the whole scene. Therefore, make sure that the colors you use and the beds or borders are wide enough and long enough to stay in proportion or contrast to your home and lot. Flower beds are for display

"Annuals are the elves of the flowering world, the lovable jesters of the queen's court."

and should stand alone, while a border is a guide-line or facing for other plants. As a rule, neither should be used for cut flowers. Cut flower beds should be placed next to a fence to support the tallest growers and should never be so wide that you can't cut the farthest row with ease. If you plant the tallest to the rear and the tiniest in front, no plant in any bed will ever be in another plant's shadow. Check your catalogs to determine height, color, habit, and needs for each plant as you plan. You can group by size, by color, or to draw attention. Beds can be orderly or casual, but borders lend themselves to rows and neatness.

Avoid laying out flower beds that have sharp corners or are full circles: taking care of these shapes is hard to do easily and without damage. Try to get your hose around a sharp corner or all around a circle without snapping off some blooms! Soft flowing lines give a natural appearance to your garden—gently drawing the eye along—and allow the lawn mower to follow the contours more easily, leaving smooth cutting lines behind instead of tire tracks all over the flower bed and turf. When you plant borders put the flowers far enough back so they won't be damaged by lawnmower wheels. If you allow three to four inches from the edge of the bed, you can trim the edge with the mower, saving you the problem of trimming on bended knees. Also, by setting your plants back far enough in a border, you will eliminate the problem of happily growing plants growing out of their beds and onto the lawn where they smother the grass.

"Flower beds are for display and should stand alone."

BEGIN WITH THE BEST

Once you decide which guest is going to share which spot with whom, you're ready to send out the invitations. To avoid hurting anyone's feelings, I suggest any pregrown nursery plants be carefully checked for disease. Invite only the fresh, strong, good-looking ones. No discrimination intended, but for their own health, the weak ones are safer left behind at the nursery. If you're going to raise the babies yourself by growing plants from seed, then I suggest you check the birth records to make sure they were recently born: the date on the package. Only current-year's seeds will do.

No matter how good your plants look when they arrive or how fresh the seed you purchase, their success depends upon how well you prepared the soil in the beds. The best soil condition you can give the plants is one that will hold moisture but let extra water run off. For twenty-five pounds of garden food, add half a pound of sugar, fifty pounds of gypsum, and six bushels of compost, if available, and then blend and mix well. Use this mix to fill a bed 20 × 20 feet, then rake and level. Leave no buried stones, glass, wood, or cans to plague you or your flowers later. When the blending job is done, the plants can move in.

THE WONDER OF THE KNEELESS WEEDER

Science has come up with a real winner in the form of a pre-emergent weed killer for gardens. It eliminates the job of weeding on bended knees, which has never been one of my favorite pastimes. All the major garden product manufacturers have a pre-emergent garden weeder. They all contain a chemical that does not interfere with any plant that is above the ground, but prevents any further germination, so there's no new growth coming through—namely, weeds. Applying one of these weed killers as soon as you've planted your flowers or as soon as your new seed has sprouted and after you've removed any existing weeds. Provided you don't disturb the surface of the soil, you won't be plagued by weeds the rest of the summer. But don't use a pre-emergent weed killer where you'll plant seeds, including grass, or you're just throwing money away.

PLANNING THE MENU

"Lively" annuals burn up a great deal of energy by constant flowering, and they need to eat hearty to keep it up. I've found that hand spreading garden food once every three weeks, with a side order of fish emulsion in between, keeps them in tip-top condition. Use the all-purpose tonic from page 65.

Since the plants grow so fast, they require a drink from time to time, except during the rainy season. It's a good idea to give them a soaking, rather than a sprinkling. Aim at their toes rather than the tips of their noses! And don't sprinkle their clothes!

Annuals are prone to insect attack, so it's important to give them a soap-and-water shower with an ounce of liquid dish detergent in ten gallons of water. Keep your eyes open for insects. At the first sign of insect damage, use any multifruit tree spray according to package directions. If there's something nibbling at their feet, use Diazinon as directed on the package. From time to time a little mildew may appear on the foliage, especially on the zinnias. A soap-and-water shower and an after-bath powdering with tomato and vegetable dust will help clear it up.

Your little annual friends are constant climbers, creepers, and crawlers, and it becomes necessary to pinch them back to keep them alert and in their own backyard. I let them bloom the first time and then I cut some of them back with grass shears to encourage more blooms. I do this again just before I go on vacation, since I won't be around and I'd miss the flowers. Petunias need this trimming most often.

YOU NEED A SCORECARD TO KNOW THE PLAYERS

Here are some helpful lists for plants for different needs.

For Borders:

Ageratum	Larkspur
Alyssum	Marigold
Balsam	Nicotiana
Bells-of-Ireland	Petunia
Centaurea (Bachelor's-button)	Salvia
Cleome	Snapdragon
Cosmos	Statice
Cynoglossum	Zinnia

For Foliage:

Amaranthus	Coleus
Basil	Dusty miller
Canna	Kochia
Castor bean	Perilla

For Partial Shade:

Balsam	Lobelia
Begonia	Myosotis
Browallia	Nicotiana
Calendula	Pansy
Coleus	Salvia
Impatiens	Torenia

For the Seaside:

Alyssum	Lupine
Dusty miller	Petunia
Hollyhock	Statice

For Window Boxes:

Alyssum	Nierembergia
Begonia semperflorens	Petunias, cascade
Coleus	
Lobelia	Thunbergia

For Cut Flowers:

Aster
Bells-of-Ireland
Carnation
Celosia
Centaurea (Bachelor's-button)
Cosmos
Cynoglossum
Dahlia
Gaillardia
Gerbera
Gomphrena
Larkspur

Marigold
Nasturtium
Petunias
Rudbeckia
Salpiglossis
Salvia
Scabiosa
Snapdragons
Statice
Tahoka-Daisy
Verbena
Zinnia

Ground Covers:

Cobaea
Creeping Zinnia
Lobelia
Mesembryanthemum
Morning glory
Myosotis
Nasturtium

Nierembergia
Portulaca
Sweet alyssum
Sweet peas
Thunbergia
Verbena
Vinca

For the Rock Garden:

Alyssum
Candytuft
Gazania
Mesembryanthemum

Pansy
Verbena
(Or use ground
    covers)

Low Growers, Up to 18 Inches Tall:

Ageratum, 6 to 12 inches
Alyssum, 4 to 6 inches
Begonia, 4 to 12 inches
Calendula, 12 inches
Candytuft, 8 inches
Celosia (dwarf varieties such as Fiery Feather or
    Jewel Box), 4 to 12 inches

Centaurea (dwarf Bachelor's-button), 10 to 12 inches
Coleus, 12 to 15 inches
Dianthus, 12 inches
Dusty miller (such as *Centaurea candidissima* and *Cineraria maritima* 'Diamond'), 6 to 10 inches
Gazania, 8 inches
Gomphrena, 9 inches
Heliotrope, 12 to 15 inches
Impatiens, 6 to 8 inches
Lobelia, 8 inches
Mesembryanthemum, 6 inches
Myosotis, 12 inches
Nierembergia, 6 inches
Pansy, 6 to 8 inches
Petunia, 12 to 15 inches
Phlox, 7 to 15 inches
Portulaca, 4 to 6 inches
Snapdragon (Floral Carpet), 6 to 8 inches
Torenia, 8 to 12 inches
Verbena, 8 to 12 inches
Vinca, 10 inches
Zinnia (dwarf varieties), 6 to 12 inches

Medium Growers, 1 to 3 Feet Tall
Balsam, 15 inches
Basil, 15 inches
Bells-of-Ireland, 24 inches
Carnation, 15 to 20 inches
Celosia (such as Fireglow), 20 to 24 inches
Cynoglossum, 18 inches
Dahlia (such as Unwin's Dwarf Mix), 20 to 24 inches
Dusty miller, 12 to 24 inches
Gaillardia, 24 to 30 inches
Gomphrena, 18 inches
Helichrysum, 24 to 30 inches
Impatiens, 15 to 18 inches

Marigold, 30 to 36 inches
Nicotiana, 15 to 24 inches
Petunias, 12 to 15 inches
Rudbeckia, 16 to 18 inches
Salpiglossis, 20 to 30 inches
Salvia, 18 to 30 inches
Snapdragons, 15 to 24 inches
Statice, 30 inches
Verbena, 12 to 24 inches
Zinnia, 18 to 30 inches

Tall Growers, 3 to 4 Feet Tall

Amaranthus, 36 to 48 inches
Aster, 36 inches
Castor bean 96 to 120 inches
Celosia (such as Forest Fire), 30 to 48 inches
Centaurea (Bachelor's-button), 30 inches
Cleome, 36 to 48 inches
Cosmos, 36 inches
Dahlia (such as cactus and giant flowered types), 30 to 48 inches
Hollyhock, 48 to 60 inches
Larkspur, 24 to 36 inches
Scabiosa, 24 to 36 inches
Snapdragon, (such as Rockets), 30 to 36 inches
Zinnia, 30 to 36 inches

FLOWER GARDENS

• •

I can honestly say I've never met a person who doesn't enjoy the beauty of a flower garden. The colors, shapes, and fragrances stimulate our imagination. Many of the newer commercial buildings have been designed with gardens built into a central area to provide a place for employees to relax and just enjoy viewing. And architects often design a new home around a garden or patio area.

Flowers provide more than just something to take up space. They provide continuity among the other elements of the garden; they can act as a border or to control traffic; some flowers protect other plants from insects; flowers enhance the architectural elements of a building's design; they provide us with fragrance and color both indoors and out. There are even flowers that can be eaten. Roses are great for making jelly, wine, and in salads. Mums are used in Oriental cooking; daylily buds are used to thicken soup; violets, pansies, and roses can be candied.

If you plan and plant properly, you can have flowers outdoors from February through November and blooms indoors every month of the year.

Flower growing is probably one of the simplest things you can do in gardening; most flowers can pretty well take care of themselves if you plant them properly. Almost all annual flowers—whether grown from seed, plants, bulbs, or clumps—need good, rich medium to well-drained soil (they don't like to stand in water) and full sunlight for most to medium shade for some. Most flowers need but one good feeding a year and very little if any weeding or cultivating; they give minimum worry from insects and disease if you wash them occasionally with soap and water and a touch of Malathion. Whenever or wherever possible I use grass clippings to mulch my flowers; two inches of mulch is usually sufficient.

"Happiness is all right here. I can get high and happy just mowing the lawn or tending the roses."

"I talk to plants all the time while I'm planting them. It keeps them calm, and me, too."

PERENNIALS AND BIENNIALS

. . . .

The perennials, by virtue of their longevity, have come to be known as the stewards of the garden: they're the neat, prim, straitlaced, no-nonsense members of the garden kingdom. Since they'll be with you year in and year out, consult with them before adding any more work or guests to your garden. After all, they're the mainstays who keep things neat and tidy. The delphinium is the head man, and his assistant is the chrysanthemum. The peony is the chambermaid, the iris is the butler guiding the way through the garden, and artemisia is the doorman, often seen but seldom noted. You're not out there alone: you've got plenty of managerial assistance, whether you like it or not!

"Perennials are the neat, prim, straitlaced, no-nonsense members of the garden kingdom. Consult with them before adding any more work or guests to your garden."

The perennials live up to Webster's definition: "Persistent for several years." They continue to return year after year, multiplying and paying their way as they go. They seldom complain, and their general health is usually excellent. Once you plant them, you don't have to keep your eye on them too much. The biennials, half brothers to the perennials, only stay around for a couple of years. They tend to be a little restless and make good plants for spots where you haven't quite decided what you want permanently.

Let's go back to your master plan for a moment. Remember, perennials are practically forever, just like trees, shrubs, and evergreens; be sure you want what you want where you want it before you plant. After all, it's no pleasure to tell an employee you don't need his help any longer, which is how you feel when you have to let a perennial go. Ask your nurseryman for perennials suggestions and check them out thoroughly before finally selecting and placing your perennials in their permanent positions.

PERMANENT POSITION

Plants are just like people; they can relax and feel more secure when their name is painted on the door of their own office. Plant your perennials for permanence and give each individual plant some working space of its own.

Perennials can be purchased in small soil bags in the spring, in tar-paper pots in early summer, or full grown in boxes or baskets in midsummer or sometimes late spring. I had to retire an old delphinium recently, and it left a big gap in my organization. So I replaced it with a big strapping new blue one. From the action around the garden, it's clear that the others thought they'd be able to loaf—until they found out what kind of a boss he was going to be! By the way, he is working out fine.

Perennials like the same soil and food conditions as annuals, and so the soil preparation is the same. Mix together twenty-five pounds of garden food, a half pound of sugar, fifty pounds of gypsum, and six bushels of compost. Fill perennial beds or planting holes with this mix and level with a rake. Then apply pre-emergent weed killer according to package directions, and mulch. Plant perennials in a hole wider than the plant and only as deep as the soil line from the nursery indicates.

Many perennials have very particular planting requirements. Read all about them in catalogs, in the material mail-order firms send with perennials, or ask at the nursery where you buy them.

Since perennials are heavy bloomers, you need to feed them on a regular basis. Give them a handful of garden food a month, and in between, give them the same dessert you give the annuals—fish emulsion.

DON'T CROWD

. . . .

Many perennials—such as iris, peonies, and mums—can be divided. Dividing is done in the early spring, either to start new plants or to give new vigor and more room to the older ones. Always dig and divide carefully.

To divide mums, dig out the whole clump and gently pull off each new plant individually. Replant the plants wherever you wish, but keep in mind that each will grow as large as a bushel basket, so leave room for expansion. One clump of mums should yield at least thirty to fifty plants.

Peonies are cut in half or into thirds with a sharp spade and replanted in new and sunny spots in fall.

Iris are dug up as a clump in late August. Remove the soil and then cut off each corm with a sharp knife. You'll be able to recognize these even if you're a beginner because each corm, or root section, will have a foliage shoot at the top. Each corm can start a new iris plant.

Although perennials generally need little maintenance, insects and disease can bother these "flower folk" from time to time. Wash them down regularly with soap and water and use a fruit tree spray or all-purpose spray according to package directions when a problem arises. Also, poor watering practices can prevent perennials from doing their best: a deep soaking once a week will do wonders for them.

Following is a list to help you make a wise selection of perennials for your garden:

Tall Perennials

Alcea (double and single hollyhock)
Anchusa (azurea)
Delphinium
Digitalis (foxglove)
Eremurus (giant desert-candle)
Helenium
Hemerocallis
Iris (Japanese iris)
Lilium
Lythrum
Penstemon
Rudbeckia
Yucca

Medium Perennials

Aquilegia (columbine)
Chrysanthemum
Chrysanthemum coccineum (painted daisy)
Coreopsis (grandiflora)
Gaillardia (grandiflora)
Gypsophila (Baby's-breath)
Iris (bearded)
Lupinus (Russel)
Lychnis (chalcedonica)
Paeonia (peony)
Papaver (Oriental poppy)
Phlox (perennial)

Platycodon (Monk's hood)
Veronica (longifolia)

Short Perennials

Alyssum (saxatile compactum)
Arabis alpina
Armeria (sea pink)
Aster alpinus
Aubrieta
Aurinia (saxatilis)
Campanula carpatica
Dianthus (perennial pinks)
Phlox subulata (carpet)

● BULBS

We've all heard that the best gifts come in small packages. That's never more true than for bulb stock! I've never been able to understand why God hid such beautiful things as tulips, crocuses, or daffodils in such ugly shells, but then, some of the most beautiful people I know are not the best-looking physically. I also remember that "beauty is more than skin deep."

Planting bulbs is just like burying a treasure. Once a bulb is in the ground, it's there to stay until we decide to move it. And it never really loses its value. As a matter of fact, the longer bulbs remain in the ground, the more valuable they become. If you plan properly, you can have spring beauty from February to June. In snow country bulbs break through the ice and snow with the early varieties called snowdrops. In warm climates they bring early spring color after the dismal rains. When you plant bulbs and your friends ask what's in that mound of soil, you can truthfully say, "There's gold in that thar hill!"

As with any buried treasure, you must make a map so you don't forget where the valuables are buried. You already have the map; it's the paper bag plan you used to start your garden. All you have to do now is mark where you planted which bulbs so you don't accidentally dig them up before they pop up their heads. (I also mark my bulbs with long thin bamboo stakes with aluminum flags on which I write the variety's name and when I can expect it to bloom.)

No gardener can complain that there aren't enough colors, sizes, or shapes to choose from in Mother Nature's jewel box of bulbs: she has something inside there to satisfy everyone's taste. Take just a few moments to look over the blooming time of each kind of bulb. With a little planning, you'll be able to fill in the voids until the perennials and annuals appear or you put in annuals.

In the last few years, the popularity of imported Dutch bulbs has dwindled to a trickle of what it used to be, and that's a pity. You younger gardeners haven't seen anything until you see snowdrops, winter aconite, or Siberian squill poke their nose through the snow in late February to smile at the world and say, "Spring is just around the corner!" As for you more experienced green thumbs, shame on you—look at all the extra beauty you're letting pass you if you don't put bulbs in. I'm prouder of my garden in the early spring than at any other time of the season; my posies are in full swing when other folks in the neighborhood still have a sleepy landscape to look at.

Here are a few suggestions to get you back in the treasure hunt and make you button-poppin', suspender-snappin' proud of your early spring garden. In the order of their blooming, there's snowdrop, winter aconite, crocus, Siberian squill, *Iris reticulata*, Chrionodoxa, *Puschkinia libanotica*,

"Bulbs are like buried treasure."

early tulips (kaufmanniana and fosteriana), followed by grape hyacinths, trumpet daffodils, the single and double early tulips, regular hyacinths, medium daffodils, Darwin and triumph tulips, short daffodils, poet's narcissus, and jonquils. Then there are the late tulips—parrot, cottage, lily-flowered, double lates, Darwin, and breeder. Now ask yourself, what more could I ask of Mother Nature than this garden gallery of glorious colors from the last weeks of snow to the fullness of spring?

PLANT IN ADVANCE

Spring-flowering bulbs are planted in the fall and winter from coast to coast. I don't know any place where these beauties won't grow; it's simply a matter of planting at the right time. The "little" bulbs such as crocus, scilla, and snowdrops, should be planted as soon as they're available in snow country, and in early December in the South and West. Tulips should be planted as soon as the weather cools and on through the fall and early winter until the ground freezes. In the South and West, bulbs can be placed in the refrigerator at 45 degrees for five to six weeks and then planted in January.

THE PROBLEM SOLVERS

The biggest problem most gardeners have is what to plant in damp, shady spots. The bulbs solve this problem, because that's where they grow the best. Once planted, they need to be kept damp. I mulch my bulbs with leaves until they begin to poke their noses through. Then I move the mulch just enough to let them finish their climb to the sunshine but keep their feet cool.

DON'T BURY YOUR TREASURE TOO DEEP

Your buried treasures do not like to be too deep nor too crowded. Plant the little bulbs three inches deep and three inches apart. Hyacinths and tulips, as well as daffodils, are to be planted six inches deep and six inches apart. There is a top and bottom to each bulb, and they sure would appreciate it if you would not plant them standing on their heads. Plant the bulb with the point up. They will grow either way, but it seems to weaken the stem when they have to turn that first corner underground in order to come out right side up.

If you plant a large bed of bulbs or several different kinds in the same bed to bloom one after the other, I suggest that you dig out the bed you intend to plant to a depth of eight inches. With the soil removed, mix into the bed two pounds of bonemeal per bushel of soil, five pounds of gypsum per bushel of soil, and fifty pounds of peat moss for each four bushels of soil. Mix well. Use this mixture to refill the bulb bed as you plant. Plant the bulbs that go deepest on the bottom and then cover them up with a light layer of the soil mix. Lay the next bulb layer in but not directly over any bulbs below, and place a layer of soil mix over it, continuing until all of the bulbs are planted and covered. Now mulch the top with leaves or light bark chips, pine or redwood.

A bulb has a built-in lunch bucket, but there's not enough lunch in it to carry it all the way through the season. Mix fifty pounds of garden food, 4-12-4 or 5-10-5, with a pound of sugar. As the bulbs begin to show through the soil, scatter a half-handful of this garden food mix over the top of the soil. Feeding tulips before they bloom will keep them blooming longer and stronger. It will also help them to produce more bulbs.

The insects that wake up early will be delighted with your foresight in supplying them with such a pleasant dinner. To discourage them, I suggest that you give the young plants a shower with an ounce of liquid dish detergent in ten gallons of water before the blooms appear, and spray the soil with Dursban according to package directions if there are any signs of insect damage. Apart from that, you shouldn't have too much trouble with insects.

After the tulips have bloomed to their fullest, cut off the stems and let the foliage alone until it has turned yellow and begun to dry; then cut it off just above the ground. To hide the fading foliage, I turn it down and place a small rubber band around it to screen it from the rest of the world.

S N E A K
P R E V I E W

• •

Bulbs can be grown indoors since they need very little effort to burst into beautiful, fragrant bloom in January and February. Tulips, hyacinths, daffodils, and narcissi, as well as crocuses, can be planted in the fall in pots, to be brought into the house to bloom. After you've bought your bulbs, buy a commercial planting mix—the type used for house plants—at your local garden center and five- or six-inch clay pots. Place a piece of broken crockery or a flat beer cap over the drain hole in the bottom of the pot. Put the bulb or bulbs in the pot, making sure the bulbs don't touch. Begin to fill the pot with soil until the bulbs' tops are just above the soil line. Continue to fill the pots until only a quarter to a half inch of the bulbs remain above the soil.

After you've planted all of your bulbs, water them thoroughly, wrap the entire pot in newspaper, and bury six to eight inches deep in your garden. The newspaper is placed around the pots to keep them clean for bringing into the house. Leave the pots in the ground for eight to ten weeks. Then bring them into the basement where they can get some light but remain at 60 to 65 degrees. Keep them there until the foliage is two to three inches high. At this point, bring them into full light in your house. Keep them damp and warm and watch the magic that follows. There's no room deodorizer that can compare with the fragrance of real hyacinths in full bloom. What an excellent experience for both children and adults! You don't have to bury the pots; you can keep them in a garage or even a spare refrigerator where the temperature will be 40 to 50 degrees, but you must keep the bulbs dark and damp.

When we think of bulbs, we forget there are other bulb types, like the tubers and corms, dahlias, glads, and lilies. A little study on your part with the seed catalogs will help you learn how to fit in a few of each.

"I tend to lean toward Holland bulbs, but I think that's only due to Hans Brinker."

STEP-BY-STEP
FLOWER CARE

....

SPRING AND SUMMER

....

Step 1. Most home flower gardens are a hodge-podge of annuals, perennials, and bulbs all planted together. Keep each type of flowering plant separated with open cylinders, bottomless pots, or permanent barriers to make it easier and safer to move or plant them.

Step 2. Remove all winter covers, trash, and spent stems as soon as possible.

Step 3. Bathe perennials and bulb foliage to remove dirt and pollution from foliage surfaces. Fill your ten-gallon sprayer with a half cup of children's shampoo, a half cup of tobacco juice, a half cup of brown mouthwash, and two drops of Tabasco sauce. Fill with warm water.

Step 4. Before you turn over the flower bed to put in annuals and summer-flowering bulbs, put a deep layer of mowed leaves, grass clippings, and other organic materials over the soil.

Step 5. Mix ten pounds of any garden food with the following:

2 cups of diatomaceous earth
2 cups of bonemeal
3 cups of oatmeal

½ pound of Epsom salts
½ pound of sugar

Use a hand-held spreader to apply this mixture over the organic material in step 4.

Step 6. Spade deep; allow to rest for three days.

Step 7. Place a thin layer of fresh grass clippings over the spaded area; till very, very well.

Step 8. Before planting bulbs, tubers or corms, dust them in medicated foot powder.

Step 9. Sprinkle crushed paradichlorobenzene moth crystals mixed with chili powder into the bulb holes, two tablespoons of chili powder to a cup of moth crystals.

Step 10. Pencil sharpening shavings (which are made of cedar) will discourage insects as well.

Step 11. After bulbs are planted, spray soil with a mixture of a tablespoon of household ammonia and a tablespoon of liquid dish detergent in ten gallons of water.

Step 12. A week after planting annuals, begin to feed them on a three-week cycle, using this all-purpose tonic, applied before noon with the twenty-gallon hand-held sprayer. In the quart container of the sprayer, mix together:

1 can of beer
1 cup of children's shampoo
½ cup of molasses
1 ounce of liquid seaweed
1 cup of liquid lawn food

Fill the balance of the jar with household ammonia and use with twenty gallons of water.

Step 13. Wash all flowers down on a two-week, evening schedule using the following solution and your twenty-gallon hand-held sprayer. In the quart jar of your sprayer mix:

1 cup of laundry bar soap solution
1 cup of chewing tobacco juice
1 cup of brown mouthwash

(See page 7 to learn how to make laundry bar soap solution and chewing tobacco juice.)

Step 14. Mulch the soil with grass clippings after applying a layer of Preen.

Step 15. Constantly remove dead blossoms. This step is probably the most important of all. Also, cut back long or leggy foliage just before you go on vacation.

Step 16. Spray foliage with Cloud Cover before heat sets in to retain moisture and keep plants healthy.

FALL

●●●

Step 17. Plant bulbs after the first killing frost.

Step 18. Summer-flowering bulbs are removed from the soil. Wash them in a mild laundry bar soap bath, let them dry thoroughly, dust them with foot powder, and store them by hanging in old onion or potato bags where they'll get air circulation.

Step 19. Follow steps 8, 9, and 10 for fall-planted bulbs.

Step 20. Cover your perennials with a light layer of straw after a killing frost.

QUESTIONS AND ANSWERS ....

Q. *How much sun is necessary for lots of blooms?*
A. I have my best luck with five to six hours of morning sun, but the afternoon sun won't hurt.

Q. *What is meant by a hardy annual?*
A. This is a tough little fellow that's planted in the fall to come up and bloom the following spring.

Q. *When is the best time to preserve flowers?*
A. Right when they are at their peak. Cut them in the morning, never after a rain. To preserve or dry annuals, cover them with silica gel, available at most garden centers.

Q. *Why can't I mix annuals with perennial flowers?*
A. I don't know why you can't. I've done it for years and Grandma Putt did it for many years before that. You can mix and match annuals, perennials, and bulbs, and biennials. That's the real secret to a beautiful garden.

Q. *If I want a big, big, splashy flower bed for a shopping center mall, what would I plant? We're a garden club that has undertaken a beautification project.*
A. You can select several of the following: ageratum, alyssum, asters, lobelia, marigolds, petunias, phlox, verbena, zinnias.

Q. *I've heard that marigolds will keep mosquitoes away, but I tried and had no luck.*

A. If you plant the giant, old-fashioned marigolds in pots and place them on patios at night, they'll work. (Even *I* can't stand the smell.) The newer varieties don't work as well because they have no odor.

Q. *When do you start seed indoors in Illinois?*

A. The first part of January or early February. Germinate the seeds in a sandy soil mix, then thin and plant them in individual pots.

Q. *Why do they recommend that you burn the dead floral foliage in the fall?*

A. I didn't know they did. I think you'll find they're referring only to sick or diseased plants. The rest go into the compost pile to make next year's garden food.

Q. *Which annuals will live in damp soil?*

A. Begonia, impatiens, and nicotiana. Coleus will also tolerate some dampness.

Q. *What do you suggest for a hot, dry location around the Southwest? We just bought a retirement home there.*

A. You should have luck with portulaca, aster, and zinnia.

Q. *I love bouquets on the table at mealtime. Any suggestions?*

A. I always have a suggestion. We have a fenceful of sweet peas, with a backup of zinnias, asters, cosmos, stock, larkspur, and snapdragons (both tall and dwarf).

Q. *Can I collect seed from this year's annuals?*
A. You can, but hybrids won't give you a good flower, and that's what most of today's annuals are.

Q. *Should I mulch my annual flower bed?*
A. Yes, by all means. After you remove the weeds and apply one of the pre-emergent weed killers, cover the surface with four to six inches of grass clippings.

Q. *I love hanging baskets, but they're so messy to water. Are there any plants that would make it neater?*
A. Stick with the same plants; just change the method of watering. Drop four or five ice cubes into the baskets every couple of days.

Q. *I've been told when you buy nursery-grown flowers for the garden, you want short green ones with no color showing. True or false?*
A. True. If you buy long, tall plants, they soon grow out of proportion. Short, fat plants can be more easily controlled.

Q. *Can you give me the name of a good flower to cascade down a wall but not be a nuisance for the rest of our lives?*
A. Try trailing nasturtiums for something different.

Q. *How do you force petunias to flower?*
A. Hold back on the water and run them a bit dry.

Q. *What annual flower variety is the most popular?*
A. Petunias are by far the number one favorite among both amateur and professional growers. They're followed closely by marigolds.

Q. *What are Epsom salts used for in the garden?*
A. Epsom salts (magnesium sulphates) are used to deepen the color, thicken the petals, and increase roots in plants. Use one-quarter cup of Epsom salts per four square feet of flower or vegetable garden in May.

Q. *We've just moved into a brand-new home in a new subdivision, which I'm sure is a branch of Interstate 75 since all the clay (blue, black, brown, and gray) was used to build up our grade. But then even that wasn't enough, so they hauled in sand, muck, and heck knows what else. My problem is I have large pockets of each. How can I have a good flower garden?*
A. What are you complaining about? You ought to send one of your first bouquets to your developer with a note of thanks for providing you with the richest growing media. Clay is the richest soil in the world if you can break it up. Begin by taking some of the sand and muck along with grass and leaves and garden gypsum. Till and spade it into the clay area. Take clay, muck, leaves, and grass and till into the sandy area. Add sand, leaves, and grass to the muck and quit your complaining.

Q. *We've built a good porous base on our clay property, but the water backs up from beneath. What's the solution?*
A. Buy, rent, or borrow a tree auger that can be used on an electric drill or hand brace and drill holes two to three feet deep all over your garden and fill the holes with gravel. These holes, called "French wells," should carry off excess water.

Q. *Can I really use household ammonia as a fertilizer without hurting my plants?*
A. Be darn careful: Use a half teaspoonful per gallon of water.

Q. *What makes green moss grow in my flower beds?*
A. Poor drainage. I'm sure not many of your flowers do too well. French wells, in addition to adding good compost base (grass and leaves), will help there. (See page 257.)

Q. *Do all flowers like the same soil or is it true that perennials and bulbs like clay better than rich soil?*
A. Clay is rich soil. All plants want loose, porous, well-drained soil.

Q. *How long will flowers last when you dry them?*
A. If you spray them with five or six coats of hair spray, you should get a couple of years or more out of them.

Q. *What's the best way to dry flowers?*
A. I use three cups of borax and a cup of cornmeal mixed together. Place freshly picked flowers in a container that can be sealed. Cover with the mixture, seal, and let stand for four to five days.

Q. *What are some good projects for children using plants and flowers?*
A. I like using fruit in such projects with kids. Cut oranges, grapefruit, limes, or lemons in half, clean out the meat, and punch two or three small holes in the skin. Fill the half shell with soil, place a seed taken from the fruit into the soil-filled shell, and treat it like any other houseplant. The peel will harden up and become the pot.

Q. *Is it a good idea to use plastic as a mulch in flower beds?*
A. I use plastic only in my perennial beds, as I seldom move them. I don't use plastic in my annual

and bulb area; I use grass clippings or roofing paper (tar paper) rather than plastic as it seems to last longer and work better.

Q. *Can I buy one kind of fertilizer for all flowers?*
A. Yeah! I use any garden food that's low in nitrogen, and high in potash and phosphorus. For bulbs and perennials I add stinky bonemeal to the soil. During the growing season you can add liquefied table scraps to the flower beds.

Q. *Is a homemade greenhouse as good as a prefabricated one?*
A. I have seen some awfully good homemade ones, but, then, I have also seen some awfully bad ones. If they get the job done, then they are all okay. I sure do like those prefabs, though.

Q. *What is saltpeter used for in a garden?*
A. As a rule it's the base used in stump removers. A half teaspoonful per gallon of water can be used to stimulate root growth. It's purchased as potassium nitrate in most drugstores. I suggest you keep a sense of humor when you go to buy it.

Q. *I was given a gallon of seaweed plant food. Is it really plant food?*
A. It sure is and a darn good one, very mild and slow acting. A friend of mine in Boston, Massachusetts, uses real seaweed as a mulch compost and has terrific luck.

Q. *How good is horse manure in a flower garden?*
A. Not really good unless it's a couple of years old. Man, it's mean stuff if it's too young. Horse manure is full of weeds and humus foliage and makes my plants too tall.

Q. *How often do you feed flowers?*
A. I feed everything in the spring and then during the season I hand-sprinkle a light meal once a month.

Q. *How much and how often do you use lime in a flower garden?*
A. Same as in a vegetable garden: one pound per one hundred square feet once every three years.

Q. *Our town offers free sludge. Is it good and safe for my plants and my family?*
A. I have followed closely the sludge testing being conducted by the Environmental Protection Agency and leading universities, and it is working out absolutely great. Use it; you can't beat the price. Sludge breaks up clay and makes grass, trees, and evergreens grow to beat the band; vegetables, too.

Q. *Why do my annuals dry out so much faster than my bulbs and perennials?*
A. Because annuals are rooted more shallowly than bulbs and perennials. Mulch or water annuals lightly but more often.

Q. *Why do my flowers look so dismal after I water them. Some even get a white powder on them?*
A. The white stuff is mildew and comes from poor water care. I find that watering with a soaker about one o'clock each afternoon, avoiding top watering, makes my flowers happy and clean looking.

Q. *You always hear about people who have a brown thumb with houseplants, but have you ever heard of an outdoor brown thumb?*
A. Knock it off! Neither you nor anyone else has a nongrower's thumb. To have a green thumb outdoors, just remember the big four: 1. Pick good,

fresh seed of a plant variety that's recommended for your soil and your part of the country. 2. Make sure your soil drains well and is rich and loose with leaves, grass, and compost. 3. Feed your plants regularly with a proper garden food. 4. Make darn sure you understand when, where, and how to water. That's it.

Q. *What the dickens is the difference between garden food and any other plant food?*
A. Garden food is for girl plants (as I've explained earlier, that's anything that flowers or fruits), and they want more potash and phosphorus and less nitrogen. The formulas of dry garden food would be 4-12-4, 5-10-5, 6-10-4, and so on; and a liquid like the one I use from Science Products is 10-52-17. Plants that just have foliage (boy plants) need lots of nitrogen, so I use a lawn food for trees, grass, and evergreens.

Q. *We live at Cape Cod. What will stand the salty sea breeze?*
A. Alyssum, petunias, lupine, dusty miller.

Q. *How many different kinds of annuals are there?*
A. There are literally hundreds of kinds of cross combinations of varieties, so you should have no problem satisfying your taste. If you mean is there more than one kind of an annual, the answer is no. An annual is a plant that lives its full life cycle in one season. A biennial is a plant that lives a lifetime in two years (maybe three if it's tough).

Q. *Please give me a list of flowering annuals that like shade.*
A. Why not try coleus, impatiens, lobelia, myosotis, calendula, browallia, nicotiana, pansy, salvia, balsam, begonia?

Q. *Which annuals can you grow inside as houseplants?*
A. Any that will grow outside if you recreate in your home the same conditions as on a June day.

Q. *Which plants are biennial?*
A. The most popular are pansies, hollyhocks, forget-me-nots, and foxgloves. These are planted in the fall, covered with soil and topped with straw, and bloom in the spring.

Q. *Aren't perennials really weeds? Or wild flowers?*
A. There is no such thing as a weed: it's just a plant we haven't found a use for yet. Yes, perennials once were wild flowers, and in some parts of the country some of them still are.

Q. *I've stayed away from perennials because I've been told they spread all over your garden, almost like weeds.*
A. It's a shame that you haven't enjoyed the beauty of perennials; they're the best flowering investment you can make. They do multiply, increasing your investment, but they only go where you let them.

Q. *When do you plant perennials?*
A. In a warm climate, any time they're available. In cold country, I prefer May for the most part. Plant in good, rich, well-drained composted loam containing leaves, sand, grass, and sawdust.

Q. *What's the blooming order of perennials?*
A. *Early:* primrose, Sweet William, violets, pinks, candytuft, creeping phlox, and bleeding heart. *Early Summer:* iris, shasta daisy, carnation, columbine, astilbe, peony, poppy, and gaillardia. *Mid-summer:* lavender, heliotrope, platycodon, baby's-

breath, delphinium, and daylily. **Fall:** chrysanthemum, aster, lythrum, and helianthus.

Q. *When is the best time to divide or move perennials?*
A. In the spring where it's cold and in the fall in warm areas. I have my own way of dividing. First, my spade is razor sharp. I keep my shovels that way with a file. In the late fall I take my spade and cut right through the perennials I'm going to transplant, pull the spade out, and lightly cover the plant with light straw for the winter. In the spring I dig up only the half I'm going to move; no shock, no mess. That way, I don't give up a season of blooms.

Q. *How do you keep the weeds out of a perennial bed?*
A. I use a chemical pre-emergent weed killer or tar-paper mulch with decorative stones on top.

Q. *Which are the best bulbs to buy—Japanese or Dutch?*
A. Bulbs originally came from the Orient, and we're starting to see them coming from the East again. I have good luck with both. I tend to lean toward Holland bulbs, but I think that's only due to Hans Brinker.

Q. *For the last three years, our tulips have started to grow in the winter but haven't bloomed. What are we doing wrong?*
A. It's not what you're doing; it's what you did. Odds are you planted the bulbs too close to a heated wall or planted them too early. Also, they might not be planted deeply enough. Plant bulbs after a good frost in open, well-drained, fertile soil that's well composted. I suggest you dig them up and start over.

Q. *When's the best time to plant spring-flowering bulbs?*
A. Never plant them before there's been a good, killing frost in the North, and not before they've been refrigerated for ten weeks in warm-weather areas.

Q. *Can you really plant bulbs too deep?*
A. You really can, and by the same token you can plant them not deep enough. Daffodils and hyacinths are planted six inches deep, tulips five inches deep, and small bulbs three inches deep.

Q. *My lilies just rot every year. Can they be diseased?*
A. I would say that your lily patch is in a wet spot; lilies can't stand water.

Q. *The stems on my tulips are big enough but don't seem to have enough support. Why?*
A. I'd say you're guilty of planting your bulbs upside down. I've been asked on behalf of bulbs everywhere to tell folks like you to plant the head up, bottom down.

Q. *What is bulb food, and is it necessary to use a special one?*
A. Bulb food is usually an ordinary garden food with a liberal supply of bonemeal and, no, it's not necessary. But you must feed your bulbs when they're blooming.

Q. *How often do you have to dig up tulips?*
A. I do it every three years, unless my bulbs aren't flowering or have only small flowers. Then I move them.

Q. *Do you have any suggestions for a plant in a hanging basket? I'd prefer a bulb so I can use it over and over.*
A. My favorite is widow's tears (*Achimenes*). It loves hot weather but must come in before frost; it grows from a rhizome.

Q. *Can amaryllis be grown outside?*
A. There are two types of amaryllis: belladonna lily and hippeastrum. Belladonna is for outside and hippeastrum for indoors.

Q. *What's the most durable of the bulb-type plants?*
A. You just can't beat the begonia, any type. They also make great houseplants.

Q. *When's the best time to plant tiger lily?*
A. In early May, when the soil is warming up, as you would any lily. You can replant your Easter lily and expect blooms in July and August.

Q. *When do you transplant lilies?*
A. The early fall is the best time. Dig up and separate the clump carefully. Replant and feed with a mild liquid garden food.

Q. *Do iris, lilies, glads, and begonias have to be dug up in the fall?*
A. Only begonias and gladioluses.

Q. *What can you do to bulb roots so they don't rot or dry out when they are stored?*
A. When the foliage is yellow, dig up the root and remove the soil. Then wash in a weak solution and let dry for four to five weeks, put them in a paper bag with Thiram, a fungicide, and shake like donuts. Now place them in a box of dry peat moss and store at 50 degrees.

Q. *I just can't afford all the dusts and sprays necessary for flowers. Is there just one I can use?*
A. It's not a good idea to have too many sprays lying around, anyway. I use a multipurpose garden dust from Science Products that can be made into a spray as well and is for food and flowers. The medication used is Malathion and methoxychlor and captan. For soil problems, I use Diazinon.

Q. *When do you take cuttings from geraniums?*
A. Any time during the season if you're planning to grow them as houseplants. You must take the last ones before frost gets them. Cuttings are taken from young growth four to five inches long. Take off all the leaves so the slip looks like a piece of asparagus. Dip an inch and a half of the cut end into Rootone and then place the slip in a three-inch clay pot filled with African violet soil mix. Feed and water until the cutting is growing well. Then transplant to a four-inch pot and bury the pot in the ground. Before frost, remove the pot and bring it inside.

Q. *How do you save geraniums?*
A. Pull them out by the roots and store them upside down in your garage until March 15. At that time you can cut two-thirds off the top and back and one-third off the roots. Pot and begin to feed and water. When the threat of frost is gone, plant in the ground.

Q. *Can you transplant caladium for indoors?*
A. Yeah, you can—but, boy, they look awful.

Q. *Can geraniums be planted from seed?*
A. Yes, they can. They germinate slowly, so start them indoors. They're called "Carefree," the seed is not in every seed rack.

Q. *Does the tea-and-refrigerator soaking really speed up flower seed?*
A. I am the guy who pushes it the most. Soak for at least eighteen hours—makes a world of difference.

Q. *Can you take cuttings from coleus?*
A. Pull a leaf and root it in sharp sand. In the fall, dig out the whole plant and pot it. The same goes for impatiens.

Q. *When do you start seed inside for annual flowers?*
A. If you have a specially designed tray with a plastic dome and soil-heating cable unit, available at any garden store, start seeds in March; if not, in February, transplanting three times to insure stronger plants. Feed new and old plants with Garden Life soluble plant food (10-52-17) by Science Products.

Q. *Which flowers are considered bug chasers?*
A. The most common are marigolds, asters, nasturtiums, and mums.

Q. *We have a large assortment of evergreens, mostly junipers. Which perennial do you suggest I use in the open spots?*
A. I love the differently colored painted daisies.

Q. *When's the best time to plant perennials?*
A. I was taught that fall is one of the best times to plant iris, peonies, and mums, and early spring for the rest.

Q. *Will perennials do well in acid soil?*
A. I would add lime every three years, but, as a rule, perennials will do well in soil that's somewhat on the acid side.

Q. *When's the best time to sow seed for perennials?*
A. I sow perennial seed in the fall, then cover it over with straw for protection. Biennials like pansies and hollyhocks must be planted in the fall.

Q. *Will peonies survive in clay?*
A. Not as a rule; they prefer loose, fertile soil.

Q. *I've heard there's a poppy that's short and stout.*
A. Iceland is the name, and they're great as cut flowers.

Q. *What can I feed peonies to keep them from drooping?*
A. You have to stake peonies. Tie them with pieces of old nylon hose.

Q. *How do you make delphiniums bloom a second time?*
A. Cut the bloom off when it's just about done and feed the plant. Don't let the flowers die on the vine. The same advice goes for the other perennials.

Q. *When's the best time to transplant perennials that must be moved?*
A. I've found that early spring is generally the best time.

Q. *What is speedwell?*
A. A very bushy, beautiful perennial, also called veronica.

Q. *How close together should I plant mums?*
A. That depends on what purpose you have in mind. I don't let them touch, if I can help it.

Q. *Is the aster an annual or a perennial?*
A. It's both; it depends which you buy. Italian aster is the perennial.

Q. *How do you save Chinese lanterns?*
A. Cut them off and hang them upside down.

Q. *What is statice used for?*
A. It's a great flower to cut and dry. It grows eighteen inches high and eighteen inches across and is also called sea lavender.

Q. *How tall do lupines grow?*
A. Three to five feet. They should be planted in the back row.

Q. *I am totally confused about which are bulbs and which are corms or tubers, or whatever they call them. How do you tell?*
A. Why bother? They're either bulbs or bulb types. The way I mulch and the way I recommend you do, you can plant any of them in the fall and let the chips fall where they may.

Q. *I have seen crocuses planted in the lawn. How do you take care of them?*
A. Just plant them, and they'll look out for themselves. When they're finished blooming, mow the tops off. The crocuses will return the following year almost without fail.

Q. *What makes tulips stop blooming?*
A. They're probably too crowded. Dig them up and separate them.

Q. *Should you cut the mushy, gray spots out of bulbs before you plant them?*
A. No, you should take them back and get new ones or your money back. The ones you have are diseased.

Q. *What's the best mulch for bulbs and corms?*
A. Oak leaf mulch makes the best mulch because it acts as a natural insect barrier. It also doesn't pack down and smother growth, as maple leaves would.

Q. *When should you plant gladiolus bulbs?*
A. Start in the early spring and then continue planting them in groups two weeks apart through July 1.

Q. *Can I leave glad bulbs in the ground all winter?*
A. Not as a rule, because glads freeze, so you should dig them up and store them. However, I have left them in the ground with four inches of mulch and had three good years out of them.

Q. *Should you cut tulips for bouquets?*
A. What kind of a question is that? Certainly, you should. Tulips make lots of folks happy, and that's what Mother Nature has in mind.

Q. *Does the size of the bulb have any effect on the size of the flowers?*
A. Bulbs are graded by size, so the bigger the better.

Q. *What do you do to bulbs after they've bloomed?*
A. Remember where they are planted and feed them once in a while. In the fall, begin to water where the bulbs are planted, and add new mulch.

Q. *Will bulbs interfere with the roots of trees?*
A. I've never heard a tree in my garden complain. As a matter of fact, my bulbs and trees are the best of friends.

ROSES

∙∙

The rose is by far the most popular flower in the world. In the United States alone over fifty million rose bushes are sold each year through garden centers and department and grocery stores. About forty-nine million of these are destined to die, all needlessly.

Roses are the easiest plant in your garden to care for. The rose is also the most prestigious plant you can have growing. If you can grow roses, folks will be sure that you're an expert in all kinds of gardening. If I had to pick the toughest plant in the garden, I would pick the rose. Right now you're looking out your window at some poor sickly looking rose bush and saying, "My rose bush, tough? It doesn't look like it could fight its way out of a wet paper bag!" Remember, I did not say they were indestructible—but with a little effort on your part, roses will pay their share of the rent faster than any other bloomer you can think of.

Roses want a bright, sunny spot with rich, loose soil and excellent drainage. That's what they want. What they get is heavy clay, plenty of shade, and a hole full of water. Also, roses are seldom fed. What they would like is to be fed a handful of garden food once a month, watered from below, and given a soap-and-water shower once a week to discourage insects and disease.

"I have yet to see a garden where I couldn't find a place for at least one rose."

LONG LIVE THE QUEEN

The rose has been a popular flower for thousands and thousands of years; it's America's national flower. According to geologists, fossils have been found indicating that roses were growing thousands of years before Christ. The rose is the very symbol of romance, has influenced our religion, health and history, and is often regarded as a living tranquilizer. In the United States alone, from forty to fifty million roses are sold each year, in a color range that virtually spans the rainbow. The flowers themselves range from very delicate thumb-size blooms to giant hybrid teas, with a wide variety of fragrances.

Most home gardeners just take the rose at face value. Little do they realize the versatility of this glorious lady. Her bright and fragrant flowers can flood a room with the sight and smell of spring love. Her petals can provide tasty food for party snacks and can be fermented into one of the finest wines you'll ever savor. Dried, those same petals can add scent to silks and linens. Roses can lift the spirit of the sick in heart or body. I belong to many garden societies, but the American Rose Society is my favorite.

A ROSE FOR
EVERY
GARDEN

· ·

I have yet to see a garden where I couldn't find a place for at least one rose. And since the rose is the queen of the Plant Kingdom, it's only right that we find a proper place. Roses are grouped into several classifications, and you need to understand these classifications before you can begin your selection. All roses are named after a person, place, or characteristic.

Roses are classified by the way they grow. Thus, we have hybrid tea, floribunda, grandiflora, hybrid polyantha, polyantha, hybrid perpetual, tree, and, in common circles, climbers.

Hybrid tea: The most popular because of its straight stems, large buds, and giant blooms, this bush will grow three feet high and four feet across in a single season. Use it as a specimen plant.

Floribunda: This type is a cross between polyantha and hybrid tea and produces a good, full, healthy bush loaded with stems of single and double flowers. It's best used for borders and group plantings.

Grandiflora: A group of roses that's not very old, it has large clusters of flowers on long stems. The easiest rose to take care of is the grandiflora. This is a rose that can be planted by itself as a property divider or in a formal bed.

Hybrid polyantha: The same rose classification as the floribunda but, because of a technicality, the Rose Society would not officially adopt the name floribunda. Either of these names on a label mean the same thing.

Hybrid perpetual: One of our oldest types of roses, of which the American beauty was the most popular, these perpetuals are often called the "June bloomers." They grow a tall bush not generally seen anymore.

Miniature roses: A group of roses too often overlooked, miniatures begin to bloom in May and continue 'til Jack Frost paints them out. They grow between twelve and eighteen inches high and are an excellent border rose.

Climbers: This is the group of roses that most of us picture when we mention the rose. Cottage walls, trellises, and garden fences are the home for these active young ladies.

Tree roses: This is one of my favorite groups because tree roses stand above all the other small evergreens and shrubs to show off color and character, like the true royalty they are.

Any bush-type rose—including some climbers—can be made into a tree rose. The ordinary commercial rose is budded onto a wild understock. The tree rose can also be budded onto a wild understock, but only after the cane is three to four feet tall. A great deal more work goes into the tree roses you buy than into other roses. This accounts for the additional cost.

My favorites are the dark red Chrysler Imperial, the orange Sutter's Gold, the yellow Diamond Jubilee and the deep pink Charlotte Armstrong. If you want a couple of really beautiful weeping rose trees, try Cherry Chase, a dark red. Rose trees have one drawback in the colder parts of the country: the whole tree must be buried beneath the ground.

When you're planning your landscape, make

"Roses are royalty, and royalty always gets the favored spot. Make sure you plan a front row seat for your roses."

sure that you plan a front row seat for your roses, because they love to see what's going on and love to be seen. After all, they're royalty, and royalty always gets the favored spot. Dinah Shore, the lovely songstress, says roses are her favorite flowers. When I visited her garden, I was delighted by the many different rose varieties I saw there. Too many gardeners concentrate on one type and miss out on the beautiful blendings that come from mixing varieties when planting.

HOW DOES YOUR (ROSE) GARDEN GROW?

I'm sick and tired of the so-called rose experts telling everybody how difficult it is to grow roses when, in reality, the rose is one of the easiest plants to care for. The real secret is sunshine. Roses must have a half-dozen hours of sunshine in the early part of the day, plus shade from the hot afternoon sun. If you plant a rose where you would be comfortable sitting out all day, you'll have the best bloomers on the block!

The rose works so hard producing those great big, beautiful, fragrant flowers and that rich, green, waxy foliage that it just can't take time out to play ground hog or mole and burrow through heavy soil. It's up to you to give it a helping hand. The queen would like you to prepare her court in loose, fertile, well-drained soil, not heavy, wet clay.

When preparing a hundred-square-foot rose bed, add five pounds of rose or garden food to the soil surface, fifty pounds of peat moss, twenty-five pounds of gypsum, and three bushels of 60-40 gravel. Now spade it all in. Make sure that all of the soil builders are mixed in well.

The best time to plant a rose is when you can get a spade in the ground. If you plant your roses in the fall in the zones below freezing, then don't bother to cut the wood back. Plant them the day you bring them home. Don't go off and leave them in the trunk of your car or in the garage and expect them to be bright eyed and bushy tailed two or three days later. If they're worth buying, then they're worth the time to plant them.

All too often the home gardener takes the term "bury" too seriously. Plants are alive, and we intend to keep them that way. With roses, all I want you to do is plant the bush.

Dig the hole just as you would for bare-root trees and shrubs. (See page 115.) Place the mound of soil in the bottom and spread out the roots. Next, begin to refill the hole, pushing the soil down firmly with your foot as you go. All roses follow one rule about the large bump or bulge above the roots: make sure it's two inches below the soil. Then, if dieback occurs in the early spring, some of the grafted stock will survive. When the rose is planted and tamped down, build a small dirt wall around the outside to hold water. For both fall- and spring-planted roses, cover the plant with a light mix of soil, leaves, and peat moss. Pile the mix as high as it will go without falling off. Or simply cover with a grocery bag. Leave the roses buried ten days for spring-planted roses and all winter for fall-planted roses. After ten days or when the threat of frost has passed, depending on when you planted, remove the soil mix and mulch with wood chips or buckwheat hulls. Another important thing you can do is add a half cup of Epsom salts to the soil surface to promote richer color, thicker petals, and stronger roots. To plant balled-in-burlap, potted, or

"If you plant a rose where you would be comfortable sitting all day, you'll have the best bloomers on the block."

canned stock, follow shrub and tree planting directions given on page 115–18, but cover the plant with a light soil mixture as described above. Plant wild garlic nearby to ward off insects.

FIT FOR A QUEEN

· ·

If you don't feed roses, then you can't expect many flowers. Give roses a handful of any rose food once a month. An excellent method to feed and water roses at the same time is to cut both ends out of a ten-ounce frozen fruit juice container and push it all the way into the ground between two rosebushes. Then half fill the container with pea-sized pebbles and once a month or so add a small amount of rose food to the can. Water into the juice container for deep penetration feeding.

"The rose is the queen of the garden, the grand lady of the plant kingdom."

Roses don't like regular sprinkling; they prefer deep watering from the end of an open hose about twice a week. Deep watering is necessary because a healthy rose can take three to five gallons of moisture from the soil during a hot July or August day. Use the soap solution in step 8 on page 282 to wash her pretty face.

Since a rose is a woman, it is a good idea to keep her looking sharp. Gather all ye rosebuds and flowers, put them in your house, or give them to friends. Don't let them die on the vine as this is bad for the plant. Whenever you cut a rose, always cut just above a five-leaflet cluster of leaves; this is where the next break will come from. Always keep the plant's center open to sunlight: cut out any foliage there. Roses like to be covered up in the winter with a light mix of leaves, soil, and peat moss.

Pile this mix as high as it can go without falling off. Then cut the bush tops just to make them look neat. When all danger of frost is past—in May in snow country—remove the mulch and cut the plant back to just above an outside eye—that is, a foliage bud that points to the outside. All in all, not much work to have blooms all summer long.

Climbers are a hardy variety and do not need mulching, but you must remove suckers and dead wood at once. Suckers are growth that comes from below the graft and will not bloom.

"When watering flowers, aim at their toes rather than the tips of their noses. And don't sprinkle their clothes."

BUGS ARE NO BOTHER

If the roses are healthy and happy—well fed, bathed regularly with soap, and planted with wild garlic—you won't have to worry about insects. Use these guidelines if you should run into a bug that just won't go away.

The rose is not only our favorite, she is a tasty and delicate feast for the insect world. If you use soap and water, feed well, mulch and water, you will discourage most of the winged warriors. But, should one or two penetrate your defenses, here are the chemical controls recommended:

Thrips: Tiny, slender pests only a sixteenth of an inch long puncture buds and cause discoloration and failure to open.

Leaf rollers: Also called rose-leaf tiers, these small green caterpillars feed on, roll up, and tie together upper leaves, thus distorting growth. Hand pick the caterpillars or crush the leaves to kill hidden caterpillars.

Aphids: Greenish yellow, black, or red plant lice, these insects cluster on the bud stems and suck their juices. They secrete a sticky substance often called honeydew. Aphids multiply rapidly. Controls must actually touch aphids. Plant wild garlic between roses to keep aphids away. Spray with soapy water to control. If that's not successful, use nicotine dust or nicotine sulphate spray according to package directions.

Tarnished plant bugs: Brassy, flat insects that are a quarter-inch long, these bugs puncture new growth and distort surrounding plant tissues. Cultivate soil cleanly to eliminate them.

Rose chafers: Iridescent beetles three-eighths of an inch long, they appear in great numbers. Feeding on buds, open flowers, and foliage, rose chafers show a preference for lighter-colored flowers. They're prevalent in sandy soil. Hand pick the insects or dust every third day with rose dust during their usual month-long onslaught, using paradichlorobenzene on the soil in the late spring when insects are breeding.

Rose slugs: Small green caterpillarlike pests, rose slugs bore into new shoots and the pith of pruned canes to rapidly mutilate foliage. Seal newly cut ends of canes and cut below the wilted portions of others to control.

Fullers rose beetles: These crawling gray beetles are three-eighths of an inch long. They feed at night, leaving unsightly black excrement behind. Treat with fruit tree spray.

Rose scale: These dirty white, scalelike sucking insects don't look like insects as they encrust stems. Use a dormant oil spray in spring, and soap and water after the leaves drop. Burn dead stems.

Red spider mites: These very tiny mites hide on the undersides of leaves. They're prevalent when the weather is dry and hot. They suck the plant's juices, turning leaves yellow and stunting plants. Treat with fruit tree spray.

Cane borers: Entering the stems, borers kill shoots by hollowing out their pith. Cut off infested shoots. Spray the foliage from June to July; seal ends after pruning, then treat with fruit tree spray.

Rust: Protect foliage subject to moist air. Wash with soap and water. Pick off infected leaves.

Rose canker: In spring, rose canker causes showy brown patches to appear; no further growth starts above. Prune out all visible cankers, taking a one-inch margin for safety. If a plant is seriously infected, you must dispose of it.

Black spot: Black spots first show up on leaves in early summer but grow progressively worse. Feed the bush to promote active growth. Pick off black-spotted leaves promptly and burn them.

Harlequin bugs: Brilliantly marked, three-eighths-inch-long bugs are bad pests in the South from California to Virginia, less so in the North. Attacked branches turn brown as if scalded. Hand pick the bugs and egg masses.

Mildew: A whitish fungus growth that covers leaves and young flower beds and stems, mildew is prevalent from coast to coast. Wash with soap and water; pick off infected leaves.

Leaf-cutting bees: Although they disfigure foliage, the main damage these bees cause is done by larvae that bore into the ends of pruned stems. Prune the stunted stem tips and wax the stem ends with a crayon.

Twelve-spotted cucumber beetles: These yellow-green, one-quarter-inch-long beetles have twelve black spots on their back. They eat blooms late in season. Treat with fruit tree spray.

Japanese beetles: If you keep your plants clean, these beetles won't be too big a problem.

Rose midges: Minute pests, these tiny midges

attack buds, causing necks to crook at right angles and buds to blight. If you've had rose midges in the past, spray your rosebushes with fruit tree spray before new growth is six inches tall. After buds show, apply fruit-tree spray at seven-day intervals, following package directions.

Most folks who try their hand at rose care usually become discouraged by insects and diseases. Don't! Plain old good housekeeping is the secret. Keep the beds free of weeds, cut off spent flowers and remove them. If a leaf looks funny, remove it.

My rose gets a weekly bath with the FSS, the full soap solution of tobacco juice and brown mouthwash spray, described on page 7. If I have a problem, I use a fruit tree spray that combines an insecticide, pesticide, and fungicide at two-week intervals.

STEP-BY-STEP ROSE CARE

. . . .

SPRING

. . . .

Step 1. I've never seen a bad rosebush for sale. The price is right if I have the time and patience to repair, plant, and care for it. Bottom line? Buy bargains.

Step 2. If you purchase a bare-root rose, wash the entire bush—roots and all—in a bucket of warm water with the following added:

2 ounces of children's shampoo or flea and tick
shampoo
1 tablespoon of brown mouthwash
¼ teaspoon of liquid bleach

If the plant is in a container and the foliage has not emerged yet, wash the container also.

Step 3. Soak bare-root roses in warm, soapy water for half an hour. Make it a clean bucket and add:

1 teaspoon of children's shampoo
1 tablespoon of household ammonia
2 tablespoons of clear corn syrup

Step 4. Make plant hole wider than necessary and plant the grafting knob two inches below the soil level.

Step 5. Sprinkle a mixture of 75 percent bone-meal, 25 percent Epsom salts, and one-half teaspoon of sugar for each four handfuls of mix.

Step 6. Mix three handfuls of human hair to the soil used to plant roses.

Step 7. Cover newly planted roses with a grocery bag for a week after planting.

Step 8. Wash down all rosebushes in the spring before you prune them back for their spring start. Fill your ten-gallon hand-held sprayer with warm water and:

½ cup of laundry bar soap
½ cup tobacco juice
½ cup of brown mouthwash (see page 7 for the tonic).

Step 9. Cut roses back to just above the lowest outside break; seal with latex paint.

Step 10. Cover with grocery bag for a week.

Step 11. Feed with a mixture of:

>5# any garden food
>1 cup of Epsom salts
>1 cup of sugar
>4 pulverized, dried banana peels
>2 cups of bonemeal

SUMMER

....

Step 12. Bathe roses every two weeks in the evening with the spray from step 8.

Step 13. Feed every three weeks in the morning with the all-purpose tonic. Use your twenty-gallon hand-held sprayer and add:

>1 can of beer (Bockbeer is great)
>1 cup of children's shampoo
>½ cup of molasses
>1 ounce of seaweed
>1 cup of liquid lawn food

Fill the balance of the container with household ammonia.

Step 14. Keep cutting roses to promote more blooms. Make sure you cut the stem just above a five-leaflet cluster. Seal wound or cut with nail polish and sprinkle dirt on top.

FALL

....

Step 15. Tie rose canes together with a nylon stocking before you mulch, cover, or heel in for winter.

Step 16. Bathe the roses before you cover them with the solution from step 8.

Step 17. Sprinkle a handful of Epsom salts around each rosebush before you cover it.

Step 18. Cover the roses with a light soil mix of soil, peat moss and leaves when the temperature has been below freezing for two to three weeks. Pile the mix as high as it will go without falling over. Or cover with a grocery bag.

Step 19. Spray exposed rose canes with Repel to prevent mouse damage.

QUESTIONS AND ANSWERS............................

Q. *Why don't my roses look like the ones you get from the florist?*

A. Probably because they're not the same class. Cutting roses are hybrid teas, which produce one, sometimes two roses per stem, with some fragrance. They've been crossed with the tea rose of China. You can purchase, plant, and harvest hybrid teas in your yard as pretty as theirs.

Q. *Can you disbud floribundas and come up with a large, long-stem rose?*

A. Yeah, but why would you want to go to all that trouble? Just plant tea roses instead. Floribundas grow their flowers in clusters; the plant is an excellent accent plant, as well as being displayed by itself. Grow tea roses if you want fewer long-stem roses.

Q. *What kind of rose can you use in a rather small rose garden and still get the most color and flowers for house use?*

A. Any of the grandifloras. These are really big mamas, with color galore and big flowers—and they're strong as hell.

Q. *Are potted roses better than packaged roses?*

A. No, but they're more expensive. With potted roses, you can plant instant flowers at any time of the season.

Q. *Are bare-root roses safe to buy?*

A. Yes, they're safe to buy, but they're not always cheaper. When roses are harvested, they're pulled from the ground, the soil is taken from their roots, and they're stored in cool, damp cellars in the fall. They're then shipped to your nurseryman and mail-order houses bare-root. Mail-order houses then put straw or shavings around the roots, slip on a plastic bag to keep the roots damp, and send them to you. Your nurseryman pots his in plantable containers and grows them to sell you started roses. If you can buy bare-root, you save handling charges.

Q. *Are tree roses tough to take care of?*

A. I don't think so, if you'll just remember to protect the graft (knob) at the top. I use newspaper and tape, plus straw. Some folks bend them over and bury them. I find that, more often than not, the darn trunk breaks.

Q. *I'd like to know the name of an ever-blooming climber that really does bloom all season and not just once.*

A. If any climber is properly planted in good, rich, light soil, fed once a month with a rose or garden food, and is in bright sun and watered well, it will bloom all season. It's just as important to cut the spent flowers from a climber as it is from any other type of rose. Climbing Show Garden is far and away the best climber. She is pink. Improved Blaze, Amethyst Rose, and Gladiator are my choices.

Q. *Can you really grow roses in a rock garden?*
A. You sure can, and boy, do they ever look great. I suggest that you use any of the climbing flori-bundas. You can use climbers to cascade down a wall, as well.

Q. *My neighbor only buys her roses by mail from Jackson & Perkins, Armstrong, or Star. She says they have better roses than you can buy in stores. Is this true?*
A. Those just happen to be three of the most repu-table mail-order houses in the world, so you can't go too far wrong. You can buy top-quality roses from local merchants. I find that newer varieties are available through the mail-order houses sooner. I buy from both.

Q. *Should you buy packaged roses with lots of growth or none?*
A. None, if at all possible. Don't select packaged roses with any length of growth, just little breaks or buds. After all, you're going to cut two-thirds of the top off before planting, just above an outside break. New growth saps the strength of your new bush if it's not in the ground.

Q. *Why do they put wax on the canes of rose bushes? The ones I buy this way seem to die more often than ones that aren't waxed.*
A. Canes are waxed to keep moisture in the wood. I don't like to buy waxed canes if I can help it, but

if I must, I pull the wax away from all the little breaks or buds.

Q. *Is it necessary to soak the roots of roses before you plant?*
A. I always give them a drink and maybe just a tiny bite of food. See page 65.

Q. *Do you really have to place a mound in the bottom of the hole when planting roses?*
A. Absolutely! First, dig a $5 hole for a fifty cent plant—the wider the better. Then make a cone-shaped mound for the rose to sit on, spreading out its roots and covering them firmly with good, rich light soil.

Q. *Should you dig a deeper hole for roses in clay than you do for those in well-drained soil?*
A. That's a darn good idea, but go a step further and mound-plant your rose. The well—that's what the deeper hole becomes—lowers the water level; if you plant your rose on a mound of soil above the regular grade, you double the safety factor.

Q. *When do you cut roses back?*
A. In the spring when they begin their new growth. I never cut my roses all the way back in fall, I simply mulch them with leaves and straw mixed with soil up as high as I can, two feet, preferably. In the spring when May flowers start up, I uncover and cut back to just below the lowest outside shoot.

Q. *When do you prune climbing roses?*
A. Suckers should be pruned out at any time; prune other growth in the early spring when new growth appears, same as the other roses.

Q. *Why don't you have to mulch climbers?*
A. I always mulch my root stock and shield my climbers from a southwest wind with burlap.

Q. *When do you mulch roses?*
A. When they get cold. I wait till the temperature goes below freezing.

Q. *If your roses were small and the leaves yellow last season, what was wrong?*
A. The plant was probably starving to death. Feed every three or four weeks, up until August 15 in snow country.

Q. *Should you spray with dormant oil in the spring as well as in the fall?*
A. And how! Spray with Volk oil and lime sulphur in the fall before you mulch, and then again in the spring.

Q. *When is the best time to move a rosebush?*
A. I like to move them in September, if at all possible, or as early in the spring as I can get a shovel in the soil. Always water right after you move older plants, and for a week or two if you move them in the spring. As a matter of fact, you can mulch them for three weeks just as you would for winter.

Q. *What's the best mulch for roses?*
A. I just can't see wasting anything that's worth using, so I find ground-up leaves are the best. I rake my leaves into a row, put the grass catcher on my mower, and mow the leaves. It grinds them up fine. Then I use them mixed with a little soil to hold them down, or put a chicken-wire basket around them half filled with the leaves.

Q. *Can soil wear out from roses?*
A. Yes, though it's not the roses that cause it, it's just lack of attention. In the spring add one-half cup of Epsom salts per four square feet; add bone-meal in the fall.

Q. *Can you mulch under your roses?*
A. Absolutely! Saves work and roses. I use tar paper and cover with decorative bark or stone.

Q. *Why do they say the more you cut roses, the more you get?*
A. If you cut in the right spot you force the rose to throw another flowering spur. The right spot is just above a five-leaf cluster. If you cut wrong, the rose has to grow another stem and then throw a flower spur for a five-leaf, so it takes longer. Also, the flower that is fading is still taking food for a "hip" seed pod, which is a waste of food unless you use the hips for tea, jam, or soup.

Q. *What's all this foolishness about outside eyes?*
A. It's not foolishness. It's honest Injuns! To have healthy, full roses you must keep the center open, which means forcing the foliage to grow away from the center. This is accomplished by cutting just above an outside bud in the spring and above an outside five-leaflet cluster when cutting and pruning roses for bouquets or spent blooms.

Q. *Should you cultivate under roses?*
A. If you don't use a mulch, it's a good idea to work up the soil from time to time.

Q. *Does it hurt to plant other flowers with roses?*
A. I don't mind—nor does the rose as long as you don't plant bulbs. That's just not fair to either one.

Q. *My roses' leaves are never really dark green. They're sort of pale and the ribs are greener. What's wrong?*
A. That's an iron deficiency and can be remedied with Green-Gard micronized iron in the spring.

Q. *Can you take a cutting from a rose and get a plant?*
A. Take a cutting—young branches eight inches long. Remove all the leaves except the top two, bury half of the stem in a bright, sunny, well-drained location, and cover with a mason jar. When new growth appears, remove the jar.

Q. *How do you layer a rosebush?*
A. Pull a one-year-old cane down so it touches the soil. Now, dig a shallow pocket two inches deep and place the cane in the pocket. Pin it down, cover with soil, leaving six to eight inches of the bud above the ground, and place a brick on top of the soil to keep it down. When it roots, cut the cane off and plant it where you want it.

Q. *Can you really eat rose petals?*
A. I love them in tossed salads with Italian dressing. The light colors are best. As you do when eating lettuce, break off the heavy base of the petal and only eat the tender part. They really dress up salads.

Q. *Why do the leaves curl up on my roses?*
A. Probably because you have a visitor called a leaf roller. He's a small green worm that ties leaves together and rolls them up while he eats. Spray with Malathion or rose and flower dust made into a spray.

Q. *Why don't my rose buds open?*
A. Look for a little, hairy bug called a thrip. He punches a hole in the buds. To stop him, dust often with rose dust or make a spray.

Q. *Does planting garlic by roses keep aphids away?*
A. Does a pretty darn good job, and a bath with soap and water and Malathion really insures control.

Q. *What causes roses to get rusty leaves?*
A. Not enough sunshine; usually, it's shaded roses that get rusty.

Q. *I like to order my roses early because I get a better selection. How early can I purchase and safely store them?*
A. If you have room to store them at between 35 and 40 degrees, you can order at any time.

Q. *Solve an argument. My wife says you should buy skinny rose bushes and I say big, fat ones! Who is right?*
A. Bow to the lady, she's right. Purchase roses with canes the size of a pencil.

Q. *Why do you have to cut new roses back so far?*
A. To give them a better-than-halfway chance to get a good start. The less top growth the newly planted roots have to supply food to, the better chance of quick rooting.

Q. *When is the better time to plant roses, fall or spring?*
A. I plant most of my roses around September 15 and cover them with a mix of leaves and soil. I also get my best buys then. If potted roses are planted in the fall, treat them just like any other growing rose.

Q. *Do you have to seal every cane you cut?*
A. By all means. It's worth the time it takes. Use nail polish or a bug by the name of rose slug will burrow into newly pruned canes. Pruning paint is a must for any gardener.

Q. *How deep do you plant packaged or bare-root roses?*
A. I bury the graft (big knob) below the ground, and on potted stock I mound soil up over the graft.

Q. *Should you use the sawdust that the plant is wrapped in when planting?*
A. Not on your plant's life. You have no idea what may be lurking in that stuff. Throw it away.

Q. *What grade rose will give me the best luck?*
A. Grade one, two years old, with three to four canes the size of a pencil. Most home gardeners mistakenly buy those great big thick canes. Do not purchase packaged roses that have soft white or light yellow-green growth on the stems. Most non-trained garden salespeople and management think these thin roses are runts and mark them down, so I waltz in and do them a favor (ha!) and take them off their hands.

Q. *Can I put stone around my roses?*
A. I prefer something that will do them some good. Stone is for our viewing benefit, and since the rose is already working overtime to give you beauty, why not give her a break?

Q. *I have trouble keeping my roses blooming late in the season. Can I give them a hand?*
A. Your postmark is from Oakland, California, so I would say that you should leave your roses alone after the first of October. Cut down on the water

and let them rest until the first of the year; then prune and begin again. January through June is also the best time to plant roses in Southern California.

Q. *Can I take cuttings from my roses?*
A. You certainly can, and you'll get more pride and enjoyment from these than from ones you buy. Take the cutting in late May from a flower stem about four inches long with at least two breaks. Take your cuttings from the middle of the branch. Dip them in water, then into Rootone and place them upright into damp, sharp sand. Keep shaded for a few days. When well rooted, remove and plant in soil.

Q. *Is there any place in this country that roses won't grow?*
A. Not if they can get sunshine, water, food, and plenty of love and affection.

Q. *What do you think of ground covers on rose beds?*
A. Not much. This is one queen who won't be happy with someone kneeling in front of her all the time.

Q. *I would like a mass planting of roses in both rear corners of our yard. How far apart should I plant them?*
A. Wide enough for you to get into the farthest one to work. Stagger each row and do not let them touch.

Q. *I would like the name of a good fence rose.*
A. I think you will be satisfied with County Fair. Consult the rose catalogs for some others.

Q. *Do you buy roses from catalogs?*

A. Sure I do, just to see if the firms are good and the roses are true to name. I have been burned on occasion.

Q. *I have heard that there is a right time to cut roses.*

A. I would say that just before your evening meal, and just the ones whose petals are unfolding.

Q. *Are these rose collars any good?*

A. Not too bad if you can find one that is at least two feet high. Most of the commercial collars are too short for my liking.

Q. *Which is the best kind of trellis?*

A. I like redwood for effect and longevity. The aluminum fan-shaped and the wire are nice, but they just don't fit in my garden.

Q. *When is the best time to mulch roses for winter?*

A. Right after the first killing frost. I have also found that the job is still enjoyable at that time, because I don't freeze my watcha-ma-jigger doing it.

Q. *Can I protect my roses for the winter with plastic garbage bags?*

A. That's a no-no. Do not cover anything with plastic in the winter. If a rose were in the bag and the sun came out, growth could very possibly start because of the condensation inside. Then the sun goes down, and the moisture freezes and kills the growth.

Q. *How often do you water roses?*

A. Depends on where you live and what the soil conditions are. In well-drained soil or sand, twice a week. In heavy soil, once a week. And, in clay soil or extra-heavy composition, water very lightly once a week.

Q. *Our roses grow tall but have small blooms and not too much foliage. Why?*
A. Not enough sun or too much nitrogen. Roses must have five or six hours of sun. Morning sun is the best. Feed roses with a low-nitrogen garden food to promote blooms, not growth.

Q. *Can you tell me which mulches are best?*
A. I can give you my choice, but others may prefer a totally different assortment. Oak leaf mulch, wood chips, pine bark, and redwood do the job for me.

Q. *Is it okay to use my root feeder on my roses?*
A. If you're careful, yes. But too many times folks get carried away and wash the soil away from the roots and then let air in to dry them out.

Q. *What is your opinion of foliar feeding?*
A. Mother Nature teams up with Jupiter Fluvius for the only real foliar (leaf) feeding. The rest I've always considered to be hogwash.

Q. *How large should a rose bed be?*
A. I prefer a bed five feet wide. Floribundas and hybrid tea roses need three to four feet to spread out in, so you can stagger them in a five-foot bed.

VEGETABLES & HERBS

· ·

YOUR TEAM
· ·

You'd think that I've been gardening so long that I'd take the results for granted. But I never cease to become excited when I'm able to pull my first radish from the ground, or pick my first bush bean from the vine, or bite into the first tomato taken from my garden. At that moment, I feel a true sense of accomplishment.

Vegetable gardening is almost like playing baseball. Everyone on the team must work together to win the game, and if just one player fumbles along the way, or makes an error, you could well lose the ball game. It takes real teamwork to have an appetite-filling garden, and you must understand that you're not just one of the team members. As a matter of fact, because you are the manager you call all the shots. Before every season you must

"Vegetable gardening is like playing baseball. Everyone on the team must work together."

hand in a roster, and the vegetable garden team has quite a list of stars and superstars. The captain is Mother Nature, water boy is Jupiter Fluvius, the coach is nourishment and the players are the vegetables. To put together a winning team, the manager must know his players and their dispositions, as well as their limitations. From time to time, it's necessary to make a trade to strengthen the team so that it works together as one unit. There's no room for individualism if you want to win. Your team must learn to play hard but fair, even though the other team has a reputation for foul play. After all, look at what's on that other team—bugs, worms, wind and weeds, neglect. You have to respect a team like that; you don't have to like them, but you sure have to respect them. Always remember, the real pleasure is in eating the fruits of victory!

Pre-season is good for the whole team. Everybody is "up" for the coming competition. As manager, you must select the starting team and plan the strategy—lay it out on paper. Plan every step, from your starting lineup to final out, including replacement possibilities that might occur as your garden players tire. Use the off-season to get background you need on your team's health and safety. Refer to the many catalogs I've suggested to learn all you can about the dazzling array of vegetables available. Once you have acquired your starting team, you're ready to play ball!

When I was playing baseball, I always gave the groundskeeper a Christmas gift each year to inspire him to take a little better care of my particular spot on the field, so that I would have better traction for quick starts. Now that I look back, I can see how I wasted my money; because he took pride in his work, he always made sure that the *entire* field was in top shape. You must make sure that your vegetable garden is in top shape, so everyone on your team can get off to a good, fast start.

Let's begin from scratch. A good garden is begun in the late fall, by cleaning your garden area. Remove all tree stumps, rocks, cans, glass, or wood. Then apply to every one hundred square feet of garden fifty pounds of cow manure, twenty-five pounds of garden food, fifty pounds of gypsum, topped off with one hundred pounds of peat moss or composted leaves and cuttings. This concoction is left to lie all winter. In the spring, when the soil is just dry enough to crumble in your hand, all of your fall additions are spaded in and graded just like an area prepared for grass seed. The garden surface should have a slight crown at the top and taper off on all four sides, like a ball field. This will let excess water from unexpected storms run off during the growing game. Otherwise, a downpour could bog down the whole team.

Exhibition games are scheduled early in the playing season to test players' strength and condition. But beware: a player is often injured in these exhibition games because he's not in shape. Many home gardeners who attempt a vegetable garden for the first time put in seeds or plants too early. Check the roster in this chapter for vegetables that start the growing game early in the season.

LAYING OUT THE BOUNDARIES

Most instructions available for the home gardener seem to assume that everybody who wants a vegetable garden has an acre or more, with recommendations for hundred-foot rows. My friends, in my eyes that's professional gardening, and if you don't know what you're doing, you can lose lots of money, time, and effort without scoring a lot of vegetable victories. I suggest that we bring that playing field down to a maximum of twenty-five-foot-long rows for the semi-pro gardeners and ten-foot-long rows for the amateur gardeners. You must determine how much time you'll have for gardening before you can lay out your final guidelines.

In order to have a winning team in any sport, you must have *esprit de corps*. That's a spirit that members of a group have in common. Vegetables can help each other even though they have nothing in common but being planted near each other. Helping each other in this way is *symbiosis*, when two unlike organisms coexist to the mutual benefit of both. One may give off as surplus or waste material what the other plant needs as nourishment or as a protective control. By planting certain vegetables with others that make good companions, you'll end up with an almost unbeatable vegetable garden team. The Bio-Dynamic Farming and Gardening Association has issued a list of companion plants. Their research was done by Richard B. Gregg, who later wrote a book called *Companion Plants and How to Use Them*. His co-author was Helen Philbrick. Here are some of the vegetables that they suggest make excellent teammates:

Asparagus and tomatoes
Beans and carrots, cauliflower, beets, cabbage, cucumbers
Beans and potatoes
Wax beans and celery, if the celery is planted at the rate of six celery plants to one bean plant
Beets and beans, onions, kohlrabi

Cabbage and potatoes, dill, camomile, sage, rosemary, and members of the mint family

Carrots and lettuce and chives

Cauliflower and celery

Celery and leeks or tomatoes

Corn and potatoes, beans, peas, melons, squash, pumpkins, cucumbers

Cucumbers and potatoes, cabbage, radishes

Kohlrabi and lettuce

Eggplant and green beans

Kohlrabi and beets, onions

Leeks and celery

Lettuce and strawberries, carrots, radishes

Onions and beets

Peas and radishes, carrots, cucumbers, corn, beans, turnips

Potatoes and beans, cabbage, peas

Pumpkins and corn

Radishes and peas, lettuce, chervil

Spinach and strawberries

Tomatoes and asparagus, parsley, cabbage, potatoes, cucumbers

If you'll take a little time to check over your vegetable plan, you'll soon discover some winning combinations.

BACK UP YOUR TEAM

From time to time, one or two of your players could become lame or ill. It's absolutely essential that you recognize the symptoms and treat immediately. As a general rule, two or three soapy showers a season will ward off injuries to foliage above the ground;

if pests appear, use fruit and vegetable spray according to package directions. The step-by-step guide later in this chapter gives you all the details.

First I stretch Weed Blocker fabric from one end of a row to the other and anchor it with soil. I then cut small holes in the Weed Blocker to plant through. As the plants grow, they are protected by the Weed Blocker from weeds and many pests. After the plants are in, I make sure my team keeps cool by mulching everything with grass clippings.

You'll find that you'll have a few tall plants that, like many growing boys, get to a clumsy stage and fall all over themselves. To prevent falling and injuries from falling, you must stake plants like tomatoes, place chicken wire down the rows of beans and peas, and place broken branches under bush beans. These measures will protect the plants and make picking easier for you.

When a player is hot and dry, the worst thing in the world you can do is let him drink too much too fast or throw ice water in his face. The vegetable team should be given a good soaking at its feet. Don't water the foliage, especially not for tomato or melon crops. Rainwater is the best source of moisture for your vegetable garden. Soak deeply once a week.

In order for a good team to function properly, it needs room to work. So don't crowd your vegetable team. Make sure that you thin out the weak plants early. You'll need to thin radishes, carrots, beets, and parsnips to give the plants enough room. When you plant cabbage, celery, tomatoes, melons, squash, pumpkin, or cucumber, plant them with plenty of room to spread out. If you cramp them, they can't give you top performance. Seed packets and catalogs give you their space requirements.

Any team will perform better with a cheering section, so I suggest that you let your children plant some of the seeds. You'll be surprised at how closely they follow the team when they have a favorite player in the game.

Some managers make a mistake in not trying out new players. They leave some potential stars sitting on the bench simply because they've relied on the regulars for so long; then when it's time for a replacement they don't know who can fill the bill. Plant a new or different vegetable each year and you'll discover a number of future starters.

No matter how strong a player is, he can't play the whole game. It therefore becomes necessary to send in relievers. The same is true in the garden. Early bloomers should be replaced after harvest. Try these combinations:

Early peas, followed by early corn, then late snap beans
Late peas are replaced by corn and then by radishes and lettuce with spinach
Onion sets are followed by tomatoes
Cabbage then lima beans
Spinach is followed by wax beans
White radishes then snap beans
Beets are followed by peppers or parsnips

You can start any seed indoors, but as a rule only individual plants, not row crops, are started indoors: broccoli, Brussels sprouts, cabbage, cantaloupe, cauliflower, celery, collards, cucumbers, eggplant, onions, peppers, squash, tomatoes, and watermelon are the most popular. Corn can also be started indoors. You plant most of your seed in individual peat pots or clay pots in a very light planter mix. I use commercial mixes made for African violets.

VEGETABLES TO START EARLY

VARIETY	NUMBER OF DAYS TO HARVEST
Beans	60
Beets	60
Dark Red Detroit	
Brussels sprouts	90
Cabbage	
Long Island Imperial hybrid cabbage	
Stone Head	50
Jersey Queen	63
Golden Acre Resistant	65
Copenhagen Market	67
Emerald Cross	67
Marion Market	80
Early Dwarf Flat Dutch	85
Swellhead	95
Wisconsin All-Season	90
Late Flat Dutch	100
Danish Ballhead	105
Red cabbage	
Mammoth Rock Red	100
Cauliflower	
Snow King	45
Early Snowball 'A'	55
Snowball 'X'	65
Celery	
Summer Pascal	110
Corn	100
Cucumber	
Triple Purpose	54
Pioneer	55
Ball Early Hybrid	58
Spartan Valor	60

VARIETY	NUMBER OF DAYS TO HARVEST
Triumph	60
Hiyield	62
Eggplant	
Mission Bell	70
Lettuce	
Salad Bowl	45
Melon	
Mainerock	75
Honey Rock	85
Super Market	85
Samson	85–90
Saticoy Hybrid	90
Peas	
Freezonian	62
Pepper	
Canape	62
Vinedale	62
Aconcagua	65
Sweet Bull Nose	65
Merrimack Wonder	68
Bell Boy	70
Yolo Wonder	70
California Wonder Select	72
Long Red Cayenne	74
Delaware Belle	75
Pimento Perfection	75
Titan	75
Hungarian Yellow Wax	80
Mercury	80
Red Chili	84
Radish	
Cherry Belle	23
Spinach	60

VARIETY	NUMBER OF DAYS TO HARVEST
Squash	
Chefini	48
Tomato	
Early Salad	45
Tiny Tim	46
Gardener's Delight	50
Ball Extra Early (TA)	55
Fireball	60
Mocross Surprise	60–70
Burpee Big Early (TA)	62
New Yorker	62
Ball Giant Hybrid	65
Bonny Best Hybrid	65
Small Fry (TA/JC)	65
Spring Set VF	65
Earliana	66
Rushmore	66
Firesteel	68
Bonny Best	70
Break O'Day	70
Burpee Hybrid	70
Mocross Supreme	70–75
Pation (TA)	70
Super Sioux	70
Valiant	70
Wisconsin Chief	72
Terrific VFN	73
Glamour	74
Ohio-Indiana	74
Bonus	75
Campbell	75
Heinz 1350	75
Roma VF	76

VARIETY	NUMBER OF DAYS TO HARVEST
Avalanche	77
Heinz 1370	77
Heinz 1439	77
Mariglobe Supreme (TA)	77
Burpee Big Boy Hybrid (TA/JC)	78
Golden Boy	80
Gulf State Market	80
Jubilee (TA)	80
Vineripe	80
Wonder Boy (TA)	80
Floradel	82
Manalucie	82
Rutgers (TA)	82
Sunray	83
Rutgers Hybrid	85
Giant Tree	88
Oxheart	90
Ponderosa	95
Beefsteak	96
Watermelon	
Dixie Queen Hybrid	82
Sweetmeat	83

V E G E T A B L E S   A N D   S M A L L   F R U I T S

· ·

I just can't help but wonder why we took so long to learn what people in most other nations discovered centuries ago—that man must tend the earth if he expects to continue to live on it. Whenever my friends visit Great Britain, France, Germany, or another European country for the first time, they're amazed that every home or row house has a garden and almost none a lawn—just a garden. And they wonder why. A garden is for survival, not looks, for most of the Old World, and this fact has just come home to us in the past few years. Many of us now plant a garden out of necessity, because we can't afford the inflated price we pay someone else to do the hard work. Most of us have discovered that the work's not as hard as we imagined; in fact, it's fun, healthful, and rewarding—physically, psychologically, and financially.

Anyone can have a garden. Heck, I know folks who grow food in an alley 'cause that's the only place there's soil. Others grow food in trash cans or in boxes on roofs. If you have a patch of soil, you're ahead of most folks. If you're going to grow good, fresh food, try to place your garden patch in a well-lighted spot where no water stands. Make sure you remember that each plant you grow needs room, just as you do, so don't crowd your plants. Feed your plants regularly and keep them clean and neat. Watch for trouble and act at once. Remember, in a garden you must never put off until tomorrow what should be done today, or there won't be a garden tomorrow.

"Plant a new or different vegetable each year."

HERBS AND OTHER THINGS

Herbs have played a big part in man's past for generations. People have used herbs believing they could improve their health, their peace of mind, even their love life. With the increasing awareness of the effect of chemicals on our environment and our health, more and more people are returning to the use of herbs and other plants to control insects and lengthen our life span.

Herbs do have a place in our everyday life and garden. Use them for flavor and avoid the artificial additives that tenderize and jazz up food. Herbs can add the pleasure of fragrance to your garden. To really enjoy a garden, you should be able to tilt back your head, breathe deeply, and fill your lungs with fragrance: mint, bay, lavender, or rue. This is the moment when a garden really comes alive—dances, shouts and sings. To wake up your garden and your life, plant and enjoy herbs.

SPICE UP YOUR LIFE

"Herb" is the word loosely used to describe certain plants that are used as aromatics. They may be used as perfumes, garment or room deodorizers, food flavorings or medicines, or plant antagonists and pesticide bases.

With the right selection of herbs growing in your garden or on the windowsill of your kitchen, livingroom, or bath, you won't need to use aerosol room sprays. Fresh herbs can make a big improvement in the taste of your everyday cooking. Let me give you some pointers on how you can use herbs to decorate, to cook and bake, and add fragrance.

I think that every vegetable garden should have a border. A border makes your vegetable garden look neat and as though it were designed to fit into the overall landscape, rather than be a dirt

"To wake up your garden and your life, plant and enjoy herbs."

patch in the middle of a palace garden. For this border, I suggest you use a bushy herb that can be picked for use and then be trimmed to be fat and low—perhaps parsley. Check the back of the seed packets for heights. I've also used herbs as borders for my evergreen beds and flower beds. Here I look for fragrance and foliage appearance, trying to put a different smell all over the garden. I wish you could be at my home on a night when the oil torches are lit and the colored floor lights are lit throughout the trees and evergreens. I'd love to watch you wander around to the spot that has your favorite fragrance. Then you would really understand the idea of "turning on" without drugs!

Herbs can be interplanted with your flowers and vegetables to keep certain insects away or to add flavor to a second plant because of proximity. Plant chervil next to radishes if you want the radishes spicier. Plant mint near windows and doors to keep ants out of the house.

Check the list of teammates on pages 299–300 for herb and plant friends.

For sniffers, here are a few of the aromatic herbs to plant throughout your garden: rue, lavender, cotton, myrtle, bay, lad's love, rosemary, smelly verbena, balms, and bergamot. For the kitchen: fennel, chervil, basil, chives, parsley, mint, sage, thyme, caraway, and borage, along with dill. For your health (these are a few that Grandma Putt kept handy for home remedies): dill, tansy, fewerfew, wormwood, St. Johnswort, castor bean, woodruff, mustard, licorice, pennyroyal, cinnamon, and mock-ginger.

If you think you're a good cook now, try adding some fresh herbs to your soups, salads, and omelettes. Then sit back and listen to the praise!

I've been asked many times about the so-called aphrodisiacal qualities of many fruits, vegetables, and herbs. I've heard many stories of the arousing qualities of many plants, but I've learned from twenty years of marital bliss and four beautiful children that love, affection, a warm kiss, and a tender embrace are all the aphrodisiacs I'll ever need. I had a discussion recently with a doctor friend of mine about this very subject, and his comments were very interesting.

My friend informed me that if folks would eat plenty of fresh raw vegetables regularly, they would be in a good, healthy state both mentally and physically. Being healthy, they would be relaxed and comfortable with the one they love. But when you have indigestion or other discomforts, there's not much chance for this affectionate communication. So eat any and all of the fruits and vegetables that agree with you in good health—and sleep tight.

FROM THE GARDENER'S STILL

As you have already surmised from reading this book, I am not one to waste anything. I am especially diligent when it comes to my fruit and vegetable garden and try not to waste anything by throwing it out. If we cannot eat it, can it, dry it, or freeze it, we can brew it and come up with some of the finest wines this side of the Atlantic.

The vegetables, fruit, and flowers that can be used to make wine is almost endless; I'm only going to list a few of the easier and more popular recipes that my neighbors, friends, and I find tasty and worth the trouble.

There are many fine wine-making books in the library. Why not try a few more recipes? Bottoms up.

Mrs. Popoofnick's Apple Cranberry Wine

8 cups cranberries
6 pounds apples, any tart variety
2 quarts boiling water
8 cups white sugar
2 cups seedless muscat raisins, chopped
1 slice whole wheat toast
1 ounce packaged yeast

Chop the cranberries very fine and put them into a canning kettle. Pour two quarts of boiling water over them; this will set the red color of the wine. Set aside to cool. Chop the unpeeled, uncored apples very fine and add them to the cranberries in the canning kettle along with another two quarts of water. Cover the kettle and put it in a warm place to ferment for one week.

At the end of the week, strain the mixture through a jelly bag,* squeezing it very dry. Discard the solids and return the liquid to the canning kettle and add sugar; stir well until it is all dissolved. Stir in the chopped raisins. Moisten the yeast with a few drops of water and spread it on one side of the toast. Float the toast, yeast side down, on the surface of the liquid. Put the covered kettle in a warm place to ferment for two more weeks. Stir twice a week.

At the end of the second week, strain the liquid again through a jelly bag, squeezing quite dry. Return the liquid to the canning kettle to settle two more days. Then siphon off the liquid into clean,

*Or cheesecloth, if your pantry doesn't run to jelly bags.

sterilized bottles and cork lightly until fermentation ceases. After the wine has stopped all of its activity, cork them tightly and seal with paraffin. Keep for at least four months before drinking.

Yield: Four quarts of wine

Beet Wine

This recipe is compliments of Mrs. Edward Bara. Parsnips, turnips, or carrots may be substituted for beets in this recipe.

10 pounds beets
1 pound seedless raisins
3 lemons, cut up
8 pounds white sugar
½ cup lukewarm water
1 teaspoon white sugar
1 package active dry yeast

Clean and trim the beets. In a 10-quart stockpot, boil the beets in water to cover until tender. Add enough water to the beet juice to make two gallons. Stir in the raisins, lemons, and 8 pounds of sugar. Stir until all the sugar is dissolved. Set aside.

Mix together the half cup of water and teaspoon of sugar. Pour the powdered yeast on top and let stand for ten minutes. Pour the yeast mixture into the beet juice and cover. Let stand for two weeks.

After two weeks, pour the liquid through cheesecloth and into sterilized bottles.

Yield: Eight quarts of wine

Dandelion Wine

You can also make this recipe using roses, violets, clover flowers, or any other sweet blossoms.

1 quart dandelion blossoms
1 cake yeast
½ cup lukewarm water
1 pound seedless raisins
3 pounds white sugar
1 lemon, cut into small pieces including peel
1 orange, cut into small pieces including peel

Measure a generous quart of the dandelion blossoms but be careful to remove all stems. Put the blossoms and 4 quarts of water in a 6-quart saucepan and boil for thirty minutes. Pour the liquid through a strainer, then strain it through cheesecloth into a large stone jar.

Dissolve the yeast cake in ½ cup lukewarm water. When the dandelion liquid is cool, stir in the yeast dissolved in water, the raisins, sugar, and lemon and orange pieces. Stir until the sugar is dissolved. Cover and set aside.

Stir the liquid every day for two weeks. At the end of two weeks, strain the liquid through cheesecloth and let stand for a day to settle.

Now strain it carefully through cheesecloth until the liquid is clear.

Pour the wine into sterilized bottles and seal.

Yield: Four quarts of wine

Potato Champagne

Compliments of my friend Mrs. H. Swanson.

7 potatoes
7 oranges
7 lemons
7 pounds white sugar
1 pound seedless raisins, ground
1 package active dry yeast
1 slice toast

Peel and slice the potatoes, oranges, and lemons. Place them in a 3-gallon crock and add the sugar and raisins. Pour in 7 quarts of water and mix well with a wooden spoon. Mix the yeast with a spoonful of warm water and spread the yeast on the toast. Float the toast yeast side down. Cover and set aside for one week. Remove the bread.

Let the crock sit another week. Strain the liquid and set aside for 3 days.

Strain the liquid again. Let the liquid sit another 3 days, then strain it again and pour it into sterilized bottles. Seal.

Yield: Seven quarts of champagne

Mint Wine

1 quart fresh mint leaves
4 pounds white sugar

Pour one gallon of cold water over the mint leaves, stir in the sugar, and cover. Let stand for ten days. Stir each day.

Strain the liquid through the cheesecloth and pour into sterilized quart bottles. Put a balloon over the neck of the bottle. When gas from the wine enlarges the balloon, let it out and put the balloon back over the bottle neck. Repeat the process until no more gas forms. Cork and seal the wine and store it. It should be ready to drink in about four months.

Yield: Four quarts of wine

STEP-BY-STEP VEGETABLE CARE

Step 1. Do yourself a favor and lay out your garden on a brown paper grocery bag or large sheet of paper.

Step 2. Always locate your garden in a bright, sunny, well-drained location.

Step 3. Always start with a clean soil surface. Remove all of last year's garden foliage to the compost bin.

Step 4. Dig a trench a spade's-length deep and two feet wide, the length of your garden starting at one edge. Fill this trench with leaves, grass, and any other compost, then cover it with the next two feet of soil and repeat. Use the first soil removed to cover the last trench.

Step 5. Overdress your vegetable garden surface with a mixture of fifty pounds of garden food, one pound of sugar, one pound of Epsom salts per one hundred square feet of garden. Apply this mix with the hand-held spreader on a two-pound setting.

Step 6. Till the garden food in with a light layer

of mowed grass and chopped leaves in several directions and as deep as you can.

Step 7. Cover the soil with Weed Blocker mulch fabric if you're using transplants. Then cover this material with six inches of grass clippings.

Step 8. Plant your garden from west to east, making sure you plant corn or sunflowers as a windbreak on the west.

Step 9. Stake plants using only metal poles and tie with pieces of nylon pantyhose.

Step 10. Feed your garden every three weeks in the morning with this all-purpose tonic and using your twenty-gallon sprayer:

1 can beer
1 cup children's shampoo
½ cup molasses
1 ounce liquid seaweed
1 cup liquid lawn food

Fill the jar to the top with household ammonia.

Step 11. Water with an old pair of socks, one inside the other, attached to end of your hose to use as a soaker. Lay the soaker over your garden's mulch from about 2 to 3 in the afternoon, three times a week.

Step 12. As vegetables begin to form, place rotting apples on the mulch to help set fruit.

Step 13. Bathe your garden every two weeks in the evening after you've mowed your lawn. In the jar of your twenty-gallon sprayer mix:

1 cup of laundry bar soap solution
1 cup chewing tobacco juice
1 cup of brown mouthwash

Spray with twenty gallons of water. (Recipes are on page 7.)

"Never put off until tomorrow what should be done today in a garden. Or there won't be a garden tomorrow."

Step 14. Harvest all of your garden crops as they ripen. If you have more than you can use, share your bounty.

Step 15. If rabbits are a nuisance, spray around the garden with a mixture of:

1 tablespoon ammonia
1 tablespoon of Fels-Naphtha solution

per gallon of water. Use a hand-held sprayer or ten-gallon sprayer. (See page 7 to make laundry bar soap solution.)

Step 16. Plastic cats, owls, snakes, and huge yellow balls with an ugly eye drawn on them will all scare the heck out of pests if you move them around the garden from time to time.

QUESTIONS AND
ANSWERS

Q. *Every time we put pepper or tomato plants in the ground, something breaks them off at the soil line.*
A. That something is cut worms. Place aluminum-foil collars two inches high around the stems, making sure that one inch is below the soil. Mulch with oak leaf mulch.

Q. *Is it necessary to add lime every year to my table garden?*
A. It's not necessary unless the soil has become acid. Don't ever use anything that isn't necessary.

Q. *Can you suggest a tomato that I can grow in a small area?*
A. You'll be delighted with F_1 hybrid patio tomato. I grow them between my evergreens with great results.

Q. *How do I keep rabbits out of my garden?*
A. Plant old-fashioned marigolds around the vegetable garden, use the spray in step 15 on page 317, or, as a last resort, use Hinder according to package directions.

Q. *Is it true that you shouldn't cultivate around tomatoes?*
A. It's a good idea not to disturb the roots if at all possible. A two-inch layer of mulch will eliminate the necessity of having to use a hoe.

Q. *When I was a youngster, my uncle grew giant pumpkins. What were they?*
A. I would say it was the variety called Jack-o'-lantern. Make sure you give this roamer plenty of room.

Q. *How much sun is necessary for a good vegetable garden?*
A. If you want any kind of results at all, you'd better find a spot where your garden will get six to eight hours of good sunshine.

Q. *We have trouble with grubs in the garden soil; our carrots and radishes are lost each season. Is there any control?*
A. The problem sounds like root maggots. These pests can be controlled by using Dursban as directed in the soil before you plant.

Q. *What causes tomatoes to turn gray or black on the top just before they ripen?*

A. Blossom-end rot, and it's the result of hot, humid weather. Not enough water gets to the fruit. Well-mulched plants with a sound irrigation program are seldom bothered. Six inches of grass clippings is the best mulch. Put it down four weeks after you plant your tomatoes.

Q. *Which vegetables grow the fastest?*

A. For those of you who want to have two or three different gardens a season, try these selections for speed: leaf lettuce, radishes, bush beans, onion sets, mustard and turnip greens, beets, and peas.

Q. *How important is crop rotation in a small garden?*

A. A lot more important than in a large garden. I always recommend that crops be rotated, with the exception of tomatoes, which can stay in one spot for three years.

Q. *How can we keep cabbage worms from eating more cabbage than we get?*

A. You can sprinkle the heads with ordinary table salt a couple of times a season, or use caterpillar killer according to package directions.

Q. *Which vegetable can we grow on the porch of our apartment? We live in the Central Park area of New York.*

A. It doesn't matter if you live in Oregon, Texas, Florida, Maine, or Michigan, you can grow a garden on a porch and be the talk of the building. Start with a bag of Redi-Earth planter mix and a redwood tub or two. In one tub plant a seed potato and a patio tomato. Results: seven pounds of potatoes and a half bushel of tomatoes. In another, plant pole beans and leaf lettuce, and in another cucumbers and radishes. You'll need a pole for support in the center of each tub.

Q. *Our cucumbers get all eaten up, and I am too old to dust every week. Any green thumb magic?*
A. There is no magic, lotion, motion or potion in gardening, but interplanting sure resembles it. Plant a few radishes in each cucumber mound.

Q. *I have heard that you can pinch tomatoes to make them climb, instead of spread out. Where do you pinch?*
A. If you're going to train your tomatoes to grow up a stake, you should pinch out the side shoots that grow out of the crook of the main side stems.

Q. *What variety of cucumber won't give you gas?*
A. If you like cucumbers, but they don't like you, try the ones they call lemon cucumbers.

Q. *Where is the best place to grow vegetables?*
A. Any place that gets six to eight hours of sun a day and where you can get an eight- to ten-inch depth of soil together—wooden boxes, wastepaper baskets, tubs, cement blocks, wooden frames, on a roof, driveway, or walk.

Q. *What kind of dirt do you need for a good garden?*
A. To begin with, the word is soil, not dirt. Soil is a productive composition of decayed materials such as leaves, grass clippings, sawdust, weeds, and fallen trees, while dirt is a collection of filth. Any well-drained soil will do nicely. While water should not stand in pockets on top neither should the soil be pure sand, which will not hold any moisture at all.

Q. *I live in a new subdivision where heavy clay was used as backfill, and I just can't get a good garden started. What will really break up the clay?*
A. You can dig in fifty pounds of garden gypsum por one thousand square feet in the fall and in the spring. In the fall, cover the soil with a mixture of leaves, grass clippings, ashes, wood chips, builders' sand and peat moss to a depth of six inches and sprinkle with fifteen pounds of garden food per five hundred square feet. Let this mix sit all winter. In the spring, spade or rototill very well into the clay.

Q. *What can you do to make sand hold water?*
A. Add everything listed in the previous answer except the sand.

Q. *When do you add compost to a garden?*
A. In the fall. Let it sit on top 'til spring, when you work it in very well.

Q. *If you spade a garden in the fall, do you have to do it again in the spring?*
A. I only spade or rototill in the fall if I need the exercise, and I do that before I add my compost or other rakings. I always spade again in the spring; that's a must. Soil becomes compacted or pushed down from snow and rain. If you just scuff it up with a rake, you don't give the new seeds and plants a fair start.

Q. *When is the best time to dig up your garden?*
A. If you have never had a garden in a certain spot before, remove the sod and throw it into your compost pile in the fall. Next put a six-inch-deep layer of leaves, grass clippings, ashes, wood chips, builder's sand, and peat moss on the cleared area and wait until spring to spade it in. Don't cultivate

a garden until the soil will crumble in your hand after being squeezed firmly.

Q. *What good do eggshells and coffee grounds do for garden dirt?*
A. It's soil, and they help to break up heavy soil or clay.

Q. *We have adobe soil. What can we do for it?*
A. Add a six-inch-deep layer of organic material—leaves, grass clippings, ashes, wood chips, builder's sand, and peat moss—after working in fifty pounds of gypsum per one thousand square feet. Let the layer sit until spring, then work it in very well.

Q. *How much and when do you add lime to your garden?*
A. You should lime once every three years at a rate of one quart jar per one hundred square feet applied in the fall, or apply two ounces of liquid lime per one hundred square feet in the spring.

Q. *Should you add fertilizer to the soil before you plant?*
A. I add about a pound of garden food per one hundred square feet in the fall and then feed my garden with a liquid garden food right after I plant in the spring.

Q. *Every year my garden has been carried away by root maggots, cutworms, corn borers, and so on. When, how, and with what can I save my garden?*
A. Apply Dursban or Diazinon to the soil in the fall according to package directions.

Q. *How do you build a raised garden?*
A. Make a frame out of 2 X 10 timbers or with cement blocks and fill it with good garden soil. A

raised garden can be built right on top of clay, cement, a tarred roof—anywhere you can find with full, open sun that will support the massive weight of all that soil. It's also a good idea to use a wood preservative available at a paint store to keep the wood from rotting.

Q. *What can you grow in a raised garden?*
A. Anything you can grow in a regular garden, if you have the room.

Q. *What grows best in tubs and big planters?*
A. Anything you'd grow in your regular garden, except that close to the house I like to use planters for vegetables that we use in salads. They look nice on a patio—parsley, leaf lettuce, Swiss chard, spinach—and they're right at hand for picking.

Q. *Most of my garden is in the sun, but about 25 percent is in some shade. What can I grow in the shade?*
A. Beans and cabbage don't do too badly in the shade, but you must watch out for insects a little more in shady spots than in the sun. Bugs like a cool spot on a hot day just as you and I do.

Q. *How do you plant on the side of a hill?*
A. Very carefully, or your garden will wash away. We call it contour planting: the rows follow the curve around the hill, not up and down the slope. All gardens should have about a 5-degree slope to the southeast.

Q. *What is the best location for a garden?*
A. An open area with no trees to shade it and a 5-degree slope to the southeast is the best; any other spots that are in full sun are great.

Q. *If you have a good spot to grow a garden, but it's very small and you want flowers as well as vegetables and berries, can you plant them all together without altering the flavor of food or fragrance of flowers?*

A. Absolutely; I never give it a thought. I use salad greens, spinach, mustard, lettuce, and red cabbage as borders in front of evergreens while growing pole beans up my downspouts near my roses, and I mix carrots and parsnips with marigolds as sidewalk borders.

Q. *Do strawberries, raspberries, and blueberries need a different soil and location from my regular garden? Can they really be grown with each other?*

A. They aren't any different from any other member of the garden team; they can and should be grown together.

Q. *How do you figure how much space you need for a vegetable garden for the size family you have?*

A. The way my Grandma Putt taught me was to add together the heights of each of my family members—rounded off, in feet—then square that number, and that's the number of square feet you need for your home garden. That's the garden space I would need to cultivate to provide food for my family for one year, whether that food is fresh, frozen, stored, or dried.

Q. *How many rows or how many plants of each vegetable should you plant?*

A. You always plant more of the things you like than the things you don't; that stands to reason. But here's a formula I use as an all-around rule. Row crops—carrots, radishes, parsnips—are planted in a row whose length equals your height, or a six-foot row for sons over thirteen years of age and for fathers; one-half that length for mothers and daughters over fifteen; a third that length for any children under fifteen. There should be three tomato and pepper plants for dad and one each for each other family member.

Q. *Do you really have to draw a picture of your garden?*
A. No, you don't have to, but it sure does make it easier to remember where you had what this year when you want to know that information three years from now when you're rotating your crops. I use a large paper grocery bag. I cut the bag, and draw in the crops in color. Then I write notes on the bag all season: it becomes my garden diary.

Q. *Are seeds you send away for as good as the ones you buy in the seed racks in your grocery store?*
A. Yes. Whoever started the rumor that they aren't should have his mouth washed out with soap. Use both sources. The mail-order seed men often have a larger and newer selection than you'll find on the racks because there may not be a large enough quantity for the packet-seed market yet. There are lots of small, specialized mail-order seed houses that never send seeds to a general market. If you want the unusual or the unique, you're more likely to find it in a catalog than a hardware store.

Q. *I have some two-year-old seed. Is it still good?*
A. Test it by sprinkling five or six seeds on top of a pot of damp soil. Cover the soil and see if they germinate. If they do, it is; if they don't, it's not. Better to test it now than wait three or four weeks to see if it comes up in your garden—only to find out you lost time and space.

Q. *Which seeds go in early and how early?*
A. The vegetable and fruit plants I call tough are asparagus, broccoli, Brussels sprouts, cabbage, celery, collards, garlic, kale, kohlrabi, mustard, onion sets and all other onions, peas, radishes, rhubarb, rutabaga, spinach, strawberries, and turnips. When I say early I mean these can go in from a month to two weeks before the last frost in your area.

Q. *Is it true that the best time to plant corn is on Memorial Day?*
A. That's as good a guide date as any for snow country planting. You can also add artichokes, beans, cantaloupe, eggplant, okra, peanuts, peppers, pumpkins, squash, tomatoes, and watermelon on that date for snow country.

Q. *How early can you plant the lettuces?*
A. I generally gamble and plant lettuce as well as beets, carrots, cauliflower, endive, parsley, parsnips, potatoes, and Swiss chard about a week before the last frost date. Then I hold my breath.

Q. *How deep do you plant corn? The birds always seem to get mine.*
A. All the large seeds are planted two inches deep. Beans and onion sets should be two inches deep as well. Beets, cucumbers, melons, peas, and squash are planted at one inch deep; broccoli, Brussels sprouts, cabbage, carrots, cauliflower, celery, eggplant, lettuce, mustard, parsnips, peppers, radishes, spinach, and turnips are happy with a half-inch soil blanket; tomatoes only want a quarter inch.

Q. *Is it true that you should always plant cucumbers on the east side of a garden?*
A. As far as I know, it's true, but I carry it a step further. All vine crops—cantaloupe and water-

melon, not to mention squash—are planted at the east end of my garden because these plants always grow toward the east and will run over the top of other plants.

Q. *Do you really have to plant so many kernels of corn to the mound in order to get corn?*
A. Yep! According to my teachers, all old experts, you must plant four seeds to the mound. If you're planting in rows, plant seed nine to twelve inches apart and two feet between the rows with at least three rows. And always plant on the west side of your garden so the corn can protect the other plants from warm, dry winds.

Q. *How often should you feed corn?*
A. Never use garden food with newly planted seed or it will rot. I feed corn the first time when it's a foot high with any lawn food and again when its beard or silk shows.

Q. *What good does soaking corn seed do?*
A. Improves the odds on its growing in your favor. I soak all vegetable seed in a cup of tea in the refrigerator for twenty-four hours before I plant. The results are worth the effort and extra time.

Q. *Corn takes up so darn much space for so long a time with little return. Can I grow something along with it?*
A. Sure you can, but be kind to both groups. I interplant pole beans. The beans grow up the stalks and don't hurt a thing.

Q. *If farmers grow pumpkins in cornfields, why can't I?*
A. There's no reason on earth why you can't, but how many pumpkins can you use? I've found that

corn and cucumbers become great friends. You see, lots of folks don't know it but corn likes its feet in the shade and its top in the sun. So my cucumbers, melons, and squash can be a growing mulch for my corn. That may seem contrary to what I said earlier about planting vines only at the east, but it's not. I said the vines would grow over the other small plants, but corn is not one of them.

Q. *How often should you cultivate corn?*
A. Are you kidding? Me? Cultivate corn? That's too much trouble, my friend. Eight or nine inches of straw or grass clippings down the rows and through the plants does all the cultivating needed.

Q. *I just can't seem to get beans to grow for me because I have such heavy soil. What can I do?*
A. First, break up the clay as directed on page 298. Next, dig a trench ten inches deep and five inches wide and fill it with an equal mixture of sharp sand and peat moss: that will give the beans a good start. Next, drive metal stakes six feet tall into the ground and stretch wires between them at the top and the bottom. Every place you plant a seed, fix an upright wire for pole beans. I grow bush beans by using a large fruit juice can with top and bottom cut out; I push the can into the soil about two or three inches, and the beans grow up through the can.

Q. *What do you feed beans?*
A. Garden food in the early spring. Beans give more nitrogen back to the earth than they eat.

Q. *How do you keep the damn 'coons, mice, birds, squirrels, or whatever from digging up your beans?*
A. The same way my Grandma Putt cured me from biting my fingernails. She always cleaned out

gourds by drilling a hole in them with her potato peeler and then saved the seeds for next year. She also saved the juice and flesh, added water to them, and kept the mixture in a jar. She would put some of this juice on my nails, and the rest she poured on corn and other big seeds just as she planted them. It's the bitterest juice you ever tasted, and I reckon the varmints must hate it as much as I did.

Q. *When do you thin beans?*
A. Never; I plant pole beans two feet apart and bush beans nine inches apart. The seeds are large enough to plant separately.

Q. *Why do my lima beans get so leggy and not have many beans?*
A. You must pick the beans just as quickly as they mature. They want a sunny, warm location, with good drainage; very little food is necessary. Beans and peas are the best investment a gardener can make, as they give the biggest return for space and time invested.

Q. *I think I have every seed catalog offered, and the more I look at them the more confused I become. Each company says their seeds are new and improved. Which are and which aren't, and which bean would you recommend in each category?*
A. I wish to give the seed growers a pat on the back because they're all working hard to develop varieties that will resist bugs and diseases and need less water, food, and care—all for our benefit. To answer the first part of your question, they're all improved. In my opinion, Top-Crop snapbean is a great bush bean, and you just can't seem to beat Kentucky Wonder as a reliable, tasty, heavy producing pole bean. And I always recommend Clark's Green-seeded Bush lima bean.

Q. *Why don't my beets ever get any bigger than a Ping-Pong ball?*
A. The soil is too heavy, probably clay; beets like light, loose soil. In heavy soil, dig a trench four inches wide and eight inches deep and fill with chopped or mowed leaves and sawdust. Beets need heat, light soil, and sand.

Q. *Can beets be started indoors?*
A. Can they ever! I use the cup part of paper egg cartons filled with light houseplant soil. My favorite variety is named after my home town, Detroit Dark Red beet.

Q. *I want to grow my beets organically. What kind of food do you recommend?*
A. Take your table scraps (not meat or bones) and place them in your blender. Add water to fill up your blender and liquefy the scraps. Pour this liquid onto your beets and the rest of your garden, then Watch It Grow!

Q. *What do you feed beets?*
A. Any garden food in the spring.

Q. *What's the earliest and the latest you can plant beets?*
A. The earliest is as soon as you can work the soil, and the latest is around August 15 in the East and Midwest, and July 15 in the North.

Q. *How do you grow broccoli so that the heads don't grow all over the place?*
A. It depends on the variety you grow. I use Green Comet because it's a tight headed variety.

Q. *What kind of soil does broccoli like?*
A. It can stand some dampness but not a lot.

Q. *Can I plant my broccoli, cabbage, and Brussels sprouts together?*

A. I would so I could give them all the same care and watch them for the same insects. As a matter of fact, it's an excellent idea. Broccoli, cabbage, cauliflower, and Brussels sprouts are all in the same family, and as a rule take up a hell of a lot of room, so remember that when you plan your garden.

Q. *How early should you start your Brussels sprouts, cabbage, broccoli, and cauliflower?*

A. Start them indoors five weeks before you plan to set them out.

Q. *Can I safely mulch cabbage without inviting insects?*

A. I mulch my whole garden, lock, stock, and barrel, with grass clippings, straw, corn cobs, buckwheat hulls, sawdust, and so on, and I don't have any more trouble with bugs than anyone who doesn't mulch.

Q. *My neighbor said you can use grass fertilizer to feed cabbage! Can you?*

A. Your neighbor is right. I use grass food for anything that grows above the ground except tomatoes.

Q. *Why do my carrots always grow all gnarled up, short and fat, or not at all?*

A. Your carrots are probably in heavy soil. Carrots like rich, light soil that's eight to ten inches deep. If your soil is clay, just dig an eight- to ten-inch trench and fill it with sand, peat, leaves, and sawdust. Carrots don't do well in shade and prefer bright, sunny areas. Feed them with any garden food after foliage appears. I plant my seeds three inches apart, one at a time. I would rather do the separating work in the beginning than thin them later.

Q. *Can you really plant cucumbers in hanging baskets?*
A. Yes, and they also make great houseplants. The only problem with growing them in hanging baskets is that they like cool, slightly damp and shaded areas.

Q. *Should you let cucumbers run on the ground or stake them?*
A. I like to grow them up fences or trellises and mulch their feet.

Q. *Are eggplants hard to grow?*
A. Not as a rule, but what most folks forget is that eggplants never stop eating. Eggplants like rich, light soil and a sunny location. Plant seeds a half inch deep, two feet apart with two feet between rows. Feed regularly with liquefied table scraps.

Q. *How do you know when to pick kohlrabi?*
A. That's a super question! Do you know that most folks who've grown it for years don't know the answer? Kohlrabi is part of the cabbage family, but you eat the base, not the foliage or the root. Pick as soon as it's the size of a handball or it'll be like eating a croquet ball—woody.

Q. *What makes lettuce get mushy and slimy?*
A. This usually happens when lettuce is planted too late in the spring. Lettuce does not like warm weather, but it can be grown in hot weather if it's grown in light shade. Lettuce is a very shallow rooted plant that needs plenty of food and must be kept damp.

Q. *Why do melons rot on the ground side or take so long to ripen?*
A. Heat speeds up the ripening. Place young mel-

ons on a brick while they're still attached to the vine and you'll speed up their ripening.

Q. *How come melon seed doesn't sprout as well as other seed?*
A. Because melon seeds have a large case with a soft center, they're more often injured or crushed in handling or shipping than a smaller, uniformly harder seed would be. Cantaloupe, pumpkin, watermelon, cucumber, and squash seeds all have this problem. To avoid disappointment, why don't you soak your seed to speed germination and let it sprout before you plant? Soak the seed in a cup of lukewarm tea for two hours, then soak a big old bath towel in weak tea and wring out well. Now place a row of seed in the middle of the towel and fold the towel over the seed. Place the whole shebang in a plastic garbage bag and keep it at 70 degrees for six days. Then remove the seed and plant the sprouted seed in the garden.

Q. *Can mustard greens be grown indoors?*
A. They sure can. Put them in large pots on a sunny windowsill, and they're usually ready to eat in five to six weeks after planting—that's the same length of time as grown outside. Remember, you can plant mustard greens early and then again in August to September, as they like cool weather. For those of you who've never eaten greens, you don't know what you're missing. Their taste is a great addition to any salad bowl.

Q. *I heard that you don't have to plant peas in soil but can plant them in straw. Is that true?*
A. Sort of. You can sow peas in lightly tilled soil, near a fence or chicken wire screen, and cover the peas with ten to twelve inches of straw, and they

grow great! Peas like to grow up something, so give them a hand.

Q. *How do you get onion sets to be big onions for storing?*
A. Onions can be grown from seed or sets, both of which are tough little fellows that can be planted as early as you can get into the garden. Plant early sets or seeds four inches apart and let them grow. Eat every other one as you hanker to. Never let a seed pod form on top; pinch it off. In late August or early September, bend the tops over to stop the top growth. Soon the bulb will get bigger. Pull it up and let it dry in the sun for two or three weeks and then store.

Q. *Is it true that parsnips grow all winter in frozen ground?*
A. Well, it's almost true. They don't grow after a hard frost, but you can leave them in the ground all winter—even if the ground freezes—and dig them up as you need them. They taste better after a heavy frost. Parsnips grow and like the same soil as their cousins, the carrots. Parsnips are my very favorite vegetable and make super wine.

Q. *Why don't peppers grown from seed planted right in the garden do well?*
A. It's probably due to you, your garden location, and the soil, not the seed. It's true that vegetables you put in as plants do better than those put in as seed, but that's because pregrown plants have a head start and so are stronger. Give peppers a dry, light soil in a sunny spot, and they'll do fine.

Q. *What plant can't you put near pumpkins?*
A. Squash! These two plants crosspollinate when

together, leaving you with some pretty odd-looking offspring.

Q. *I want to grow my own potatoes. Where do I begin?*
A. You can begin by deciding if you want to grow only enough to harvest and eat or enough to store some, as well. Buy good seed potatoes from your local garden center in March or April and plant them in good, well-drained soil. You can plant in mounds or in a foot of marsh hay or straw piled on top of the soil—my favorite way. Cut seed potatoes into pieces with at least two eyes each and plant in April, May, and on June 1.

Q. *Why won't radishes grow well in the middle of summer?*
A. Because they like cool weather. Early spring and late fall are best to grow radishes, but if you plant them in light shade, they'll provide a pretty good selection of sizes for eating.

Q. *If you use spinach as a border planting under evergreens, won't it pick up a strange flavor?*
A. I've never had that problem, and I use spinach as a border all the time. Spinach loves shade, where it's cool and damp. Feed spinach a little lawn food every three weeks.

Q. *Can you plant more than one kind of squash on a mound?*
A. You sure can. It's only pumpkins and squash that get each other in trouble. I grow zucchini and yellow summer squash back to back in a mound with a round clay sewer tile pushed a third of its length into the soil so I can water easily. Acorn and butternut are a must with winter squash. So many good squash varieties are available that I try a dif-

ferent one each season. Remember, squash likes sandy, gravelly soil, so make heavy soil light by adding sand and gravel or make foot-high mounds of sandy loam.

Q. *When do you start tomato seeds indoors so that they don't get too tall and leggy and fall over?*
A. I start mine six weeks before it's time to go outside in commercial African violet growing medium. When the new plants are two and a half to three inches tall, I plant them deeper in paper cups. As a matter of fact, I leave only the top layer of leaves above the soil. I let this plantlet grow until it's nine inches high and again transplant. This time the plant goes into a four-inch clay pot without disturbing the root ball and gets planted deeper than it was in the cup.

Q. *Is it really necessary to stake tomatoes?*
A. It is unless you like sore backs and rotten tomatoes. There are lots of ways to keep tomatoes off the ground without staking. Old fencing made up of large squares, wooden frames, and plastic pails with the top and bottom cut out all do fine as supports. I still like stakes. Me, I drive a six-foot metal pole—only metal will do—into the same hole and at the same time I plant my tomatoes. As the plants grow, I tie them to the stake with pieces of nylon pantyhose, not rope or twistums. I use metal poles and nylon because they attract static electricity, which makes stronger, greener plants, and deeper fruit.

Q. *Do you have to take suckers off tomatoes?*
A. No, you don't have to, and most folks don't want to go to the trouble. I do because I plant fewer plants and want more fruit. I remove free-loading suckers that ride along for a free meal and don't produce.

Q. *What makes the bottoms of my tomatoes turn soft and grayish black every year?*
A. It's caused by improper distribution of water to the plant. If you will wait until about four weeks after you plant your tomatoes and cover the roots with four or five inches of grass clippings or straw, you should never be bothered by blossom end rot.

Q. *What makes tomatoes stop growing in the middle of the summer? The fruit falls off, the leaves curl up, and the plant dies.*
A. This is called fusarium wilt and can be prevented by spraying the soil in the fall and early spring with the fungicide Benomyl. If you had the problem last season, treat it before you plant again 'cause it sure as hell ain't going away by itself.

Q. *Is it true that pipe, cigar, and cigarette smoke can ruin a tomato crop?*
A. That's the truth, friend. I suggest that you smokers wash your hands well before working in the garden. The disease you could be transmitting is called tobacco mosaic; it also loves potatoes.

Q. *Is liquid cow manure good for tomatoes?*
A. Only if the cows don't step on the tomatoes! Sure it is, and so is fish fertilizer, garden food, and any of the labeled tomato foods. I use one called Tomato Gro (10-52-17).

Q. *Can tomatoes grow in shade?*
A. Not very well; they like a bright spot in your garden. And there is a bright spot—they don't mind fairly heavy soil.

Q. *We love turnip greens, but they don't do too well in the summer. How come?*
A. 'Cause they don't like hot weather. Plant early

in May and again in August. You can have some luck in the summer if you plant them in partial shade, but don't expect wonders.

Q. *We just don't have any luck with watermelons, and I've tried all kinds. We have good, rich black soil. Why don't they like us?*
A. It's not you; it's your garden location! If you planted on a sunny hillside your watermelons would grow to the bottom of the hill before you could get there. Dry soil, in a sunny location, with real good drainage is what they love. And don't forget to remove any sick or dried blossoms.

Q. *Is it true that there's a yellow watermelon?*
A. It's true—the meat is red, but the hide turns yellow when it's ripe. It's called Golden Midget; and it's super for growing in the North in small areas. It takes sixty-five days! Not bad, eh?

Q. *Is it a fact that rhubarb leaves are poisonous?*
A. 'Tis a fact, so don't eat the leaves. But don't let this scare you away from planting some. Plant a root in the spring and don't expect any rhubarb till the following year.

Q. *When do you plant raspberries for best results?*
A. In the spring, in good, well-drained soil, twelve inches apart and four feet between rows. Trim the roots some when you plant and then mulch with grass or straw. Feed three weeks later with any liquid plant food. I use Tomato Gro. Every spring after I have fruit, I feed again and cut back to three inches off the ground. Move the mulch and look for young shoots. Cut out all but the strongest and you'll always have a garden full of raspberries—big, fat, and sweet. Please grow some.

Q. *Are these garden weeders any good, or will they kill my vegetables or hurt my pets or me and my family?*

A. I swear by them. They're pre-emergent weed killers, and they do a great job. If you use them in combination with mulch, you should have nothing to do but water, feed, and harvest.

Q. *How long can I count on my strawberries to produce?*

A. For years and years if you do it right! Buy good, healthy, fresh plants for your good, rich, tilled, light soil. As soon as you can get your tools into the soil in the spring, set the plants twelve inches apart with rows at least four feet apart. I use my long-handled bulb planter to make holes and then spread the roots out over a small stone or ball of soil the size of a golf ball. Don't set the plant any deeper than it was at the nursery or in its container. Now feed with liquid garden food or a good dry food and pick off any blossoms the first year. Cover the plants loosely with straw in the fall and uncover them in the early spring. The main plant will grow babies on runners. Let them go but don't let them bunch up; spread them out all around the mother plant. Thin out some babies if you have to. At the end of three years, spade the original plants under and let the grown-up kids do their thing, growing babies back over where Grandma used to grow. You have to get varieties that grow well in your area because strawberries are more sensitive to where they grow than most plants. A Northern variety may not produce in the South. Your nurseryman will help you select. Also, use Berry Set as directed.

Q. *What can I do to control the eight jillion bugs that drive me and my garden nuts?*

A. I think you just about hit the number on the

head; it's a shame we can't do the same to all the bugs. I can't list every insect I've been asked about because both of us would get tired—me of writing, which I do by hand, and you of reading. So let's make it easy on us and hard on the bugs. If they crawl, fly, hop, skitter, or slink on, over, or around your garden, use an all-purpose fruit tree spray or tomato-vegetable dust made into a spray. As for the creeps that hide in the soil and pick on our poor defenseless plants from below, Diazinon or Dursban can usually handle the toughest of them. Of course, you might want to try a tonic first, before bringing in the heavy artillery. (See p. 65.)

Q. *I want to grow an herb garden. What's the best location?*
A. Generally where nothing else likes to grow. Herbs as a rule like sandy or gravelly soil, since most of them are in the same family as many a weed.

Q. *Does an herb garden have to be formal?*
A. Of course not; where did you ever get that idea? Plant herbs for convenience: put some of the more fragrant ones close to the patio and the ones you use for cooking near the house while dill, the gangly one, is usually hidden. You've probably seen the pictures of a wagon wheel buried in the ground and different herbs planted between the spokes. Let your imagination be your guide.

Q. *Which are the best herbs to plant for the average home?*
A. There is no such place as an average home; each home is special. Here's a list of herbs you might get the most out of: chives, parsley, dill, thyme, sage, mint, fennel, chervil, borage, basil, anise, rosemary, tarragon, sweet marjoram, savory,

and coriander. That ought to keep your home, kitchen, and life spiced up.

Q. *Which herbs do you use for preparing wildfowl?*
A. Hunters use dirty hands, but you can try marjoram and sage.

Q. *Is the marigold really an herb?*
A. Why not? It used to be used to color butter, and it makes great wine.

Q. *What is meant by balloon-sealing wine?*
A. Instead of using the old-fashioned method of water sealing, which consisted of a complicated apparatus of corks and glass tubing to enable the gasses to escape, we now just place a child's balloon over the neck of the bottle. When the gasses fill the balloon, causing it to enlarge, we let them out and put the balloon over the bottle neck again. This process is repeated until no more gasses form, at which time the wine can be corked and stored.

Q. *Can I use any kind of barrel to make wine?*
A. The best kind of cask, as it is called by my good Italian wine making teacher, is a new white oak barrel. Don't buy one that is charred or waxed inside. If you use either of these types you will smother the wine, and it will sour.

Q. *Can you grow herbs in a barrel?*
A. Sure you can—or in an old crock, a wagon wheel, a rubber tire, an iron kettle, or any other imaginative container.

Q. *What medicinal purpose does ginger serve?*
A. My grandma used to give us a cup of ginger tea after she'd rubbed our chests with camphorated oil to sweat out a cold, and then she put us to bed.

Q. *I'd like to grow herbs on my apartment's patio in New York City.*
A. It wouldn't matter if you lived in Timbuktu. You can grow herbs anyplace. Why don't you get a clay strawberry pot and plant parsley, chives, mint, sage, rosemary for fragrance, and thyme in the pockets.

Q. *We have a wildflower growing in our rock garden. It's got a tag on it, with the name* Galeopsis terrahit. *Can it be grown inside as a kitchen herb?*
A. The real name is common hemp nettle, and if you have any plans for spicing up your life with this, forget it. You'll get stung harvesting it and sick from the results.

Q. *What are the three best salad herbs?*
A. My wife makes super salads, and she adds thyme, basil, and tarragon. Yummmmm. Tarragon will probably be your first choice because it doesn't dry well.

Q. *What's the herb that tastes so strong in most Italian food?*
A. Probably oregano. I like it in scrambled eggs and on fish when they're freshly caught and pan fried.

Q. *Can I make up my own curry powder from an herb garden?*
A. Well, you could, but you might run into trouble with an herb called turmeric. But here are some other ingredients you can use: coriander, black pepper, mustard seeds, ginger, cumin, allspice, cardamom, cloves, and anise.

HOUSEPLANTS

··

LIVING ROOM
LANDSCAPES

··

The way interest in houseplants has grown in the last few years is just astounding! Fifteen or twenty years ago, there were very few indoor gardeners. Those who were around had a very limited selection of plants to work with. In those days, indoor gardening meant having a plant collection on a windowsill or in a vestibule. Things sure have changed. There are now more houseplants than people, and the assortment is virtually unlimited as to color range, size, and shape. With the proper selection of plants, you can accent a piece of furniture, change the character of a room, or flatter an entire interior. With recent improvements in heating and lighting in today's homes and apartments, anyone can raise houseplants, even without

343

the proverbial green thumb! You only need a little knowledge and common sense.

CHOOSE CAREFULLY

There are five basic types of houseplants to choose from: foliage plants, flowering houseplants, flowering pot plants, bulbs and corms, and cacti. The foliage plants and flowering houseplants, like African violets, are permanent residents. Flowering houseplants and bulb or corm plants are often holiday or special occasion plants that are temporary visitors. The cacti are the fun plants and collectors' items.

The fun of indoor gardening is in choosing the most suitable plants from the large selection available. But first let's lay down some ground rules. Rule number one: Make sure that the plants you pick appeal to you and that you don't select them just because a person or book recommends them. Rule two: Make sure that these plants are suitable for the conditions they must live in. Rule three: Be sure that they don't call for more time and experience than you have to offer. Ask yourself these questions before you make your final selection:

1. What shape plant do I want? Upright, bushy, trailing, or climbing? The uprights consist of aphelandra, codiaeum, cordyline, dracaena, *Ficus elastica* (rubber plant), *Ficus lyrata*, grevillea, pandanus, and sansevieria.

The bushy plants are adiantum, azalea, begonia, coleus, fatsia, fittonia, maranta, neanthe, and saintpaulia (African violet).

Trailing plants consist of *Begonia glaucophylla,*

Campanula isophylla, columnea, *Ficus pumila, Fuchsia pendula*, helxine, *Saxifraga sarmentosa*, tradescantia, zebrina.

The climbing plants are cissus, *Cobaea scandens, Ficus pumila*, hedera, hoya, *Philodendron scandens*, rhoicissus, scindapsus, and tetrastigma.

2. Do I want the plant to live in the same room permanently? If the answer is yes, avoid flowering pot plants: they only bloom indoors for a short while.

3. Do I want a plant with colorful foliage? Lots of houseplants have colorful foliage and variegated leaves. (Variegated simply means that the leaves are multicolored.) If you want color, choose from this list: sansevieria, *Peperomia magnoliaefolia variegata*, dracaena, *Hedera helix, Zebrina pendula*, or *Ficus pumila*. These plants require plenty of light. Other colors are available with nidularium, maranta, coleus, *Begonia rex*, codiaeum, cordyline, aphelandra, and *Cissus discolor*.

4. How much time and effort will I be able to give? Some houseplants are almost indestructible, while others are best left to experienced green thumbs. If you're a newcomer to the Plant Kingdom, or you're interested in plants mostly for interior design, then I'd recommend you select plants from the "easy group," plants that can stand a little cool weather and a certain amount of neglect or poor management.

The easy plants are hedera, *Cissus antarctica, Rhoicissus rhomboidea, Ficus pumila, Ficus elastica* (rubber plant), sansevieria (mother-in-law's tongue), *Philodendron scandens*, chlorophytum, tradescantia, cyperus, scindapsus, *Monstera deliciosa*, fatshedera, fatsia, helxine, grevillea, tolmiea, *Saxifraga sarmentosa*.

Easy flowering plants are billbergia, clivia, geraniums, impatiens, fuchsia, and all of the cactus plants.

5. What kind of living conditions am I going to offer my foliage friends? Here's a general description of growing conditions that we might find in most homes and apartments and the plants that will best fit those conditions.

Dim and cool: aspidistra, dizygothica, fatshedera, fatsia, ferns, *Ficus pumila*, hedera, helxine, maranta, and philodendron. When I say cool, I mean in the 50- to 55-degree range, not cold like 40 degrees.

Bright but no sunlight: *Cissus antarctica*, columnea, fuchsia, *Monstera deliciosa, Rhoicissus rhomboidea*, scindapsus, tetrastigma, tolmiea, foliage houseplants with variegated leaves and most of the holiday plants.

Some sunlight each day: chlorophytum, cordyline, *Ficus elastica*, peperomia, sansevieria, and most flowering houseplants.

Bright sunny window: beloperone, cobaea, coleus, genista, geranium, impatiens, passiflora, cacti and succulents.

Little heat in the winter: aspidistra, billbergia, *Cissus antarctica*, chlorophytum, fatshedera, fatsia, hedera, *Philodendron scandens, Saxifraga sarmentosa*, zebrina.

Homes with gas heat: Least affected by fumes are thick-leaved foliage houseplants. All flowering plants (except impatiens and billbergia) should be avoided.

Poor humidity, dry: aechmea, billbergia, chlorophytum, clivia, *Ficus elastica*, grevillea, pilea, sansevieria, vriesia, zebrina, cacti and succulents. It is absolutely essential for you to determine exactly what the climatic conditions of your home are and not to hedge on your evaluation. Should you have any doubts, choose another plant to avoid disappointment for both you and the plant.

BE A TIRE
KICKER

· ·

When you go to buy a houseplant, be as choosy as you would be if you were buying a new car. You must remember that houseplants are raised in greenhouses where the air is warm and humid. The world outside is far less accommodating, so always buy from a reputable supplier who will have made sure that the plants have been properly "hardened off" and are able to stand the shock of the change to living in a home. Of course, houseplants can be bought at any time of the year, but it's best to buy delicate varieties in late spring or summer, when taking them outside to take them home won't hurt them. Look over the plant carefully before buying; it should be sturdy with no damaged leaves, and it should be free from insects.

Have the nursery wrap up your purchase before you leave, and treat it gently for about a week. Keep it out of direct sunlight and drafts and be careful not to give it too much heat or water. After a week it can be placed in its permanent quarters and treated normally. Plants that are purchased in flower during the winter months, like azalea and cyclamen, require different treatment. Put them in their permanent quarters immediately and give them as much light as possible.

LANDSCAPING YOUR LIVING SPACE

Every room in your house can accommodate a plant, planter, or vase, but you should know which plant will best fit in each room. Plants serve a more important purpose in our lives than mere decoration. They promote our good health by purifying the air around us. Plants can brighten our spirits when we're down; busy our hands when we're idle; sharpen our creative abilities; keep us company when we're lonely, and be a sounding board when we're mad.

Plants are an everyday part of our lives. Just look around. Here are some brief suggestions of how to use plants indoors:

A *plant window* is one of the most spectacular ways of displaying houseplants. Instead of a windowsill, a plant trough runs along the length of a large picture window. Into this trough go a variety of flowering and/or foliage plants, the largest specimens often being used to frame the two sides. Blinds are usually installed in the window to protect the plants against both sun and frost damage. The floor-to-ceiling plant window is the most satisfactory method known of blending room and garden together, bringing the outside in.

A *climbing display* can frame a window or cover a metal or bamboo room divider. Where a dense screen is required, use tetrastigma or *Cissus antarctica*. If you merely want to decorate the supports of a screen and not cut out light or hide the view, then choose a small-leaved climber like *Ficus pumila* or *Hedera helix*. Some climbing plants are self supporting; others may require tying loosely with raffia to the support.

A *miniature garden* is an indoor garden that uses smaller plants and attempts to reproduce garden features on a small scale—paths, pools, mossy turf, even windmills and figurines! Cacti and succulents are sometimes used for miniature or dish gardens, but they should not be mixed with other types of indoor plants because they need dry conditions.

A *single flowering plant* can be used to provide a splash of vivid color against pastel furnishings; a large foliage plant could provide an ideal focal point. Single plants are generally larger or more dramatic. Pots with drainage holes should stand on unobtrusive saucers deep enough to prevent water from running onto the surface beneath. Pots without drainage holes should have a bottom layer of broken crockery or small charcoal lumps. Be careful not to overwater.

Some flowering plants are seen to best advantages when not surrounded by other plants. Small- and medium-sized foliage types, however, should be grouped together for best effect and not kept strung out as isolated pots on shelf, table, or windowsill.

Planters come in many forms. You can buy containers made of wire, split cane, pottery, or plastic to hide ordinary clay pots, or you can use household objects like copper bowls and pans for that purpose.

The best planter to choose is a matter of personal taste, but remember that the plant should not have to compete with the pot hider for attention, so pick a container that is simple in shape and not too brightly colored. A pot hider should be taller than the pot it contains and, when suitable, the space between them should be filled with damp peat.

MAKE YOUR GUESTS AT HOME

● ●

I don't understand why most folks have so much trouble understanding the temperature range that plants like indoors. You only have to remember plants will be uncomfortable when you would be. They prefer the same comfort range most people do: 65 to 75 degrees. They don't like drafts, cold or hot. To check for drafts, place a lighted candle on a saucer where you intend to keep your plant, and watch the flame. If the flame blows out or blows in one direction for a long time, any plant calling that spot home will surely perish. When leaf edges are brown or black, your plant is in a draft and has caught cold. Move it!

No matter how much light you have in a room, it's not the same as sunlight. When your plants all bend over in the same direction, you can bet they're trying to look out the window. Turn your plants a little every few days so that all sides get some sunlight. But don't place plants in direct sunlight or the foliage will be burned. Filter the sunlight with a sheer curtain. If you intend to decorate your home with plants, pick colors for the walls in white or cream, light blue, aqua, or pale tan. These colors will reflect more light back into the room.

Small blooms or no blooms, thin, tall stems, and small pale leaves are all signs that a plant is not getting enough light. I find that a 60-watt GE grow light keeps my plants happy all winter.

Dissolve a child's vitamin tablet or a One-a-

"Plants prefer the same comfort range most peple do. They don't like drafts, cold or hot."

Day with iron tablet in one quart of water and use this solution three times each winter to feed plants.

Fresh air is the best thing you can give houseplants. On a mild day, open doors and windows. In the summer, send your plants off to camp. The east side of your home is the best camping spot—warm, fresh morning sunshine that's not too hot in the afternoon. Plants become stiff when they've been in all winter. To give them a little exercise, place the smaller ones on top of your radio or stereo from time to time. The base vibrations will keep the circulation moving—and besides, plants love music.

PLANTS GET THIRSTY

Without water your plants will die, and it'll be on your conscience, since they can't help themselves. It's best to water whenever the soil is dry to the touch, and that will be never if you water on a regular routine. A watering schedule should be based on the needs of the plant, the time of year, and the humidity in the room. If water runs right through the plant and pot, the soil has shrunk from the sides. When this happens, sink the pot over its rim in a bucket of room-temperature water with a drop of weak tea added. Let the water soak in for five or six minutes. Take out your plant, dry it off, and put it back in its place. When water will not go into the soil at all, it's caked hard. Pierce the surface of the soil with a fork and sink the pit beneath its rim in the same bucket. After a few minutes, remove it and put it back where it belongs.

The best water for your houseplants is rain or

melted snow. Water defrosted from your refrigerator is next best. The worst water for your plants is tap water. Place a layer of agricultural charcoal over the top of the soil in your plants' pot to filter out the additives we put into water; since plants don't have teeth, they can do without the fluoride. The charcoal dressing will also look nice and remove smoke and food odors from your rooms.

Houseplants love a warm shower; it starts their day out right. Your home is probably so dry that your plants wake up with their eyes stuck shut, their noses dried up, and their mouths full of cotton. Control humidity by giving them a shower or put your plants on a shallow tray covered with a layer of pebbles. Put water into the tray just below the bottom of the pot. Or you could give your foliage plants a steam bath twice a month. Place a brick or block in the middle of a bucket and put your plant on it. Then add boiling water to the bottom of the bucket. Do not let the hot water touch the pot or plant. Let the plant sit in the steam for five or six minutes, then return it to its favorite spot.

Indoor plants respire, that is, they return moisture to the atmosphere through their leaves. If your rooms are too warm or too dry or you don't pay enough attention to watering, your plants will run out of leaf moisture, dehydrate, and die. Spray all of your houseplants with Cloud Cover or Christmas Tree Saver, both the tops and bottoms of the leaves.

"I try to water houseplants in the morning, because that's when I'm thirsty."

INVITED TO DINNER

· ·

When you decide to ask the plants to live at your house, you also take on the responsibility of feeding them. All plants need food, and they must have a balanced diet. They need nitrogen to build leaves, phosphate to make roots, and potash to promote flowers. Small leaves and stunted and pale foliage say your plant's not getting enough nitrogen. Not enough feeder roots develop if your plant lacks phosphate, and the plant dies. Weak stems and small, poorly colored flowers mean there's a potash deficiency. All plants need iron, which can be added by dissolving a one-a-day vitamin with iron in a quart of water. Feed this iron to your plants three times each season. Once a winter, water your plants with a vitamin shot—a child's vitamin tablet dissolved in a quart of water.

The best time to feed plants is during the growing season when they're making flowers and new foliage. Don't feed them when they're resting or when they have draft symptoms. The best way to feed your chlorophyll colleagues is with a good organic liquid like Alaska fish fertilizer. I have a party for my plants every time I water them because I spike their water with the following mixture. Into one gallon of warm water add:

¼ teaspoon instant tea granules
½ teaspoon Knox gelatin
½ teaspoon children's shampoo
½ teaspoon household ammonia
1 capful of whiskey

10 percent of the recommended rate of any house-plant food

EXPAND YOUR HOUSEPLANT POPULATION

A great way to expend your houseplant family is by propagation—increasing the number of plants you know will grow well in your home by making more of them yourself. For the more ambitious houseplant gardener, propagation is an economical way to experiment with a variety of plants. You can start new plants from seeds or existing plants.

STARTING FROM SEED

Growing plants from seed is the easiest, most successful method of propagation because you seldom fail in the initial step: germination. Once you've gotten a seed to sprout, a routine of good general plant care—feeding, watering, and cleaning—is enough for most plants.

You can start by gathering seeds from the fruits and vegetables in your refrigerator. Few people realize that citrus and other seeds can be coaxed into producing exotic plants and a lot of conversation. Coffee, pineapple, tangerine, lemon, grapefruit, and orange seeds are the easiest to work with. These seeds can be the beginning of a terrific tabletop garden.

The seeds of tangerines, grapefruits, lemons, and oranges yield very attractive plants. Dwarf orange, grapefruit, and lemon and miniature orange plants and kumquats can also be started from seed. Citrus seeds are injured by drying, so leave them in the fruit until you're ready to plant them. The seeds usually germinate in about thirty days. Soak the seeds in warm water with a drop of weak tea for twenty-four hours before planting to help speed germination.

Plant the seeds in a half and half mixture of good soil and sphagnum moss in a flowerpot; cover the seeds with about a half inch of the mixture. Keep the soil moist but not soggy wet. A soil temperature of 70 to 80 degrees is best. The seedlings should not be exposed to direct sunlight.

During the winter, these plants do best in a southern window where they get sunshine. They prefer temperatures from 55 to 60 degrees at night and 70 to 75 degrees during the day.

Put them outdoors for the summer where they can get the morning sun. Do not take them out of their pots. These plants need a lot of water when they're bearing flowers and fruit. Sometimes the miniature oranges may have flowers, green fruit, and ripe fruit on them all at the same time.

In late fall, the plants should be kept cool and somewhat on the dry side. At other times of the year, give them a pinch of soluble fertilizer dissolved in water once a month.

Citrus plants require an acid soil, but tap water is usually alkaline. If the leaves turn yellowish but the veins remain green, your plant has an iron deficiency, which occurs when the soil is not acid enough. A pinch or two of iron chelate tablet dissolved in water will take care of this problem.

Coffee seeds take four to eight weeks to sprout. Unroasted coffee beans can be planted but even better are ripe coffee cherries from a coffee plant, like those that grow in a botanical garden. Remove the pulp from the cherries by hand. After pulping, put the seeds in a glass of water overnight. The next day, wash the beans in fresh water and plant at once.

The beans can be planted in a half and half mixture of good soil and peat moss or in shredded sphagnum moss in a flowerpot. Wet the sphagnum thoroughly and then squeeze out the excess water. Cover the beans lightly with sphagnum or soil.

If sphagnum is used, you must fertilize as soon as the seedlings appear. Give them a weak nutrient solution every week. When the seedling has four leaves, plant it in an individual pot, using the same mixture of good soil and peat.

Your coffee plant will require sunlight and should be fertilized lightly once a month during spring and summer. Water when the soil feels dry to your touch. Occasionally spray or sponge the shiny green leaves with water to rid them of dust.

In six to eight years, a coffee plant may produce fragrant white flowers and red cherries, but that isn't likely in your home because the conditions aren't as favorable as where coffee grows outdoors.

For a wider variety of seeds, check out the packaged seeds at your local garden center. For mail-order shopping, request a catalog from the Park Seed Company, Cokesbury Road, Greenwood, SC 29647-0001.

Whatever the source or variety of your packaged seeds, begin by reading the directions and any special planting instructions. Use peat pot liners in 2¼-inch clay pots. The liners should be soaked in water, then filled with a mixture of one-half soil and one-half professional potting mix. Mix two teaspoons of Epsom salts into each quart of soil blend.

Plant each seed according to package instructions, cover the pots with a sheet of clear plastic, and store in a dimly lit location. If you have to keep the pots somewhere bright, cover the plastic with a single sheet of newspaper. Every day, remove the condensation from the underside of the plastic and mist the seeds. When sprouts appear, move the pots into bright, indirect sunlight.

STARTING FROM EXISTING PLANTS

Nature provides the best methods to propagate each plant species; you'll get the best results if you follow Mother Nature's lead. Later in this chapter I describe some common houseplants and the best propagation method to reproduce each one. Here's a description of each method.

Stem cuttings. This is the most popular method of starting a new plant from an existing one, like coleus. Cut a three-inch-long piece from the plant's stem. Be sure the cutting has the top and at least four leaves on the stem. Dip the bottom one inch of the stem into Rootone. Poke a one-inch hole in the soil mix and put the stem into the hole, being careful not to disturb the Rootone.

Leaf cuttings. Simply place the stem of a leaf like ivy or geranium into the soil mix. For succulents, cut a mature leaf and place a third in damp soil, or place a small leaf on top of the soil and cover it lightly with the soil mix.

Plantlets. Plantlets are small plants that develop at the end of a flowery stem, as the spider plant does. Snip the plantlet from the parent plant and pin its roots into the soil of a new pot.

Offsets. Offsets are small plants that grow on the roots of the parent plant, like mother-in-law's tongue. Cut these off with some roots intact and plant in a separate pot.

Division. Plants that grow in several large bunches can be divided by cutting or pulling apart the large bunch and replanting each smaller bunch separately.

Cane cuttings. Cut the cane of a plant like aspidistra into three-inch sections with one good knuckle per piece. Lay a section on its side with a leaf facing up, then cover the lower two-thirds of the section with soil mix.

Air layering. Cut a V-shaped wedge in the stem of a large stem plant, such as dumb-cane or dracaena. Cover the cut with damp moss, surround the stem and the cut with foil or plastic (you may need tape to keep the plastic in place), keep the moss damp until roots appear, then cut off the new plant below the roots and plant in a separate pot.

Layering. Lay a length of a climbing or vining plant like tolmia across a bed of soil and pin it down at a joint; roots will form at this joint. Cut the plantlet from the old plant where it was pinned and plant in a new pot.

You can start plants from fruits and vegetables, too, using these methods.

Pineapple plants are easy to grow but they do have one special requirement: the cups formed by the bottom of the leaves must be kept filled with water. Pour the water on the leaves, and it will roll into the cups. The soil mixture should remain moist.

Cut off the pineapple's leafy top and place it on wet sand or vermiculite in a pot. Enclose the whole thing in a plastic bag and put in a bright place out of direct sunlight. Keep the cups at the bottom of the leaves wet. If the top seems to be slow to root, spray it once a week with a mild solution of soluble fertilizer.

A mature pineapple plant can be forced to bloom by placing it in a plastic sack with an apple for three days; the gas produced by the apple does the trick. After three days, remove the apple and the plastic bag. The pineapple should bloom two or three months after treatment.

Vegetables can make the most interesting houseplants. An onion, beet, or sweet potato placed half in and half out of a glass of water grows very quickly. The onion sends up long, slim, light green leaves, closely resembling those of its cousin, the narcissus. A sweet potato vine will remain in good condition for several months. The leaves are heart shaped and quite attractive. But you'll have no luck growing a sweet potato that's been treated to keep it from sprouting. Look for ones that have live eyes or sprouts on them.

Carrots and rutabaga tops should be sliced off with a horizontal cut two or three inches from the stem and placed in water. Beets can be grown the same way you grow carrots.

FEED HUNGRY PLANTS

Plants react differently to each plant food, so trial and error is the best way to find a good food for each plant. For best results, switch plant foods frequently.

Every time you mix plant food, use this high-powered water as your base.

1 gallon warm water
1 teaspoon liquid soap
1 teaspoon household ammonia
1 tablespoon hydrogen peroxide
½ teaspoon Knox gelatin

Combine these ingredients.

Every third batch, add a capful of whiskey or one-quarter cup of beer and a teaspoon of clear corn syrup.

Keep your hands, tools, pots, work area, and plants clean to help ensure the health of your plants. In return for a little effort to start your plants and following the three-step system of houseplant care—feeding, watering, and cleaning—you'll get a houseful of pride.

METHODS TO USE FOR COMMON HOUSEPLANTS

African violet	Seed, leaf cuttings
Aglaonema (Chinese evergreen)	Offset
Anthurium	Seed, division
Asparagus fern	Seed, division
Aspidistra	Division
Begonia	Seed, leaf cuttings
Bromeliad	Seed, offset
Caladium	Division
Coleus	Seed, stem cuttings
Croton	Stem cuttings
Cyperus (umbrella plant)	Division
Dieffenbachia	Cane cuttings, air layering
Dracaena	Cane cuttings, air layering

Fatshedera	Stem cuttings
Fatsia	Stem cuttings
Ferns	Seed, plantlets, division
Ficus	Seed, air layering
Fittonia	Division, layering
Ivy	Stem cuttings
Maranta	Division
Monstera	Stem cuttings, air layering
Palms	Seed
Petargonium (geranium)	Stem cuttings
Pellionia	Division
Peperomia	Stem cuttings
Philodendron	Stem cuttings
Pilea	Seed
Pothos	Stem cuttings
Primula	Seed
Sansevieria	Leaf cuttings, offset
Schefflera	Seed, stem cuttings
Soleirollia (baby's tears)	Division
Spider plant	Plantlets
Succulents	Leaf cuttings, offset
Syngonium	Stem cuttings
Tolmiea (piggyback)	Layering
Velvet leaf	Stem cuttings, leaf cuttings
Wandering Jew	Stem cuttings

OVER-CROWDED?

If you're kind to your plants, they'll grow right out of their pots—you'll be able to see the roots coming out of the bottom. When plants are out of room, it's time to move them. Be sure to water them the night before their move. Transplant them into the next size pot (from three-inch to a four-inch pot, for ex-

ample). Use only clay pots. Cover the hole in the bottom with a partially flattened beer cap and add enough soil to the bottom to bring the top of the plant soil up to within an inch of the top of the new pot. Place the plant on top of the soil. Then press new soil around the sides, dress with charcoal, dampen, and return to its old place.

KEEP YOUR GIFT PLANTS BLOOMING

The biggest mistake most of us make when we receive a flowering plant as a gift is to give it lots of love but not enough proper care. If you follow these suggestions for the more popular gift plants' likes and dislikes, you'll be repaid with an abundance of blooming glory.

Chrysanthemums Potted chrysanthemums are usually the longest-lasting flowering houseplants.

Keep yours in a good light and in the coolest spot you can find. Water it well and frequently, about every other day, or when the soil becomes dry to the touch. Spraying the foliage with water helps. After your plant has bloomed, cut it back to about eight inches tall and keep it moist but not wet. Hardy varieties can be planted outside, but many of the varieties you receive as flowering plants are not hardy. To be on the safe side, plant them all in well-protected spots and keep them well covered if you want to attempt to carry them over the winter outside.

Azaleas Azaleas need bright light but not strong sun. The soil should be evenly moist and the temperature kept between 55 and 65 degrees. You'll have better luck in keeping your azalea happy if you remove the foil or other covering from the pot and submerge the pot in a pan of water every other day for fifteen to twenty minutes and then allow it to drain. Spray the foliage with water three or four times a week. If you'd like to try to keep your azalea alive indoors indefinitely, give it a chance to replenish its strength after it finishes blooming. In the summer, set the pot in the ground in light shade where it is protected from hot winds. Water it regularly and feed with fertilizer for acid-loving plants. Bring it inside in early fall and place it in a cool, light location, keeping the soil moist but not wet. When you see bud activity, provide more sun, water, and fertilizer.

Easter lilies Keep your Easter lily in a cool spot, well out of the sun. Check it daily, adding water when the soil is dry and sandy on top. Water well then, being sure the moisture goes to the bottom of the pot and drains. Remove blossoms as they fade and pinch out the yellow anthers as new buds open. Keep your plant watered and growing in good light after it has flowered. When it dies down and the weather warms, plant it outside in a sunny place, pot and all. If you wish to try for bloom indoors again, replant the bulb in the fall in a pot with only two inches of soil beneath the bulb. Place the pot in your unheated garage until December, then bring it indoors and keep at a temperature no higher than 60 degrees until foliage appears. Then provide water, light, and fertilizer.

Bulb plants The blooms on your bulb plant will last longer if you place the plant in a cool, light place. Water it when the soil starts to dry out, probably every day. Remove the old flowers when they've faded, but allow the foliage to mature by continuing to water the plant. As soon as the garden soil can be worked, the bulb can be removed from the pot and planted outdoors to provide enjoyment for you again next year in the garden.

Hydrangeas Your hydrangea will bloom for a long time if you keep it well watered and out of direct sun. You'll need to water it at least twice a day, or submerge the pot in a pan of water daily, let it soak for about ten minutes, and then let it drain. After your plant has finished blooming, cut back all of the stems with flowers and then plant it in your garden in a shady area. The stems that have not bloomed will often produce blooms the same summer. If you bring the plant back inside for winter, cut it back severely after it has bloomed and repot it in fresh planter mix. Keep it in full sun, give it a great deal of water, and feed with fish tablets (pressed fish fertilizer) once a week.

Gloxinias Gloxinias are unusual houseplants with handsome, velvety foliage and flowers in striking colors. If you give them proper care, the plants will last for months. They require full light but should not be placed in direct sun. Keep the soil uniformly moist. When it starts to become dry, set the pot in about an inch of water until the soil becomes moist. If this isn't convenient, water may be applied to the top of the soil, but avoiding wetting the foliage.

Cyclamen To get the greatest enjoyment from this colorful plant, keep it in a cool, bright place. A temperature of 55 degrees at night and 70 degrees during the day is ideal. When the soil starts to dry out, supply enough water to wet it to the bottom. If it gets too dry and the flowers wilt, submerge the pot in water for about five minutes or until the soil is wet again.

Roses Place the plant in a cool, light spot. Keep the soil uniformly moist. Water thoroughly when it starts to dry out. Cut off old blooms as they fade. Treat your gift like a packaged rose when you plant it outside.

Poinsettias Poinsettias can be enjoyed longer if you check the soil every day and water when it's dry to the touch. Don't allow the soil to dry out completely or to remain soaked. Place near a warm, sunny window, but not touching the glass. If you want to enjoy the plant another season, stop watering it and store it in a cool, dry place when the leaves fall off. In spring, water it again and cut the stems back to six inches tall. Keep the stems pinched back as new leaves begin to form to make a short, compact plant. From early October until blooming starts, place the plant in a dark closet (without a single flash of light) for twelve hours out of every twenty-four at night, say 8:00 P.M. until 8:00 A.M., and keep in a sunny window for the other twelve hours of the day. Fertilize during active growth.

HOUSEPLANT IDENTIFICATION

SCIENTIFIC NAME	COMMON NAME
Adiantum	Maidenhair fern
Aglaonema commutatum	Chinese evergreen
Asparagus plumosus	Asparagus fern
Aspidistra	Parlor palm
Begonia	Begonia
Bougainvillea	Bougainvillea
Bromeliad	Bromeliad
Calathea	Calathea
Chlorophytum	Spider plant
Cissus antarctica	Kangaroo vine
Cissus discolor	Cissus discolor
Codiaeum	Croton
Coleus	Flame nettle
Cordyline	Cordyline
Cryptanthus	Earth stars
Cyperus	Umbrella plant
Dieffenbachia	Dumb-cane
Dizygotheca	Finger aralia
Dracaena	Dragon plant
Fatshedera lizei	Fathead lizzie
Fatsia japonica	Fig-leaf palm
Ficus benjamina	Weeping fig
Ficus elastica	Rubber plant
Ficus lyrata	Fiddle fig
Ficus pumila	Climbing fig
Fittonia	Fittonia
Grevillea robusta	Silver oak
Hedera	All of the ivy family
Helxine soleirolia	Mind your business
Maranta	Prayer plant
Monstera deliciosa	Swiss cheese plant
Neanthe elegans	Dwarf palm
Nidularium	Bird's nest bromeliad
Pandanus	Screw-pine

SCIENTIFIC NAME	COMMON NAME
Peperomia	Pepper elder
Philodendron	Sweetheart vine
Pilea cadierei	Aluminum plant
Platycerium bifurcatum	Staghorn fern
Rhoeo discolor	Boat lily
Rhoicissus rhomboidea	Grape ivy
Sansevieria	Mother-in-law's tongue
Saxifraga sarmentosa	Mother of thousands
Scindapsus	Devil's ivy
Setcreasea purpurea	Purple trailer
Syngonium	Goose foot
Tetrastigma voinierianum	Chestnut vine
Tolmiea menziesii	Piggyback plant
Tradescantia fluminensis	Wandering Jew
Zebrina pendula	Purple-leaf wandering Jew

MIDSUMMER REPOT

• •

I often wonder what goes through your minds as you read these pages. I wonder if you wonder if a gardener's work is ever done. The answer is NO! If I run out of chores to do around the yard or garden, I soon become bored and stalk around the yard, into the garage, and out to the potting shed looking for something to do. And I always find something. My gardening is a labor of love, not a boring burden. Yes, I get tired out from the physical effort of many of the jobs like mowing and digging, but when I rest, at least I call it rest!

In August, I repot most of my houseplants, the ones that are outdoors for the summer. Those of you who have been my garden friends for a number

"If roots are feet, pots are shoes."

of years know that I have a potting shed out back that my son Jeff and I built. On a nice bright day, I take a couple of the bigger plants back to the shed, take them out of their current pot and place them into a clean (not new in most cases) *clay* pot. I stress clay because they're my plants' favorite shoes (if roots are feet, pots are shoes). I don't increase the size of the pot unless I have a reason to do so.

Let me walk you through the steps.

1. Find a nice, cool shady spot to set up a permanent or temporary potting shed.

2. The bench should be thirty to thirty-six inches wide, waist high or high enough to place a comfortable chair under, and long enough to put your soil, pots, flats and other paraphernalia on as you work.

3. Soak new pots for a half day in a warm soapy water with some bleach added to the liquid dish detergent. Scrub them squeaky clean; use a cheap bristle brush or plastic cleaning pad.

4. Mix 75 percent Hyponex professional soil with 25 percent light garden soil to use if you need to add soil to the pots.

5. Water the repotted plants. Don't overwater when the temperature is high.

6. Shower the foliage to clean it. Keep foliage clean and cool with a daily shower.

7. Return the plants to a comfortable location, still outdoors, until it is time to move indoors.

Houseplants can be given a new lease on life if you repot them every summer, especially the temperamental fig trees.

I collect all sizes of clay pots from my friends and neighbors who don't recognize their value. Spoil yourself and build a potting shed where you can rest, relax, and make plant friends.

SNOWBIRDS CAN STILL ENJOY PLANTS

Every year, before winter's icy storms blanket their homes, many senior citizens in the northern United States and Canada pack up their belongings and head south to warmer climates. Some of these snowbirds, as they're called, set up shop in plush motor homes, while others live in permanent winter quarters. Either way, reestablishing a household usually involves opening up and airing out residences that may have been idle or unoccupied for months. One way to freshen the air and retrieve that "homey" appearance is to place a few fresh plants inside the motor home or house. An added advantage to having plants in the home is that they help clean the air that we breathe.

According to research conducted by the Florida Foliage Association, most senior citizens living in Florida during the winter months say they love plants and want to have them in their winter homes. Many of the seniors, however, say they don't have plants because they can't take the plants with them when it's time for them to travel north again. Now snowbirds can hire the services of a plant rental and/or maintenance firm.

A firm like this will place plants in your home and care for them on a regular basis. If the plant dies, then the maintenance firm is responsible for replacing it, unless you did something to cause it

"Place smallish house-plants on top of your radio or stereo from time to time. The vibrations will keep the circulation moving, and besides, they love music."

to die. If you did, it's usually your responsibility to replace the plant. When you head back, you don't have to worry about what to do with your plants. The maintenance firm either takes them back or takes care of them in your home while you're up north. You can even choose plants for a particular occasion and return them after the event. What an easy way to add special flair to any festivity!

Most plant rental/maintenance firms will accept short- or long-term rental agreements. The cost for these services varies depending on the number of plants you choose, their size and varieties. Before you sign with a plant rental company, make sure they can get the plants you want and will care for them once they're installed. What a simple alternative plant rental is!

YOUR INVITED GUEST

Seventy-five to eighty million homes and apartments have a friendly houseplant or two living or trying to live. It seems to me from my mail and conversations that the fault here is with most of you, not with the plants. Remember, you invited the plants to your house or office; they didn't tap you on the shoulder as you walked by and beg to go along. So it's your responsibility to make them feel welcome and safe. They in turn will do everything in their power to please you.

Although some people say they just can't grow plants, that's foolish. If you take the time to spend some time with your green friends, have the patience to wait for them to do their thing and, last but not least, have the persistence to stick with a sick plant 'til death do you part, anything will grow.

Plants get as hungry as you do, and the bigger they grow the more they eat. So feed them constantly. Feed foliage plants with high-nitrogen food and flowering plants with any flowering-plant food, a little bit every time you water.

PLANTS HAVE PERSONALITY

"You are the provider, protector, and confidant of your plants. Learn their language, so you can carry on an interesting conversation."

A lot's been said or written about plant sensitivity. In my opinion, and in my experience, plants do have feelings and will produce for someone they like and pout and be stubborn for someone they dislike. Anyone who doubts that plants are anything more than just a glob of green on the end of a stick need only watch the Venus flytrap in action or see the sensitivity plant open and close at the touch of a hand. Anyone who says he's grown tomatoes and not talked to them at least once or twice when they looked ill, isn't telling all. You'll be in close contact with your houseplants all winter, and you'll begin to feel an affection for each one of them. Remember, the feeling will be mutual. You're the provider, protector, and confidant of your plants. Learn their language, that you might carry on an interesting conversation!

QUESTIONS AND ANSWERS......................................

Q. *How can I turn my black thumb green?*
A. Paint it. Seriously, though, everyone has a green thumb; you were born with it. It's just that some thumbs ripen sooner than others. Pride, patience, and persistence, along with practice, are the only necessary ingredients to turn any thumb green.

Q. *Which plants are really houseplants?*
A. Any plant that grows in the house is a houseplant. If a maple tree was happy growing in your living room, it would be a houseplant. If you can recreate the normal living conditions of any plant in your home, it can survive.

Q. *Can I grow fruits and vegetables indoors?*
A. Sure you can. What do you think those little orange, lemon, and lime trees, not to mention avocado trees, tiny tomatoes, cucumbers, and so on, are doing? All you have to remember is that the plant's comfort is what counts.

Q. *Does talking to plants really work?*
A. Don't ask me; ask one of your plants. You already know where I stand—close! (My fern is hard of hearing.)

Q. *Is it true that plants for sale in supermarkets are not as good as those available in plant shops?*
A. Heck, no. They both buy from the same sources,

and that's a fact! It's what happens after they arrive that makes the difference. The produce man doesn't have the time for care that a plant man does, so the plants have to wait in line with the cabbages and the cucumbers.

Q. *Are there places inside where plants won't grow?*
A. Airtight closets, inside the oven, in a closed refrigerator, and in a hot furnace. Outside of those few places, no.

Q. *How come all plants I purchase have bugs?*
A. Because you've been visiting dirty plant shops. If a shop doesn't look clean, smell clean, and feel clean, don't go in—or if you do, don't bring anything out.

Q. *I'm on welfare and don't have much money, but I'd like some plants. Which ones don't cost much, grow fast, and won't die?*
A. The ones you're looking for are watermelon, squash, cantaloupe, cucumber, zucchini squash, any one of which makes a great houseplant. Chickweed and wandering Jew are also inexpensive plants.

Q. *Where do most tropical houseplants come from?*
A. Most of our tropical houseplants come from Honduras to Florida and California and then on to us.

Q. *What's the difference between cactus and succulents?*
A. To touch is to know; that's all, just thorns. They eat, sleep, and think the same.

Q. *Is it true you shouldn't buy plants when the temperature is below freezing?*
A. Plants should never be exposed to temperatures below 50 degrees. If you can guarantee they won't be, then you can buy and transport them at any time.

Q. *Are plants grown in plastic pots better than those grown in clay pots?*
A. If you're the commercial grower and paying the freight to ship, they are. But I prefer that you put your plants in clay work shoes and then set them down into the beautiful decorative planters, so you can easily change their wardrobe from time to time.

Q. *What do you think of buying houseplants through mail order?*
A. There are good and bad companies in any business. I have run into both, but never the same one twice.

Q. *This may seem like a stupid question, but what's the best kind of top to put on a plant counter I am building?*
A. Not to me, it's not. Cover the counter with metal, glass, plastic, or Formica so that it can be kept super clean and free of germs and insects.

Q. *What tools do you really need if you're going to have a great many indoor plants?*
A. I have three bent forks I use as rakes, five spoons in varying sizes with the sides bent over to use as shovels and scoops, two sharp knives, a pair of tweezers, a toenail clipper for cutting stems, scissors, and a razor blade in a cork. That should do you.

Q. *Can you have too many plants in a room?*
A. Only if the plants are dirty or buggy.

Q. *Have you ever seen a soil sample under a microscope? What are all those bugs?*
A. Your guess is as good as mine. Some of them are good microscopic bacteria that give the soil its grow power, while others are real pests.

Q. *Where can I find a book or a chart that tells me which plants to go with what decor?*
A. Take a look at all the home-decorating magazines. You'll see what you're looking for aesthetically, but in most cases it's deadly for the plant. Use your own imagination.

Q. *Should you test houseplant soil for anything other than acidity?*
A. No, it's not necessary.

Q. *What's the best soil-testing kit?*
A. A cheap one.

Q. *Is garden soil good for potting plants?*
A. I use it and don't have too much trouble. Just keep your eyes open for insect problems, and treat any immediately.

Q. *What's a good houseplant soil mix?*
A. Equal parts of garden soil, peat moss, or sawdust and sand or perlite. Most commercial planter mixes will do just fine.

Q. *What kind of soil does cactus like?*
A. I have pretty good luck with a heavier soil mix and sand.

Q. *Are ashes good to mix with soil for plants?*
A. Sure they are, but don't get carried away; a little goes a long way. Two handfuls are enough for a bucket of soil mix.

Q. *Can sawdust be used in place of peat moss?*
A. I know lots of growers who do use it. However, you'll have to feed a little more often until the sawdust begins to decay.

Q. *What good do coffee grounds do plants? And should you mix them into soil used for repotting?*
A. Coffee grounds help keep the soil loose and build up acidity for plants that like rich soil, such as citrus, azaleas, and gardenias.

Q. *Are eggshells good to put into the soil?*
A. They only help lighten heavy soil. Crush them as fine as powder.

Q. *Can I use sandbox sand for rooting cuttings?*
A. If you mean beach sand, no. Beach sand packs together. The plants prefer sharp sand (builder's sand).

Q. *Explain the difference between peat moss, sphagnum moss, perlite, and vermiculite, and what they're used for.*
A. Peat moss is a fine, muck-base decomposed plant material. Sphagnum moss is a coarser, fibrous moss that almost looks like dried seaweed. Perlite is an expanded rock material, and vermiculite is a layered insulation material. They are all excellent soil conditioners and rooting mediums.

Q. *How do you steam-sterilize soil?*
A. Boiling water poured over it will generally do

the trick, or steam it for two hours under a canvas cover.

Q. *Does baking soil make it clean?*
A. Sure it does, but it smells dreadful. Cook at 250 degrees for one hour.

Q. *Do you have to have several different kinds of plant food?*
A. A recent survey shows that most people have between six and eight different brands of plant food sitting on their shelves. That's a waste. I suggest you have only two—one for boy plants and one for girl plants. If a plant flowers or makes fruits or vegetables, I consider it a girl and feed it with a flowering plant food called Bloomin. If, on the other hand, the plant is all foliage, it's a boy in the garden world, and boy plants are fed with a foliage food called Substral Earth Food.

Q. *Can you make your own plant food?*
A. Sure you can, but it isn't quite a full diet for your plants; and also don't overdo. This is the one my aunt Florence uses.
To one gallon of warm water add:

½ teaspoon children's shampoo
1 teabag
10% of any houseplant food
½ teaspoon Knox gelatin
½ teaspoon household ammonia
1 capful of whiskey

Q. *How often should you feed houseplants?*
A. I feed every time I water.

Q. *I heard that birth-control pills are good for houseplants. Is this true?*

A. It's true for estrogen pills only, and then they work great on all but the African violet and other plants with hairy leaves—they bleach out the color of the leaves. To use on the rest of your plants, add one pill to three gallons of water and use once a month. Do not use on edible plants.

Q. *What do you use Epsom salts on?*

A. Epsom salts—magnesium sulphate—are used to deepen the color of flowers or colored foliage, thicken petals and foliage, and stimulate root growth. I add one-quarter teaspoon for each four-inch pot in the fall. For outside use, one-half cup per rose in the spring.

Q. *What do you think of fish emulsion plant food?*

A. I think it "stinks" (smell only), but it sure does the job on orchids and the rest of the Hawaiian group—bird of paradise, antherium, and the like. Use fish emulsion sparingly, as a little goes a long way.

Q. *How can you tell if you've overfed your plants?*

A. Generally the leaves will wilt, shrivel, and be soft. If you see these symptoms, water through the soil to flush it out, and pray.

Q. *Can I use lime on my houseplants?*

A. If you're using liquid, it's ½ teaspoon per quart of water. Dry, it's one cup per ½ bushel of soil mix, and then test.

Q. *Is gypsum a source of calcium?*

A. You bet your grass and the rest of your plants it's calcium! I add one pound per bushel of soil mix and three tablespoons per four-inch pot in spring and fall to my indoor houseplants.

Q. *What do you feed cactus?*
A. Rattlesnakes, scorpions, tarantulas—I'm just kidding. Boy cactus gets boy food and girl cactus gets girl food. You tell the difference the same way as with other plants.

Q. *What do you feed orchids?*
A. I use Substral Bloomin, and then once a month I give them a treat and serve fish.

Q. *How often do you feed poinsettia?*
A. As often as any other flowering plant. (See page 365.)

Q. *What is meant by acid plant food?*
A. That is plant food that contains more salts than others. Azaleas, citrus plants, gardenias, and rhododendrons are the acid group. I use weak coffee once a month for my indoor plants.

Q. *What type of plant food do you use if you're growing plants hydroponically?*
A. I continue to use the same plant food and in the same manner—10 percent of the recommended rate.

Q. *How many hours of light do plants need indoors?*
A. Plants need the same amount of light for the same length of time indoors as they do outdoors, but not all plants need the same amount of light for the same length of time. Plants vary in likes and dislikes as much as people do. Look in your local newspaper to find out what time the sun comes up on the longest day of the year (the first

day of summer). Then study the light requirements of plants you wish to befriend and see if you have locations to make them happy.

Q. *What kind of lights should I buy to grow plants indoors?*
A. Along with natural light, I use Duro-lites, 75- and 150-watt plant lights, as well as GE and Sylvania.

Q. *What the hell difference does it make to the plants if they get red or blue rays?*
A. The same difference it does to your body. Man, plant, and animals need sunshine to survive, and pure sunlight contains a perfect combination of violet, blue, orange, yellow, green, and red light. Red light makes the plant mature faster, while the blues tend to make the plants short, fat, and have dark green foliage without too many flowers. So we must get a good mix of both. There are at least a dozen books that go into growing plants under lights. About the best I know is one by a friend of mine, Elvin McDonald, *The Complete Book of Gardening Under Lights*, and it's in paperback.

Q. *How close should plants be to a light source?*
A. A rule of thumb is twelve to eighteen inches with forty- to sixty-watt bulbs, but then I must remind you that I could probably write a whole book on this subject. The Duro-lite Lamp Company at 17-10 Willow Street, Fairlawn, New Jersey, 07410 has a super little book for $1.

Q. *Which window exposure is best for which plants?*
A. I am only going to name a few of the more common plants for each location, so don't be offended if your favorite is not on the list.

Bright Light: South or West with a Sheer Curtain

African violet
Amaryllis
Aphelandra
Azalea
Baby's tears
Cactus and succulents
Christmas cactus
Chrysanthemum
Citrus plants (all types)
Croton *Codaeum*
Cyclamen
Gardenia
Gloxinia
Hedera (ivy)
Hibiscus
Hoya (waxplant)
Jade plant
Jerusalem cherry
Kalanchoe
Lanpranthus
Pittosporum
Poinsettia
Yucca

Medium Light: East Window

Anthurium
Asparagus fern
Begonia
Bromeliad
Caladium
Chlorophytum (spider plant)
Dieffenbachia (dumbcane)
Dracaena godseffiana, sanderiana
Fiddleleaf fig
Fuchsia
Grape ivy
Hydrangea
Matanta (prayer plant)
Nephthytis
Orchids (all)
Palms
Peperomia
Piggyback plant
Pothos (marble queen)
Rubberplant
Schefflera
Wandering Jew

Shady: North Window

Aspidistra
Bamboo palm
Dracaena marginata and *massangeana*
Kentia palm
Nephrolepis
Philodendron
Sansevieria
Spathiphyllum

Q. *How can you tell when a plant doesn't have enough light?*
A. In most cases, lack of light is indicated by pale, yellowish foliage, few flowers, and funny-shaped leaves. Leaves will begin to fall off all over; growth almost stops; buds only half open. That enough symptoms?

Q. *Can plants get too much light?*
A. I don't know why folks seem to think all plants are night owls and want light twenty-four hours a day, but I will let you in on a little secret. Plants only grow when they get proper sleep in the dark. If they stay up too long, they'll wilt just like you will, and their leaves will get burned spots on them.

Q. *What does diffused light mean?*
A. Light that's spread out or toned down; what results from putting a sheer curtain in front of a west or south window.

Q. *Which is the best exposure outdoors in the summer for my houseplants?*
A. The same exposure that's best for them inside. Just remember, when we bring them inside, we're trying to recreate the plant's normal living conditions.

Q. *Will a humidifier that I installed myself keep enough moisture in the house for most houseplants?*
A. It will help, but it's still not enough for your plants. It's lack of humidity that causes the edges of the leaves to turn yellow or brown, buds to shrivel up, and leaves to fall off all over. As a rule, a temperature of 70 degrees should be accompanied by 40 percent humidity. I suggest you get two or three inexpensive humidity gauges at your hardware store to check.

Q. *What damage does a dehumidifier do to plants?*
A. Your dehumidifier draws humidity out of the air, and houseplants need moisture in the air. By the way, the water from your dehumidifier is super for watering plants. Almost the best. Same with your air-conditioner water.

Q. *Is it true that an air conditioner is bad for plants not because of the temperature but something else?*
A. It's kind of ironic. In the summer we like our homes at 70 degrees, and so do plants, but the way an air conditioner works, it draws the humidity out of the house, which kills plants. But if you were to put 40-percent moisture into the room for the plants' sake, the air conditioner would die.

Q. *Can I use my baby's vaporizer for moisture in the air for plants?*
A. That's a great idea; we do it all the time, even in small greenhouses.

Q. *How close to my aquarium should my plants be to do any good?*
A. On top, next to, and all around—the closer the better. By the way, you can water your plants with that water.

Q. *Does spraying the foliage really help?*
A. Yep, sure does—once a day from September to December, and twice a day from January to May. I use a weak solution of tea in my Hudson Cordless electric sprayer.

Q. *Is a room humidifier as good as a central one?*
A. It is for that room, but not for the rest of the house, you, or your plants, if any of you leave that room.

Q. *Does an air purifier help or hurt plants?*
A. Heck, any time you hold dust down or eliminate it, it helps you, your plants, and your pets. You bet it helps.

Q. *Will a pan of water on a register help my plants?*
A. I kicked over many a pan of water that was sitting on the floor register at Grandma Putt's on my way to the toilet in the dark. And my Grandma was the plant expert of experts.

Q. *If the foliage dries up, how do you get moisture back into it?*
A. First, water the plant with warm water and shower the foliage with soapy warm water. Then put a brick in the bottom of a bucket, set the plant on the brick, pour boiling water into the bucket. Cover the bucket with a towel and leave for a three- to four-minute steam bath.

Q. *When is the best time to mist plants?*
A. I try to mist just before we all go to sleep (plants, kids, and me and Ilene) and again before noon. Remember to put in some tea. The tannic acid in tea helps the plants' digestive system; it's also a wetting agent.

Q. *If I give my plants a shower every day with soap or baby shampoo, will it help the foliage?*
A. Yeah, but don't get carried away. Every couple of days is enough, if you have to. I wash every two weeks unless a heavy smoker has spent some time at my house.

Q. *Is gas heat bad for plants?*
A. Not unless you've got a leak, and then it's a real killer for plants, pets, and people.

Q. *Is it true that if you burn a fire in your fireplace, houseplants will die?*

A. Heck, no! Whoever told you that? If you were to have the plant on the hearth where it could cook, then it might die; but heat is heat.

Q. *What temperature do plants like best?*

A. As a rule most house plants like between 62 degrees at night and 74 degrees during the day, and so should you.

Q. *What do people mean when they speak of proper air circulation for plants?*

A. The same thing they mean when they tell you that you should have good air circulation. It means to move the air around in a room. That's why you have cold air returns in your home. I often let a small oscillating fan run in the winter to move more air.

Q. *What makes my plants grow crooked all the time?*

A. You don't take them for a walk every day. Turn the pots at least half a turn each day so that they get the same light exposure all over.

Q. *How can you tell when it's too hot for plants?*

A. When it's too hot for you. If you feel uncomfortable, so will your plants. First, the leaves will wilt, then dry up, then they'll fall off from the top. Then the roots will rot. 70 to 74 degrees is plenty high enough for both of you.

Q. *What are the symptoms of plants that are too cold?*

A. The leaves will immediately droop and become grayish—almost black—overnight. They'll also look like they have goose bumps.

Q. *Is water from a water softener bad for plants?*
A. You can bet your pots on it 'cause that's all you are going to have left—the plants will be dead. Take the water out ahead of the softener.

Q. *How do you purify water for plants?*
A. Poke small holes in the bottom of a washed-out quart milk carton and fill it half full with agricultural charcoal. Add crushed, washed shells from a dozen eggs and run water through this. Most of the salts that cause the white powder to collect on the soil and pots will be gone.

Q. *Is water from my defroster, dehumidifier, snow, and rain all the same?*
A. Can't find much better, unless you have a pipeline to heaven.

Q. *How often do you water houseplants?*
A. When they need it. Depends on the season, your house, the plant, and your memory. As a rule, I water when the soil feels dry to the touch at least an inch or two down into the soil.

Q. *When do you water houseplants?*
A. I try to water in the morning, because that's when I'm thirsty.

Q. *Which is the best way to water—top or bottom?*
A. When it rains from hell, I will water from the bottom.

Q. *How often do you water a terrarium?*
A. When the soil looks dry, remove the cover and feel it. If you can't get your hand in, find some way to get a soil sample up.

Q. *What's the best way to water a terrarium?*
A. With a plastic straw. Mix water, food, and soap just as though you were going to water regular houseplants. Then place a straw in the water and cover the end with your thumb. Remove the straw from the water, place it down into the terrarium, and remove your thumb. Not bad, eh?

Q. *Why do you always say to add soap to water?*
A. Soap makes water wetter, bugs don't like the taste of it, and I believe in clean soil. Dirt is filthy, and my plants and I don't use dirt.

Q. *Are those water meters, gauges, and sticks any good?*
A. Darn right, they are! If you have the cents, they make lots of sense.

Q. *What's a nice, simple way to water plants when you're on vacation?*
A. With someone else's hands, or you can buy some great watering devices.

Q. *How often should you water hanging baskets?*
A. Use the same rule as for plants with no hangups.

Q. *Which plants are best indoors for hanging baskets?*
A. Any plant that grows outside can grow indoors. Plants best suited for hanging baskets are fantana, Christmas cactus, wandering Jew, fuchsia, spider plant, strawberry begonia, hoya, ivies, and any of the melon or squash plants, and a cucumber thrown in.

Q. *Which plants would you recommend for terrariums?*
A. This may seem as if I'm pulling your leg, but I'm serious. Any weed that grows under trees or shrubs like chickweed, moss, wild ferns, small toadstools, lichens, coleus, wandering Jew, begonias, African violets, and peperomias will do well.

Q. *What plants would you pick for a dark room?*
A. Aspidistra, bamboo palm, *Dracaena marginata*, *Dracaena massangeana*, Kentia palm, *Nephrolepis*, *Philodendron*, *Sansevieria*, and *Spathiphyllum*.

Q. *I am a traveling bachelor. Which plants would you recommend for me?*
A. How about a tomato? Well, I tried. Well, Don Juan, any plant that likes it cool, dim, and damp, which ends up with rex begonias, wax begonias, and ferns. A staghorn should fit your way of life or maybe a bird's-nest fern. Get the picture?

Q. *Which plants can I start indoors from seed?*
A. Any plant that has seeds you can start from seed indoors.

Q. *How do you do root cuttings?*
A. There are hardwood and softwood cuttings. For complete instructions on when, how, and why, you must purchase a package of Rootone rooting hormone, and with it you get the best instructions. Honest Injun!

Q. *How long do bulbs have to cool before you can plant them?*
A. Bulbs have got to cool at below 40 degrees for ten to twelve weeks. You can cool them in the refrigerator or underground.

Q. *Which bulbs grow indoors?*
A. All of them.

Q. *Can you give me a list of things that can go wrong with houseplants and how to spot them?*
A. I will give you a few of the common problems and how to spot them.
Ends of leaves turn black: plant was in a cold place too long.
Ends of leaves turn brown: plant was in a warm, dry draft or not enough humidity
Leaves just wilt: room is too hot, or the plant wants a drink, or you have a gas leak
Mature leaves turn yellow and fall off: plant is starving to death
Little tap leaves turn yellow: plant needs iron and more light
Leaves fall off from the bottom: you are overwatering, and the plant does not get enough light
Leaves fall off from the top: not enough water and humidity is too low
If the plant stops growing but looks pretty good: too much light and outgrowing its pot

Q. *When do you transplant a houseplant?*
A. When its roots grow out through the hole in the bottom, or when they just seem to stand still.

Q. *Why do all the plants I transplant die?*
A. Because they go into shock. Water the plant twenty-four hours before transplanting, soak the new clay pot for one hour before, and use damp soil. Feed right after with a plant hormone food.

Q. *Do plants really like music?*
A. They sure do, especially anything with a bass beat that you can feel physically.

Q. *Talking to plants is just a fake, right?*
A. Moses talked to a burning bush and Christ to a fig tree. If you can talk to a flat tire or a cake that flops, you can talk to a tree.

Q. *I saw you use a pest strip for insect control in houseplants on TV. How does it work?*
A. If you have lots of plants, just hang a strip close by. If you have a few plants spread out, cut the strip into one-inch squares. Drill a hole into the end of each and put a stick into the hole so that it looks like a lollipop. Place one in each pot.

Q. *What good does it do to give plants people names too?*
A. It makes me remember each one easier; I flunked Latin twice. Besides, you can't call them all "Hey, you!" when carrying on a conversation.

Q. *Why do the blossoms on my gardenia fall off?*
A. The gardenia (*Gardenia jasminois* or 'Veitchii') does not want the temperature to drop below 60 degrees; it wants no surprise breezes or sudden temperature drops. It likes a lot of humidity, which you don't have in the wintertime. It likes a really rich composted mixture of leaves, peat moss, sand, and manure. Gardenias are best planted in pots and set outside on the patio in the summer when the threat of frost is gone and—*wow*—will they fill the air with perfume. The younger a plant, the more flowers. Two- to three-year-olds do the best.

Q. *Why don't my African violets keep blooming after the original flowers fall off?*
A. African violets (*Saintpaulia*) are a snap to grow if you remember they're real bloomers, which means they need lots of attention but not a great deal of care—there is a difference. To begin with,

keep the soil damp, not wet, and don't let it dry out. Water from the top, just as you would any other blooming plant. Use 10 percent of the recommended rate of any African violet plant food in your watering water, with three drops of liquid dish soap detergent per quart. Rainwater, snow, water from defrosted refrigerator ice, air-conditioner runoff, or dehumidifier water are the best. You should feed the plant every time you water. Mist foliage with warm water to help humidity, which it likes at 40 to 50 percent. Heat should be 65 to 74 degrees indoors, with twelve hours of good bright light, which should be twelve inches from plants. Grow your plants in clay pots and show them off in plastic, metal, or glass. Violets love to be root bound. Any new growth (side shoots) should be cut off with a sharp knife and planted in its own shoes.

Q. *Why do the stems of the large, lower leaves on my African violet turn brown and break or rot off?*
A. You would rot or break off if your arms rubbed on a rough old pot edge for long enough. I take an old wax candle and rub the dickens out of the edge to make it smooth. I also constantly remove older foliage to start new plants.

Q. *When do you divide an African violet?*
A. I remove any new crowns that appear as soon as they look as if they can take care of themselves in a 2¼-inch clay pot, which is clean and has been soaked for at least an hour or so. Make sure that the added soil is damp and that the plant has been watered at least twenty-four hours before.

Q. *How do you divide violets?*
A. With an extremely sharp knife. Simply cut the newer crowns away from the older plant, keeping as much soil as is necessary and some roots to in-

sure a good start. I keep my newly planted violets lightly shaded for a week.

Q. *What do they mean by letting a plant rest?*
A. Producing flowers takes a lot out of a plant, so to let it rest, you can pluck off buds, take it out from under the lights, run the temperature just a little cool—65 degrees—scrub the pot, maybe give it a little shot of Epsom salts in water—one-half teaspoon per quart. Two to three weeks of rest will be enough.

Q. *Should African violets be allowed to rest and for how long?*
A. When they naturally stop blooming I let them rest, give them a physical, transplant, and then let them start again.

Q. *Can I get amaryllis bulbs to bloom more than once a year?*
A. If you want to go to a lot of trouble you can, but nine out of ten times it won't work. When the plant's through flowering, cut the foliage back to the bulb, set in a warm, bright window that's 75 degrees during the day and 70 degrees at night, feed and water as any flowering plant. When you have full-grown new leaves, stop food, water, and shut off the lights. The foliage will dry up. Cut it off and leave the plant in the dark; moisten it from time to time until you see growth start again. Then move it into the light, feed and water it, and pray.

Q. *Can you grow amaryllis from seed?*
A. Yes, but be prepared for a two- or three-year wait for flowers.

Q. *Is an avocado the same as a Calavo?*
A. Yes, the California growers promote avocados;

Florida saw a need for merchandising their product under a different name, Calavo.

Q. *What's the best way to start and grow an avocado tree?*

A. Since the fruit is good tasting and good for you, buy and eat several. (By the way, the Florida fruit is just as good as the California fruit.) Next, remove the brown hide from the pit. Place one or two pits in a glass of weak tea at room temperature, with a dash of Epsom salts, making sure that the liquid is just an inch from the butt (the point is the head). Support the pit with toothpicks. Place in a dark cupboard for five days. Now, move into sun and let it grow until the root hits the bottom of the glass and top growth has two real leaves. Transplant into a four-inch clay pot that has been soaked then filled with warm, damp African violet soil, leaving about a fourth of the pit above the soil line. Water, feed, and treat like any other houseplant. When growth is ten to twelve inches high, pick out the middle growth and watch the plant branch. Let that grow to six inches and pinch it, and so on. The others you can try by planting directly into soil to begin. Keep the soil damp. High humidity is a must.

Q. *Why do the spikes of my aloe plant get soft and spongy?*

A. *Aloe vera* is also known as the first-aid plant, hangover plant, and beauty plant. When the leaves are soft it means the plant needs water. When the leaves are firm and hard it has enough water. Aloe likes lot of light (a western exposure), dry air, and it does not like the temperature to go below 55 degrees. Feed with any foliage food added to your water.

Q. *Why won't azaleas bloom again in the house?*
A. The azalea is a flowering shrub that blooms when the temperature is cool. Most of our homes are not. To keep the flowers longer, maintain the temperature at 50 to 65 degrees; keep the soil damp, not wet. Feed it with any blooming plant food in your watering water. Azaleas can be planted in your garden and then brought into the house in the fall.

Q. *Will aglaonema do well in the shade?*
A. Yes, all of them; there are several in the family—*commutatum, fransher*, pewter plant, and silver king. It's an excellent selection for low-light rooms, but it does well in sunlight too. Don't let room temperature go below 60 degrees and keep the soil damp; feed with foliage food.

Q. *Why can't I keep baby's-tears going in my house?*
A. Baby's-tears are a weed—granted, an expensive one, but nonetheless a w-e-e-d. All you have to do to understand how to grow this popular weed is to have chickweed in your lawn. It grows under shrubs and trees where it is cool, damp, and slightly dark. May I suggest that you dig your chickweed up and tell people it's baby's-tears—they'll never know the difference, and you'll save money.

Q. *Now look! I'm not a nut, but I've just got to know if someone is pulling my leg. Is there such a thing as the singer's begonia, the Hitler begonia, and the critics' choice begonia?*
A. They are stretching the truth a little on Hitler. The singer's begonia is an orange angel wing begonia called Wayne Newton and, like the guy himself, is super. The so-called Hitler begonia is an Iron Cross begonia, and the critics' choice is a rex begonia, referring to the film critic Rex Reed. The bego-

nia is one of the most versatile plants available. All begonias prefer plenty of light and do well inside or out; they must be kept damp but not sopping wet and fed with flowering plant food. I say they're versatile because they're great for slightly shady rooms; they need 50 percent humidity and a minimum night temperature of 65 degrees.

Q. *How long do you have to wait for a bird-of-paradise to bloom?*
A. About as long as you do for a little girl—twelve years—though some develop earlier than others; seven years seems to be about average. Birds-of-paradise like warm, humid, bright living conditions. Keep them slightly damp and add your plant food to the regular watering water—15 percent of any flowering plant food.

Q. *How long after a bromeliad blooms can I expect a new shoot?*
A. I sure hope you have lots of patience, because a year to a year and a half is average. Bromeliads, of which pineapple is the most famous, like it warm—74 degrees, humidity at 50 percent and up, plenty of bright light. Feed regularly with any flowering plant food. The soil should be light and loose; wood shavings and peat are best.

Q. *If cactus is so easy to grow, why do I have so much trouble with mine?*
A. Probably because you haven't gotten the point yet. Cactus is best ignored, placed in a bright western window near heat. Water well and then don't water again until the meat feels soft (I use a blunt stick to gently poke). Succulents are the same. Keep the humidity down with cactus and feed with foliage plant food. The soil mix should be a sandy loam.

LET'S GET SERIOUS

● ●

In 1970 When I wrote the original *Plants Are Like People*, I wrote about a thousand words in chapter 16 called "Solution to Pollution." I pointed out the shortcomings of the home gardeners' attitude toward getting a handle on the ever-increasing environmental pollution problem and now, twenty years later, the attitude of the masses has not changed. They're more complacent now than they were then. Ordinary everyday litter is a disgrace along our highways and byways in the rural areas as well as the urban and suburban communities. Litter laws are ignored by the public and seldom, if ever, enforced. Solid waste has become a financial problem for communities that appease their consciences by banning the bagging of grass clippings—what a joke!

The political arenas are filled with rhetoric supplied by special interest groups, and the blame for lack of progress is on the overworked, understaffed EPA.

Is there a solution to pollution? Not in the near future; at least not that I can see.

Garden chemicals, weed killers, and bug sprays have garnered their share of media attention, with hearings and investigations by local, state, and federal governments, and unfounded charges directed at the professional lawn chemical appliers and chemical manufacturers.

Auto emissions, uncontrolled industrial waste, and airborne pollution account for more danger to the environment than an application of weed killer. The industrial moguls rape the environment every day and very few are ever punished. Let's face it: If there's any hope, it must begin with each of us doing our own soul searching for our own shortcomings as they relate to environmental house keeping.

Just the fact that you're a gardener is step one; the rest of the steps are simple. Keep your little corner of the world clean and green. Don't use chemicals to prevent a problem you don't yet have. Read and follow directions exactly. Look for sound, proven, safe, economical, commonsense ways to solve garden problems and complete your chores. "Actions speak louder than words" has never been more appropriate.

We should all just try to remember that here and now, as well as in the hereafter, we and we alone are responsible for our actions. No one can push us into hell nor pull us into heaven. We do either all by ourselves.

Do what you know is right!

THE ORGANIC MISUNDER- STANDING

Who said leopards can't change their spots? Last year's critics of the organic "nut" down the street are now piling onto the environmental bandwagon by the thousands. Calling themselves practicing ecologists, they're tooting the horn for every biological control that the Madison Avenue crowd can find a hook to hang on and sell to millions of confused home gardeners who're simply trying to keep their little corner of the world clean, green, and safe. Well, folks, it's a con designed to stampede you and your local governments into passing ordinances that will harm, rather than help, the environment.

Our leading agricultural colleges have been engaged in research for a century or more looking for controls and stimulants that will produce more and healthier foods to feed this planet. At the same time, researchers in the medical and pharmaceutical fields are finding more and more uses for natural medications—to prolong the average life expectancy closer and closer to a one-hundred-year average. I want to personally thank both schools of the academic community for this wonderful world we live in, and I look forward to each of their new discoveries.

Now for my point. Chemical garden applications are not bad or dangerous; the appliers are. Insecticides, pesticides, and herbicides do not pollute and they never have. Man pollutes through misuse and abuse. TLC, common sense, hands in pockets, and mouth shut will solve most maladies. A garden chemical or human medicine, when properly prescribed and properly used, is good for both human and environment.

When I think that a medication is needed—be it chemical cure or control—I recommend it. In some cases, it may be very strong medicine for a very strong problem, but the application will be the necessary strength for the necessary period of time.

The proper description for my type of garden practice is the "natural commonsense method."

In each issue of my newsletter, I try very hard to nudge my readers into practicing commonsense controls with commonsense products that are usually gentle, safe, low cost, effective, and, above all, environmentally friendly. Yes, I sometimes rub both the academics and the industry the wrong way because I am a "preventive gardenist." Although many of my tips, tricks, tonics, motions, potions, and lotions are entertaining and may seem a bit foolish, they all seem to work, and that's the bottom line!

FIRST LINE OF DEFENSE FOR A GARDENER IS CAUTION

By now you know that I wait until I see the whites of their eyes, the point of their stinger, or the slimy path of their travels before I bring out the heavy garden guns. I want you to become so attuned to keeping your yard, gardens, and plants clean and happy that simple natural formulas or mild medications can head off a real big battle. Here, once again, is a reminder of the line of defense.

Plants grown in soil rich in humus and minerals are less likely to be attacked by insects and disease. Some plants are labeled disease resistant; buy these whenever possible. Following are lists of biological, mechanical, and chemical insect controls.

BIOLOGICAL INSECT CONTROL

1. *Bacillus thuringiencis* (B.T., Thurcide, AT-TACK, Dipel) is a seed that causes a fatal disease in any caterpillar. B.T. is sprayed or dusted onto the plant, then eaten by the caterpillar (it soon stops feeding), which then dies in about twenty-four hours. B.T. is not toxic to humans.

2. *Bacillus popilliae* (milky spore disease) "seeds" are applied to garden, flowers, or lawn where they're eaten by grubs of the Japanese beetle, rose chafer, and others, which become diseased and die. This helps reduce the food supply of moles.

3. Dormant ladybugs may be purchased by mail and released into the garden. Adults and larvae eat aphids, mites, scale insects, among others.

4. Praying mantis egg cases may also be purchased by mail and tied to plants about a foot above soil level. Eggs hatch into carnivorous insects that eat most types of insects, especially the larva and caterpillar forms.

5. Toads eat many insects; birds are good insect

catchers, as well. A water supply for both will encourage their presence.

6. Planting chives at the base of fruit trees discourages insects from climbing up the trunk.

MECHANICAL INSECT CONTROL

1. Physical removal of insects by hosing them with water (aphids, white fly, and so on), picking them by hand (rose chafer, tomato worms), or using a stick to remove them (for tent caterpillars and nest-worms) are all surefire methods.

2. Insect traps containing odors (like sex attractants), electric bug killers, ant traps, roach traps, all help to reduce insect populations.

3. Adhesive surfaces reduce insect populations. Sticky flypaper and yellow boards painted with adhesive attract many insects in the garden. Gypsy moth tape and traps, Tanglefoot (encircling a tree), sticky red balls hung in an apple tree—all of these protect the plant without poisoning food.

4. Netting can be used to ward off rose chafers, cabbage butterflies, birds, and other pests.

LESS TOXIC INSECTICIDES

Sometimes the insects survive in spite of our efforts. The following sprays/dusts are of a more "natural origin" and may be used in severe infestations.

1. Rotenone or pyrethrum are extracts from plants and are a stomach and contact poison for insects. These are often found in aerosol sprays, especially for those houseplants.

2. Black Leaf 40 (nicotine sulphate) is a plant extract and controls many insects. See label for directions.

3. Dormant oil sprays (like Volk oil by Ortho) can be used in the spring or fall to coat branches and leaves of dormant plants. The oily coating suffocates insects and eggs of aphids, red spider, mites, and fruit worms, as well as disease spores.

4. Sulphur (Flotox-Ortho) used as directed can help control some insects and disease. See label for directions.

5. Sevin (carbaryl) kills many insects and cutworms.

6. Bordeaux mix contains copper and is an old-style material good for controlling many diseases.

7. Insecticidal soaps are now on the market and work by dissolving the tough shells on scale insects and others. The soaps are useful for moss control, as well.

MY BAKER'S DOZEN OF SPRAYING COMMANDMENTS

1. Select the right sprayer for the job. Buy the best quality you can afford. It will make spraying easier and, with good care, your sprayer will last for years. And be sure to get one that gives you full control of spray mix and application!

2. Before you spray, be sure to read all of the sprayer directions—right down to the warranty. "Test drive" your new sprayer using water to see how it works and what it will do.

3. Mix your spray materials exactly according to instructions.

4. Choose the right pressure. Use high pressure for a fine, penetrating mist that's good for flowers. Use lower pressure if you want a heavier, wetting, nondrift spray that's best for treating weeds.

5. Spot spray; don't broadcast. Spray only to the point of runoff. Avoid drenching—and waste.

6. Spray where the trouble is. Because most trouble starts under the plant leaves, it's especially important that you spray there. Cover the entire stem system, too. Spraying on target avoids waste in time and material.

7. Use an adjustable nozzle to produce a fine, cone-shaped mist for close-up applications and a coarser spray for long-range spraying or for weeds.

8. For maximum effectiveness—not to mention less wear and tear on you—spray in the cool of the day.

9. To prevent drifting of spray to nontarget areas, don't spray when the wind is blowing.

10. If you prefer to dust plants, apply the dust in the morning or evening when the air is still and when dew on the plants make the dust stick better.

11. Dress sensibly; don't wear shorts or a bathing suit when you spray. It's a good idea to wear gloves—plastic throwaways will do—and a hat if you're spraying above your head or at eye level. Wear shoes. I recommend that you wear your golf spikes when working in the yard. The spikes do two jobs at once; they improve your traction on uneven ground, and they aerate the lawn.

12. Thoroughly drain and clean your sprayer when finished, use a mild solution of warm soap and water. Wipe your equipment dry when finished. Good care will make your equipment last for many, many seasons, making it an even better investment.

13. Store sprays and dusts out of reach of children, preferably in a locked cabinet. Keep sprays in their original containers. Be sure labels are kept on containers. Do not burn empty containers.

THE TONICS ARE FOR REAL!

Wherever I go I'm asked if I'm serious when I rattle off the recipe for one of my tonics or mixtures. When I reply yes, they want to know why, if my formulas are so good, isn't someone packaging them and making a lot of money? To begin with, they're not *my* formulas, they come from generations past. I merely update the ingredient names so that you'll try them.

For example, you'll accept and use my recommendation for the use of household ammonia as a fast temporary form of nitrogen, but if I were to tell you to use dog urine instead, you would go nuts! The fact is, they both do the same thing. We usually think of this urine as something that harms, not helps, which only goes to show you that too much of a good thing can be bad. Four grams of a natural enzyme can break down the urine in your yard and restore damage.

Children's shampoo—either a synthetic or the natural fluid from the yucca plant (SSO)—is a soil softener and washes pollution from foliage, as soaps do to our skin.

Epsom salts or magnesium mixed with your fertilizer deepen color, thicken foliage, and increases roots.

Mouthwashes are bactericides that interrupt the reproductive cycle of organic bacteria.

There is no hocus-pocus in my recommendations—just a little bit of knowledge of, and faith in, the practices of past generations who have helped us get this far.

ADMITTING WE HAVE A PROBLEM IS STEP ONE TO A CURE

"Everyone has a green thumb. It's just that some thumbs ripen sooner than others."

The solution to pollution does not lie in blaming the other guy or passing the buck. It lies in understanding what ecology, environmental control, and pollution really mean and where they begin, and then determining what steps we can take to correct them.

In concluding this book, I would like to refer to the beginning, the book of Genesis, chapter I, verses 11–13 and 26–31, which tell us that we were created in God's image and He is the *creator*!

May you enjoy the best that Mother Nature can provide, with your own helping hand.

COMPOSTING

· ·

Composting is the ultimate in recycling; it is the re-use of the earth's own waste. Most home yarde-ners talk about starting or building a compost pile, a small number begin, and very few complete the task. That's a shame.

Composting your yard, garden, and table waste is the smartest, safest, most economical way I can think of to rebuild the hard-working soil in your garden each year.

You really don't need anything other than a small space to pile the grass clippings you don't use for mulch each week. You can also add leaves to the pile and use your blender to mush up table scraps of vegetables and meat to add to the pile as well.

After you spread a layer of grass clippings, dig up a shovelful of soil and lightly sprinkle on top. Next, alternate spraying a can of regular Coca-Cola and a well-shaken can of beer. The sugar feeds the bacteria which break down the organic materials, the yeast stimulates the enzymes, and the carbonation is a breath of fresh air

Before you use the compost, cut up a shovelful at a time with a lawn mower to shred it finer.

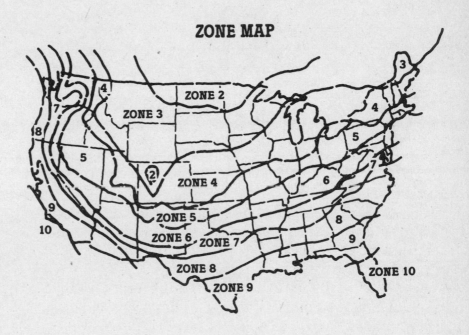

ZONE MAP

INDEX

There's an epidemic with 27 million victims. And no visible symptoms.

It's an epidemic of people who can't read.

Believe it *or* not, 27 million Americans are functionally illiterate, about one adult in five.

The solution to this problem is you… when you join the fight against illiteracy. So call the Coalition for Literacy at toll-free **1-800-228-8813** and volunteer.

Volunteer Against Illiteracy. The only degree you need is a degree of caring.